WORTHY OF JUSTICE

THE POLITICS OF VETERANS TREATMENT COURTS IN PRACTICE

JAMIE ROWEN

STANFORD UNIVERSITY PRESS
Stanford, California

Stanford University Press
Stanford, California

Library of Congress Cataloging-in-Publication Data

Names: Rowen, Jamie author

Title: Worthy of justice : the politics of veterans treatment courts in practice / Jamie Rowen.

Description: Stanford, California : Stanford University Press, 2025. | Includes bibliographical references and index.

Identifiers: LCCN 2025012689 (print) | LCCN 2025012690 (ebook) | ISBN 9781503611498 cloth | ISBN 9781503644663 paperback | ISBN 9781503644670 ebook

Subjects: LCSH: Alternatives to imprisonment—United States | Veterans—Services for—United States | Veterans—Legal status, laws, etc.—United States | Criminals—Rehabilitation—United States | Drug courts—United States | Mental health courts—United States | Criminal justice, Administration of—United States

Classification: LCC HV9304 .R69 2025 (print) | LCC HV9304 (ebook) | DDC 364.6086/97—dc23/eng/20250708

LC record available at https://lccn.loc.gov/2025012689

LC ebook record available at https://lccn.loc.gov/2025012690

Cover design: Martyn Schmoll
Cover art: iStock

The authorized representative in the EU for product safety and compliance is: Mare Nostrum Group B.V. | Mauritskade 21D | 1091 GC Amsterdam | The Netherlands | Email address: gpsr@mare-nostrum.co.uk | KVK chamber of commerce number: 96249943

WORTHY OF JUSTICE

CONTENTS

ACKNOWLEDGMENTS

This book is the culmination of ten years working with incredible advocates, research assistants, colleagues, and family members who helped me clarify what I was learning as I observed veterans treatment courts (VTCs). The opportunity to conduct research at this scale, with hundreds of hours of court observations, interviews, and documentary analysis, would not have been possible without support from the many people who generously offered their time and insights, as well as material support.

First and foremost, I extend my appreciation to the veterans whom I met along the way. This includes those veterans struggling in jail and a residential facility, who let me learn about their lives and experiences as they fought to reestablish their independence. In these settings, I met the many volunteers and paid staff who illustrate the meaning of service. I was similarly inspired by the judges and court staff who let me learn from their work. I wish I could name them, but I want to respect their anonymity. All of the arguments in this book reflect my own ideas and conclusions, and I make no representations on behalf of these generous interviewees.

The primary reason I chose to study VTCs is because I wanted to learn from people who were dedicating their lives to helping others. Although some of the stories I tell in the book illustrate the courts' struggles, these stories should not be read to impugn any individual. I continue to find that most people who work in the court system, however maligned they may be in political or some academic spaces for their participation in mass incarceration, are often in the profession to help others. Working within broken systems can be heroic, and far more challenging than sitting back and criticizing these systems. Several of these "interviewees" went above and beyond in helping me understand and learn from veterans in the criminal legal system, and illustrated how impactful individuals can be.

Second, I want to thank the Law and Science Program, part of the Social and Behavioral Sciences Directorate at National Science Foundation (NSF), and specifically Program Director Reggie Sheehan, for supporting the bulk of this research with an NSF Career Award 1845165. I initially studied VTCs thinking that this project would last a year. However, because the NSF saw the value of this work, I was able to devote six more years to understanding VTCs, and support students at three different universities who also wanted to learn about these courts. Other grants also enabled the pilot research necessary to develop this project. At UMass, I had the benefit of a School of Social and Behavioral Sciences Faculty Grant, a Healey Endowment Grant, and a Center for Racial Justice and Urban Affairs Grant. *Law and Policy* also granted permission for me to reproduce several arguments, supported by the same data, published previously in that journal.

I never would have received the NSF award were it not for Maureen Perry Jenkins and the Center for Research on Families (CRF) at the University of Massachusetts, Amherst. As a CRF fellow, Maureen and a team of methodologists and colleagues from across the university helped me translate my nascent insights about VTCs into a coherent research proposal. As part of the CRF fellowship, I was able to enlist the help of Calvin Morrill, an award-winning sociologist in the Jurisprudence and Social Policy Program at Berkeley Law School. Cal volunteered his time over many years to help me not only to develop the initial proposal but also to think through the findings. Cal's incredible research acumen was instrumental in the research design for this project as well as its findings. Likewise, Liz Chiarello from Saint Louis University inspired me with her own research design and, later, with her incisive comments on a draft manuscript.

Ryan Foley, now at New York Legal Assistance Group, was also instrumental in helping me understand veterans benefits, as well as take the lead in supervising students engaged in court observations. His professionalism and the quality of the data he oversaw was unparalleled. Over the course of this research, I employed or supervised dozens of research assistants. Several stood out for their commitment and contributions to this project. First, Alexandria Nylen, Catie Fowler, Brie McLemore, and Liliam Fiallo were outstanding graduate student assistants. At the undergraduate level, Merit Brent, Tegan Oliver, Jacqualin Fallon, Ginevra Mastrobattista, Lilian Alvino, Haley Hohensee, and Claire Healey were highly effective and diligent in data collection and analysis. Lila Stromer provided valuable editorial assistance, as did my editors at Stanford University Press, Michelle Lipinski and Marcela Maxfield, the anonymous reviewers for Stanford University Press, and other publication venues that have viewed various parts of this project.

Over the years, I have received feedback from many colleagues on this project, whether at conferences or in workshops, or over coffee or a meal. My UMass colleagues, including Paul Collins, Rebecca Hamlin, Lauren McCarthy, Youngmin Yi (now at Wellesley), Kelsey Shoub, Sindiso Mnisi Weeks, Tania Do Carmo, and Charli Carpenter, generously worked through many of my half-baked ideas to help me find the argument for this book. Portions of this research were presented at the American Political Science Association, Law and Society Association, Southern Political Science Association, and American Sociological Association Annual meetings, as well as for the University of Albany and the American Bar Foundation. At UMass, I presented this book as part of the Human Security Workshop and multiple times to the Legal Studies and Political Science Departments for feedback. Discussants and audience members always inspired me to think about various aspects of this project, with colleagues such as Victoria Piehowski, Alyx Mark, Lisa Holmes, and Mary Ellen Stitt offering additional and impactful feedback. Tamara Lave provided support throughout this research as well, making fieldwork far from home far more palatable.

Of course, no one (at least no one as social as I am) can complete a book without the support of friends and family. My husband, Chris Klimmek, is one of my favorite interlocutors. He always helps me get to the heart of my argument and, with a litigator's precision, clear up points that only make sense to me. My children were born during the course of research and provided much needed perspective and joy. My stepchildren were also critical to keeping me balanced. I had the benefit of extraordinary childcare, particularly with Ana Sofia Sanchez, Kamila Furtado, and Rocio Fuentes, which gave me the opportunity to support my family in multiple ways. My twin sister and brother-in-law supported me with lodging and great meals during multiple research trips. My parents, stepparents, brothers, and in-laws have likewise consistently expressed enthusiasm and support for my research.

Beyond my gratitude to everyone mentioned above, I extend my acknowledgments to all those who continue to support high-quality social science research that can help people who were not born with the privileges that others benefit from. I hope that those who are interested in helping veterans, or anyone struggling in the ways that people in this book are, find the resources they need.

WORTHY OF JUSTICE

One

INTRODUCING VETERANS TREATMENT COURTS

On an afternoon in June 2017, in a small rural courthouse in New England, I observed a somewhat unusual scene. Three individuals, each having pleaded guilty to their offenses, stood before a judge. But they were not sentenced, or condemned, or even criticized for their past choices. Instead, they were commended for graduating from an eighteen-month program of supervised substance abuse treatment. Friends, neighbors, program personnel, prosecutors, and a few members of the media filled the courtroom benches, and they applauded at the end. The program had not been easy to complete; these three people had to come to court regularly to check in with the judge, attend mandated regular therapy sessions, and fulfill court-ordered community service. Complying with these demands often meant missing work—perhaps risking their jobs—and passing on precious time with family. But graduating from the program conferred vital benefits: the graduates both avoided imprisonment and received release from probation. More importantly, they were sober and ready to make a clean start.

I say that this scene is only somewhat unusual because it is one example of an increasingly common institution: the treatment court. The term *treatment court* may suggest a large and stately building where legal proceedings are conducted. But treatment courts are not separate courts in a physical sense. For example, the courtroom described above is ordinarily used for criminal trials and related proceedings (e.g., arraignments, plea allocutions). Yet, one afternoon each week, this courtroom also serves as this region's veterans treatment court (VTC), a treatment court that only qualifying veterans can participate in. The VTC is better understood as a separate set of legal procedures with accompanying social supports that use a region's existing criminal legal and, where available, veterans services infrastructure. In this VTC in the Northeast, qualifying veterans who have pled guilty to crimes meet regularly with a judge to review their progress through their eighteen-month probation program, discuss any challenges they are facing, and receive support and guidance. In this court, veterans volunteer as mentors to fellow veterans participating in the program. At this graduation, the veteran mentors wore their dress uniforms, complete with medals and regalia.

This VTC is just one of the over six hundred VTCs (Rapisara et al. 2024) that operate in the United States, and operates similarly to the over three thousand adult drug treatment courts on which the VTC model is based. Over the past three decades, jurisdictions across the US have developed alternatives to traditional criminal procedures and punishments for adults accused of crimes that are associated with substance use and mental health disorders. The most common is the adult drug court, which originated in Miami in 1989 and uses an interdisciplinary team within the criminal-justice system to bring psychosocial treatment resources and techniques to people evaluated as having substance use and/or mental health disorders. A judge serves as the leader of the team, which usually includes someone from the prosecutor's office and the public defender's office, a probation or community supervision officer, and a substance abuse/ mental health treatment provider. Other specialized courts, such as those designed to address mental health disorders, prostitution, human trafficking, or impaired driving—often referred to with the broader label of "problem-solving courts," first applied a century ago to court programs for juvenile offenders— have evolved from the drug court model.

Worthy of Justice: The Politics of Veterans Treatment Courts in Practice examines this specific form of problem-solving court with the goal of exploring broader inequalities in US society. The existence and, as this book suggests, appeal of VTCs reveals how the presence of veterans in the criminal legal system, specifically veterans diagnosed with substance use and mental health disorders, has become a "problem" that courts are supposed to "solve." The first VTCs were established decades after drug treatment courts began proliferating to address the so-called War on Drugs, yet VTCs are now the second-most common form of treatment court in the country. Politicians, advocates, and even some scholars tout the novelty of VTCs as a uniquely effective criminal legal innovation.

Despite these claims of novelty, VTCs were designed from existing treatment court models and practices. What VTCs added is the availability of extensive (and free) medical and social services through the Department of Veterans Affairs (the VA) and the social and political legitimacy that comes with serving veterans. This legitimacy, however, is not a given and must constantly be negotiated with VTC stakeholders. For example, at this graduation, like other court sessions, we all stood as the security officer announced the judge's entrance and called the court into session. The judge sat above us in the same elevated space as they do in trials. The judge welcomed us and then described the efforts of the graduating program participants, who sat in the jury box, to maintain sobriety. Just as the judge did, other speakers emphasized the pride they felt helping those who served our country. The veterans who served as mentors to the participants, wearing military insignia, gave speeches comparing the value of this graduation with the value of serving. One probation officer compared this graduation to his daughter's recent professional advancement in the military. A mentor presented each graduate with a challenge coin, a military symbol for a "job well done."

Such public events appeal to program personnel and policymakers, but they are not typical sessions. When advocates or observers write about VTCs, they often discuss these formal events rather than the day-to-day hearings. They describe program participants as developing substance use or mental health disorders *because* of their military service, the cause of their criminal legal involvement. This is part of what I refer to as the *common narrative* that veterans are in VTCs because of something that happened during their service. The implication is that they would not be in these courts had they not chosen to join the military and serve their country. This narrative weaves together three interrelated rationales for VTCs: (1) veterans deserve the more favorable and supportive procedures of the VTC over traditional courts because of the sacrifices they have made for their country, (2) courts should provide these more favorable procedures to those whose criminalized behavior is in some sense the responsibility of the state, and (3) VTCs are uniquely beneficial for participants because they understand and incorporate military culture (Russell

2009; Hawkins 2009; Cartwright 2011). This narrative shapes media accounts of VTCs, public events in VTCs, and though evolving as more scholars continue to reveal the variety of ways in which VTCs have been implemented, the narrative still permeates scholarship about how VTCs originated and developed to be effective in helping veterans desist from crime and better integrate into society (Douds et al. 2017; Baldwin and Hartley 2022; Sherman 2024).

DISCOVERING TENSIONS IN THE COMMON NARRATIVE

After only a few initial court observations, I recognized that the reality of VTCs often does not fit the common narrative that justifies their existence. For example, one of this court's graduates stood out because she was the only woman in the group—most of the participants my research team and I observed over the years were men. She looked both proud and uncomfortable as the court personnel recited her specific dedication to substance abuse treatment and her successful efforts to secure work and housing. Personnel were clear in their desire that she come back as a mentor to help future participants. A few weeks after this courtroom celebration, I met with the young woman commended at her graduation from the program, when I learned that she had never completed boot camp, never served in active duty, and certainly never saw combat. She told me she was sad that she had not been able to complete boot camp, relating it to a long-standing challenge with addiction that predated her military service. Her brief experience in the military was eclipsed by the eighteen months that she spent in a VTC for a subsequent drug conviction. By some definitions—for example, the US government's criteria used for eligibility for VA benefits—this graduate was not a veteran at all, because she had not even completed boot camp. And her substance use and legal problems did not result from her short stint in the military.

This graduation ceremony also highlighted a deeper tension within the common narrative itself. The graduation celebrated the participants' military service, and the judge, mentors, and other speakers invoked the participants' prior sacrifices for their country as the rationale for the VTC. They described the court as a way to "give back" to those who gave so much through their service. Implicit in these speeches was the assumption that the rigors of military service had led to their substance use problems and eventual criminal convictions. The military was thus both celebrated and blamed for its role in these veterans' lives. This contradiction intrigued me, leading me to dig deeper into the way that VTCs grapple with the consequences of participants' military service.

The court hearings I attended at the Northeast VTC revealed another crack in the common narrative. In addition to suggesting that veterans are uniquely deserving of the criminal legal benefits VTCs offer, the common narrative is that VTCs are potentially more beneficial for participants because they incorporate military culture into their programs and offer participants the camaraderie they once had (Russell 2015; Douds and Ahlin 2019; Vaughan, Holleran, and Brooks 2019). Yet at hearings at the Northeast VTC (and at the other VTCs I subsequently studied), participants' military service, combat experience (if any), and any resulting trauma were almost never mentioned; the focus at hearings was on participants' substance use problems and how to get them treatment and social services.

Given that it was hard to see what distinguished these veterans from other criminal defendants—aside from their decision to join the military, not what they did as part of the military—I found myself wondering: What if everyone in the criminal legal system, not just those who joined the military, were treated with such care?

After a year observing the Northeast VTC, I decided to investigate other VTCs, hoping to understand whether the VTC in the Northeast was an outlier, or if there was more "military culture" in other VTCs, and how other VTCs helped veterans in their communities. I selected two more VTCs, both in urban centers: one in the Southeast and one in the West.

The differences between these three VTCs surprised me, revealing another crack in the common narrative. I studied the Southeast VTC first, which was located in a large downtown courthouse. The first time I arrived for a scheduled hearing, I wondered if I was in the wrong place. At the Northeast VTC, court participants and their mentors chat in the hallway before hearings, which generally start on time. At the Southeast VTC, after sitting alone in the hallway for half an hour, I saw some people trickle in, but few were chatting. While all participants at the Northeast VTC stayed in the courtroom for the entire session, those in this second VTC left immediately after being called in front of the judge. The most significant difference between these courtrooms was the interactions between judge and participant. In the Northeast VTC, it was unusual to see a participant argue with the judge; at the Southeast VTC, the judge had tense conversations with participants who were often argumentative and even used expletives in the courtroom. The Southeast VTC judge repeatedly tried to convince the participants that the VTC program would help them, but that they had to comply with its many requirements for sobriety if they wanted to graduate. Similar to the Northeast VTC, there were still few or frequently no references to military culture or military service in day-to-day hearings.

At the West VTC, I waited in a long line to even enter the municipal courthouse. While the urban courthouse where the Southeast VTC is located is large but fairly calm, this one was massive and active. I wound my way around service animals, well-dressed professional-looking people walking hurriedly through the hallways, and what appeared to be clients huddled with their lawyers. Like at the hearings at the other two VTCs, I found nothing here that I could identify as military culture. Half a dozen veterans sat in the jury box, all wearing orange jumpsuits indicating that they were in jail. The judge announced that there were a total of thirty current VTC participants in jail. The day's participants not in the jury box wandered in and out of the courtroom; except for the six from jail, almost no one sat still. Clinicians followed these free-roaming participants out the courtroom door to check on them: Are they meeting with their assigned treatment provider? Do they have housing? Do they want to stay in the treatment court program? Participants in both the Northeast and Southeast VTCs generally dressed nicely, even if somewhat casually, for court appearances. On the other hand, many participants at the West VTC appeared to be on the margins of society, often wearing tattered clothing and slurring their words, as if they were intoxicated or on drugs. The bailiff used no discernible order to call up participants, who were referred to as "line" plus numbers. While interactions were not nearly as orderly, respectful, or affectionate as in the Northeast VTC, they were also not nearly as tense or confrontational as hearings in the Southeast VTC. Rather, there appeared to be mutual understanding between the West VTC judge and participants that the latter were struggling; many were transient with long histories of substance abuse and mental illness. The judge, speaking in a very practiced tone, asked them what they wanted to do to help themselves, and what the court might do to assist them.

There were other significant differences among the three VTCs. Contributing to their individual hearing dynamics, each VTC has different rules for entry, different sobriety requirements, and different ways of trying to help participants. Thus, I learned that it is not only difficult to generalize about

VTCs but it can also be misleading to do so. My observations suggest that the performance and results produced by each VTC (for example, participant outcomes) are driven primarily by eligibility criteria, program requirements, and judicial personality. This means that what scholars usually focus on in assessing treatment courts—specifically their costs and benefits, or the rates at which participants commit new crimes or complete a treatment court program—is not nearly the whole story. Each court has different goals and thus strategies to achieve them. And, each court *felt* different, particularly in terms of how much court personnel and participants performed or appeared to genuinely buy into the common narrative.

Still, some general features remained constant across these three VTCs. Most notably, clinicians and court personnel in all three embraced the common narrative, describing program participants as a deserving group whose criminalized behavior is different from those who did not join the military. Another common feature was their reliance on the extensive medical and social services made available by the VA to many participants.

Several scholars have told the story of how these factors made VTCs popular, leading to their rapid growth and their different rules and regulations. Most notably, Douds and Ahlin (2019) trace the development and implementation of VTCs around the country as part of a larger movement to assist veterans. They and others point to the differences in how VTC rules and regulations are created; many courts have autonomy to design their rules, while others strictly adhere to municipal and state laws around treatment courts (Hummer et al. 2024; Rapisarda et al. 2024). Douds et al. (2017) focus on variation within one state, Pennsylvania, which reflects specificities of local courthouse and the communities they serve, while Baldwin and Hartley (2022) evaluate eight VTCs across three states, and reveal strikingly different approaches to identifying veterans, court requirements, data collection, and analysis of results.

Others examine VTCs as a distinct criminal legal reform designed to address the perceived problem of veterans in the criminal legal system. Edwards, Hinojosa, and Hassan (2019) point out the important role of the VA in facilitating their growth. Vaughan, Holleran, and Brooks (2019) illustrate how references to the military—often jokes related to military service—permeated the VTC hearings they observed in Texas, yet they conclude that VTCs appear like any other specialty courts "with military aspects." Baldwin and Brooke (2019), taking a more critical approach, point to the "rapid expansion" of these courts without evidence of their efficacy as compared to other criminal legal options that veterans might pursue (Tsai et al. 2016). This burgeoning scholarship is useful not only for those interested in how VTCs vary but also for revealing how the adult drug treatment court model has evolved to meet a variety of challenges facing people in the criminal legal system while still being limited by state legislation and funding (Hummer et al. 2024; Rapisarda et al. 2024).

This book tells a different story. Building on these scholars' work, it explores the puzzles presented by VTCs that I have sketched above. First, there is the tension between the public rationale for these courts—to address the unique needs and challenges of veterans—and the reality that the military experience of program participants is far more varied, as is the relevance of military experience in court practice. Second, there is the tension between these courts' celebration of military service and the implicit assumption of the courts: military service caused or contributed to the veterans' criminalized behaviors. Finally, while some studies show variations between courts with regard to rules and requirements, my case studies reveal more stark divergence in goals, strategies, rules, and practices among the three courts.

Digging into these smaller puzzles illuminates a larger question: How is criminal law in the United States used to manage perceived social and political problems, and what kind of inequalities does this instrumentalization of law reproduce? VTCs illustrate how the politics of crime and the politics of welfare increasingly intersect and, together, construct classes of Americans meritorious of public support. Relatedly, VTCs offer a unique lens on social inequality in the US by illustrating the convergence of two dominant institutions—the criminal legal system and the military. They provide insights into how social and political institutions are shaped by beliefs about which people deserve state resources—and which do not. As a result, understanding the purpose and practices of VTCs can inform broader questions not only about the roles and meanings of the military but also about the law in US society.

WORTHY OF JUSTICE

The central argument of this book is that the rationale for VTCs—mirrored in their practice—flows not from what veterans have *done* but from who veterans *are*. As the popularity and prevalence of the VA and related veteran benefits attest, veterans are viewed as uniquely worthy of social support, ranging from state-funded social and medical services to hiring preferences. VTCs are a logical extension of this concept of worthiness, adding a criminal legal benefit. But in VTCs, the idea of *veteran* worthiness confronts and intersects with another belief about social worth: criminals are not worthy of social benefits and support.

Like all treatment courts, VTCs have tension with the idea that those who commit crimes deserve punishment while attributing criminal behavior to things other than "unworthy" character. Drug treatment courts, for example, often characterize drug addiction and resulting criminal activities as a "disease" that infects participants rather than the product of poor choices and character defects (Tiger 2012). VTCs add the idea that their participants' criminal behavior is the result of military service rather than other personal choices. VTCs thus reflect and amplify the ideal of veteran worthiness while interrogating the idea of criminal unworthiness.

My focus on veteran worth complements and extends existing VTC explanations that focus on the public's perceptions of veterans by examining how those perceptions map onto VTC practices. In articulating the motivation to create VTCs at the national level, for example, Douds and Ahlin (2019) point to the visceral feeling of debt toward veterans. During my research into VTCs over the last decade, I frequently heard that veterans are "owed" the benefits offered by the court. The idea of debt to veterans is multifaceted. Veteran deservingness is embedded in the belief that military service is a sacrifice for the good of the country. That sacrifice needs to be repaid through special treatment in all social and political settings, including the criminal legal system. These beliefs support a cultural narrative of the noble warrior fighting noble wars. This narrative has changed over time as public opinion about wars has changed, but support for veterans remains deeply entrenched in US social identity (Appy 2015; Darda 2021).

There is also a well-founded concern about the harm that comes with military service. Baldwin and Hartley (2022) suggest that the treatment court model differs from earlier treatment courts focused on drug courts and prostitution because of the many complex needs of people returning from military engagements abroad. Compared with those who never served, military enlistees have higher rates of post-traumatic stress disorder as well as traumatic brain injury, which can contribute to challenges they face within the military and after they leave (Hartwell et al. 2014). Importantly, substance use disorders are highly correlated with criminal behavior and punishment, and an ongoing problem for veterans since the Vietnam era (Blodgett, Avoundjian, and Finlay 2015; Blonigen et al. 2016; Kessler et al. 2014). Although veterans currently have lower rates of incarceration compared to their nonveteran peers, a change over the last forty years (Holliday, Ayer, and Skrabala 2023), studies show that veterans are more likely to have criminal legal contact (one-third of veterans compared with one-fifth of nonveterans), have higher rates of violent offenses and sexual crimes, and face longer sentences than their nonveteran peers (Orak et al. 2023; Timko et al. 2020).

These different understandings about what VTCs can and should do reflect other data on what brings veterans into the criminal legal system. One suggestion is that military service leads to criminal legal behavior; for example, in 2016 there was a disproportionate number of combat veterans in prisons: about one in four male veterans in state prison (28 percent) and one in five in federal prison (21 percent) (Bureau of Justice Statistics 2021). There is also a persistent thirty-year overrepresentation of veterans among criminal legal defendants accused of sexual violence (Seamone, Holliday, and Sreenivasan 2018). This is sometimes explained with reference to the hypermasculine culture in the military, a direct contrast to the VTCs' common narrative that military culture is salutary for justice-involved veterans (Holliday et al. 2023).

These data suggest that being in the military can contribute to criminal offending which, by extension, means that the state bears some responsibility for the criminalized behavior of those who served in the military. The dilemma is that research reveals that many of the same factors that push people into the criminal legal system are the same for veterans and nonveterans, namely, the absence of social connectedness and social capital (Culp et al. 2013). Snowden et al. (2017), for example, argue that studies suggesting that veterans are more likely to have criminal legal contact focus on veterans who were unable to fit into "military culture," many of whom did not leave the military under conditions that enable them to access the full panoply of VA benefits. Musheno and Ross (2008) similarly show that veterans who struggle upon returning to civilian life struggled before joining the military. Notably, research comparing subsets of veterans in the criminal legal system shows veterans who never saw combat were more likely to have committed a violent offense, but less likely to have committed drug offenses; whereas combat veterans were more likely to commit a drug offense and less likely to commit a violent offense (Van Dyke and Orrick 2016).

Other studies suggest that neither joining the military nor being in combat is the conclusive factor behind post-traumatic stress disorder (PTSD), other mental health disorders, or being in the criminal legal system (Elbogen et al. 2012; Brooke and Gau 2018). Brewin, Andrews, and Valentine (2000) likewise found that the most consistent predictors of PTSD are childhood abuse and/ or personal or family psychiatric history. Trauma severity, low socioeconomic status, low education, low intelligence or cognitive capacity, other adverse childhood circumstances, life stressors, and lack of social support are all significant predictors of developing PTSD, although they vary in the extent of predictiveness. Brewin et al. (2000) suggest that female gender, younger age, and minority status are also significant predictors of developing PTSD. The most comprehensive national study of VTCs, albeit focused on those in the VA healthcare system, suggests that only one-third of VTC participants have PTSD, even fewer have traumatic brain injury, and many are older veterans suffering from long-term chronic homelessness (Tsai et al. 2016).

Regardless of the relationship between military service, substance use, mental health, and criminal legal involvement, VTCs are not unique among problem-solving courts in deciding that some criminal legal defendants deserve different treatment than others. However, their assumptions about the participants are distinct. All courts involve "target populations that are credited with the ability to change and reform" while also lacking agency due to life circumstances (Shdaimah, Leon, and Wiechelr 2023, 14). The most prevalent treatment court, the adult drug treatment court, rests on assumptions about addiction, pathologizing individuals in the criminal legal system as diseased (Tiger 2012; Murphy 2015).

At the same time, the courts differ in their reasoning for targeting certain populations to the exclusion of others. For example, treatment courts focused on youth assume a young person can be rehabilitated in a way that an older person may not be capable of, just as those focused on mental illness assume a person is less culpable if their crime is related to a mental health disorder (Johnston 2012). Another illustrative contrast to VTCs are problem-solving courts focused on prostitution, as both rest on the express assumption that the criminalized defendant is also a traumatized victim (Jacobson 2013). Both types of treatment try to distinguish the person in the court from the activities that may have brought them there, and the role of trauma in criminalized behaviors. However, people working in these courts still view prostitution as inherently exploitative (Shdaimah et al. 2023), the opposite of how people in VTCs view military service. Relatedly, the existence of prostitution courts rests on the fact that prostitution is criminalized. Change that law, and no more prostitution courts. The same is not true for VTCs, which draw on defendants based on their involvement in the military, not the specific acts they engaged in.

Even as a medical logics about criminalized behavior perpetuate certain stereotypes, framing certain criminal legal defendants with medical concepts has the express purpose of undoing long-standing assumptions and practices that punish. The irony, of course, is that they still rely on punishment. Further, hierarchies are inherent in these characterizations, typically based on how people perform in the courtrooms rather than what brought them there. Revier (2021), for example, notes how drug treatment courts treat some participants as "criminal-addicts" or "recovering addicts," a distinction that often maps onto the participant's race (see also Gowan and Whetstone 2012). Moore and Hirai (2014) describe the court "performances," showing how some people engage with the courts as "outcasts" or "true believers." As a subset of adult drug treatment courts, VTCs borrow this logic of pathology in a distinct blend of drug and mental health treatment courts and, as this book illustrates, have their own versions of "true believers" and "outcasts."

Further, VTCs are distinct from these other courts in that they have ideological foundations that rest on the value of military service, an ideology that has contributed to long-standing social welfare practices that treat veterans as uniquely deserving of public benefits. As Skocpol (1995) explains, "Legitimate civil war pensions were idealized as that which was justly due to the righteous core of a generation of men (and survivors of dead men)—a group that ought to be generously and constantly repaid by the nation for their sacrifices " (103). The idea that those with a "righteous core" are "justly due" public benefits encapsulates how worth and deservingness intersect, with significant policy implications.

Rather than focus on this "feeling" of debt or the challenging mental and physical health outcomes for people who served in the military, this book uses the story of VTCs to examine how ideas about these facets of military service materially manifest in the social services, and now criminal legal benefits, available to veterans. These social services, particularly those offered by the VA, are critical to understanding how VTCs work, why individual courts differ from one another, and how these courts both shift and reproduce inequalities in the broader social service and criminal legal fields. Instead of assuming the distinct capacity of VTCs to help participants because of a (difficult to define) shared military culture, as many accounts do, this book argues that the ideological and material resources available to veterans make these courts unique.

Looking to the long history of social services offered to veterans and not to other social groups, VTCs represent a unique judicial organization that integrates the vast social service bureaucracy for veterans into the criminal legal system. They reflect and reveal moral decision making about who should receive social service benefits as a general matter, and who should receive them in the criminal legal system. Regardless of whether one believes that those who engaged in military service deserve this level of public support, an idea once contested but now widely accepted, veterans' access to social welfare benefits reveals and reflects stark inequalities that are produced, diffused, assessed, and institutionalized across a range of settings throughout the US.

VETERANS AND INEQUALITIES

Understanding veteran social welfare and criminal legal benefits reveals not only their different political and social meanings but also their material implications, all of which are central to the contradictions of the populations that VTCs serve. In this book, I use the word veteran in much the same way that the courts do—an inclusive term that does not depend on the length of time or specific experience one had while in the military. The word veteran has a colloquial meaning—someone who served in the military—yet a court that calls itself a VTC often does not mention the military or adhere to legal definitions. While states have their own definitions of who qualifies as a veteran, under federal law, one is not considered a veteran if they left the military under dishonorable discharge conditions.

Yet, veterans have strikingly different experiences in the military depending on the amount of time they served, where they served, and the positions they held. These experiences may have little to do with a person's access to VA benefits, which are shaped by the "conditions" under which they left the military. Because VTCs rely so heavily on VA services for health care, these courts often reproduce the same inequalities that come with these legal military definitions and their associated benefits. Veterans in VTCs who were discharged under other than honorable conditions may have to find outside treatment services, just like civilians in the drug treatment courts, because they are not eligible for federal VA benefits.

Regardless of these distinctions, veterans hold a unique place in US society when it comes to the provision of social services. In general, the US has avoided providing social benefits beyond temporary relief for immediate hardship. The social welfare system constructed in the Great Depression distinguished between public assistance and social insurance, which contributed to ongoing distinctions between people deemed deserving of short- or long-term support (Katz 2013, 8). Social welfare policies that favor veterans reveal one answer to critical questions posed by poverty scholar Michael Katz (2013): "Resources are finite . . . Who should—and, more importantly, who should not—receive help? Answering this question means drawing lines separating individuals into categories and defending arbitrary distinctions that discriminate among people, none of whom can survive by themselves with comfort and dignity."

Neither the harms that can come from military service are arbitrary, nor is joining the military an arbitrary decision, yet the allocation of resources to veterans—a category that defines a shared employment experience—reveals the politics of resource allocation based on beliefs about the value of military service over other life choices. These beliefs about worth show up not only in the general delineation of veterans from nonveterans but also in how VTC rules and practices, because they rely on the VA, privilege some veterans over others.

Along with manifesting a distinct feeling about the US military, VTCs also reflect a unique facet of American culture: using the criminal legal system to manage vulnerable populations and govern complex social and political issues in ways that exacerbate social inequalities (Garland 2001; Simon 2007). By showing how VTCs magnify beliefs about the quality of people who join the military while also ensnaring them in the criminal legal system, this book provides deeper insights into inequality in the US beyond race and gender. Despite the institution's dogged history of racism, serving in the military has been shown to decrease long-term economic inequalities among those who enlist. Still, the vastness of US racialized inequalities in the military cannot be erased; they are manifested in veterans both who end up in the criminal legal system and who don't have access to VA benefits.

Any discussion of social worth in the justice system must of course confront the reality that the US criminal legal system reflects the implicit (and at times, explicit) view that racialized minorities—especially African Americans—are less worthy of public support and more deserving of punishment. There are many powerful books about racialized inequalities in both the criminal legal system and social services (see, e.g., Alexander 2012; Hinton 2016; Gonzalez Van Cleve 2016; Forman 2017; Miller 2021), as well as work that shows how racialized practices in the military may perpetuate harm on minoritized groups (Ray 2018). A growing body of scholarship has documented the ways in which African Americans and other "disfavored" minorities are far more likely than whites to be arrested, prosecuted, convicted, and incarcerated for the same or similar behaviors, particularly as related to substance use. Similar trends exist in treatment courts: African Americans are less likely to be referred to any type of treatment court, and those who are referred are more likely to be "terminated" for noncompliance (Cheesman, Marlowe, and Genthon 2023). Because race is central to inequality in the US, it shapes this book's subject as well. In the three VTCs that I studied, African Americans and other minorities were overrepresented as compared with percentages in their surrounding communities and (in most cases) in the military as whole. This mirrors the structural racism found throughout the entire US legal system.

However, this book is also about inequality based on having the status of veteran, which is one that includes all races, and which is legally, socially, and politically constructed in a different way than race, which I illustrate by examining how ideology and public benefits intersect. Although my research was ethnographic and does not make conclusions about participant outcomes by race, I saw a variety of racial dynamics in VTCs as related to people in other types of treatment courts. Race often seemed to drop out of the equation in day-to-day VTC proceedings, except with regard to participants' existing vulnerabilities upon entering the court. Everyone in the court was treated as worthy of the court's support, as though this status as veteran masked or overcame their status as less-than-worthy minorities. Yet, when describing what distinguishes veterans from other criminal legal defendants, personnel sometimes turned to racialized language about criminal defendants who were not in the VTC, suggesting that a person's military experience shifted their perceptions on behavior, specifically behavior associated with racialized minorities. These observations echo Darda's (2021) conclusions that the category of veteran has been constructed on the image of the white Vietnam veteran, which helped privilege veterans in the allocation of social benefits while also contributing to the marginalization of racially minoritized veteran voices. They also map onto Liebert's (2022) account of how criminal courts treat people exposed to violence in the military differently than people, disproportionately racialized minorities, exposed to violence in urban centers.

The role of gender in criminal and legal processes has also been extensively explored in scholarly and popular publications, and gender is likewise central to the story of VTCs. VTC participants were overwhelmingly, often exclusively, male, making it difficult to generalize about the few women participants I observed or how they were treated, as I could count the number of women on two hands over my ten years of research. Further, the camaraderie often touted and observed seen in VTCs has a distinctly masculine element. I often heard concerns about the lack of women in VTCs early on in my research, but by the time I was writing this book, this appeared to be an accepted fact by VTCs. The result is that, unless otherwise noted, this is largely a book about men who joined and left the military, and at some point afterward were arrested.

Similar to identities related to race and gender, which can be sources of either empowerment or exclusion (Jenkins 2000; Wimmer 2013), inequalities related to veteran identity, particularly as it relates to criminal legal involvement, are complex. Some studies find that joining the military may decrease one's likelihood to engage in criminalized activity (see Bouffard 2005; Brooke and Gau 2018), so the common narrative that military service contributes to criminalized behavior—and therefore veterans should be treated differently in the criminal legal system—reveals the irony of treating veterans differently than other criminal legal defendants. Still, there is a heavily racialized component to this criminal legal involvement. No matter their economic status, being African American puts one at the highest risk of criminal legal involvement (Zaw, Hamilton, and Darity 2016). Yet, research shows that African Americans who join the military are less likely than their civilian counterparts to engage in crime, while veterans of any race with low socioeconomic status are more likely to engage in crime than their wealthier civilian counterparts (Bouffard 2005). At the same time, African Americans are more likely than their white counterparts to be ineligible for VA benefits after serving because of dishonorable discharges, yet far more likely to have PTSD (Merians et al. 2023). The reasons for these disparities are not fully understood; they could relate to discrimination before and during military service, or possibly to the exposure and severity of stressors during combat (Dohrenwald et al. 2008). Together, these studies show

how blending the criminal legal and social welfare institutions for veterans may contribute to distinctly disparate outcomes that, like other inequalities in US institutions, are racialized. While some of these disparities are easy to observe, such as the racial disparities in discharge status (discussed later), there are more subtle racialized effects of militarism because valorization of the military may be used to silence civilian claims of inequality (Ray 2018, 165).

What is notable about the construction of veteran identity is its legal, political, and social dimensions, particularly how they cross other typical markers of inequality—such as race—while reflecting others—such as class—in the US. As a result, VTCs are useful in illustrating how the US uses its criminal legal system to manage its growing social inequalities in ways that can contribute to arbitrary distinctions between people who need help. The respectful treatment of veterans in court—regardless of their race—is helpful to show veterans' social, political, and cultural status in society. This is why Collins (2017) refers to VTCs as "status courts," arguing that they both reflect and confer social status on veterans as a group that is distinct from other criminal defendants. The fact that specialized courts have been created for veterans sends a particular message about who belongs, who matters, and who is deserving (Hall and Lamont 2013). This message offers "cultural repertoires" that individuals can mobilize to buffer themselves from negative messages about themselves, such as stigma for their arrest or conviction (Lamont et al. 2016).

This book analyzes how these messages of worth show up in explanations about the creation of VTCs as well as in their implementation, allowing us to better understand both the inequalities outlined here and the tension in how VTCs both celebrate the military and implicitly blame the military for contributing to criminalized behaviors. Through this analysis, we also see how broader social inequalities manifest in the dilemmas posed by bringing the VA into the criminal legal system, and the criminal legal system into the provision of veterans' services.

ADD VETERAN AND STIR: LEGITIMACY AND
THE POLITICS OF WORTH

The typical explanation for creating treatment courts is that they address underlying causes of criminalized behavior (Marlowe, Hardin, and Fox 2016). VTCs include an extra argument, which I call "add veteran and stir," to the treatment court model. Add veteran and stir reflects the common narrative that military service either explains or is related to the pathologies that contributed to criminal offending, and mobilizing military culture in a treatment court will make it more effective (Caine 2009; Cartwright 2011; Lucas and Hanrahan 2016; Perlin 2013; Russell 2015; Stratton and Lagarce 2012). However, to legitimate VTCs, their proponents also advance the claim that veterans should have a criminal legal benefit unavailable to other similarly situated criminal legal defendants. This requires a claim that joining the military is a worthy act, regardless of what a person does after service.

These ideas form the foundations of the politics of worth, by which I mean the structural dynamics (both material and ideological) of decision making about the allocation of resources in social and political institutions. The politics of worth operate at individual, community, state, and federal levels. Individually, judges, policymakers, and advocates think about veterans as different than similarly situated criminal legal defendants. The politics of worth also involve media and popular cultural representations that create hierarchies of value between life choices—one of which is joining the military—and between the psychological consequences of exposure to military combat violence and other types of violence.

Examining the politics of worth through the creation and implementation of VTCs reveals numerous inequalities—those that lead people to enter the military, those within the military, and those within the criminal legal system. The common narrative that military service led to VTC participants' criminalized behaviors provides cover for other US institutions by putting the onus of responsibility for veterans' criminalized behaviors on the military. Analyzing how VTCs traffic in worth highlights broader issues of inequality in US social policy, while simultaneously showing the opportunities and challenges these courts face in helping participants access social services. More broadly, the politics of worth are central to understanding inequalities in social service and criminal legal organizations, as individuals and organizations make decisions about who deserves resources and who doesn't.

Thinking of VTCs as "add veteran and stir" to drug treatment courts, their appeal makes sense. Treatment courts reflect the growing use of courts to solve entrenched social and political problems related to substance abuse, mental health, poverty, and now war and militarism (Rowen 2020). What distinguishes VTCs from these other problem-solving courts is not simply who they admit, but the resources that they have access to and the narrative they build around who is worthy of what kinds of criminal legal benefits. Yet, the result of this add veteran and stir approach to the criminal legal system is not a cleanly blended mixture. Rather, the criminal legal and social welfare bases that existed remain, simply with a layer of social services and legitimacy unavailable to non-VTC defendants.

The politics of worth both reflect and create intersecting inequalities in VTCs because of how worth operates in the criminal legal system and in the VA healthcare system. In the criminal legal system, supposed "benefits" such as the option to join a treatment court are often unavailable to those charged with felonies. This is one reason for the racial disparities in treatment court access—racialized minorities are more likely to be charged with a drug-related felony and incarcerated than their white counterparts who may engage in similar drug-related activities but be charged with a misdemeanor and avoid incarceration (O'Hear 2009). In the VA, benefits depend on discharge status, creating hierarchies of access to social services.

In addition to these intersecting institutional inequalities, the politics of worth also relate to how VTCs explain themselves to different stakeholders. This politics of worth was most evident in public events in which court personnel explained the value of their courts. In addition to media accounts of VTCs, this is where the common narrative is clearest. While most hearings were predictable discussions about how each participant was doing, occasionally the Northeast and Southeast VTCs hosted events in which politicians and media were invited to observe the courtroom. On these days, the judge and personnel described the court's many benefits, emphasizing the service that the participants gave to their country and how these VTCs offer one way for US society to give back. The court personnel appeared to be selling the VTC model to people they thought mattered—local policymakers, the media, and social service providers who help participants.

These examples illustrate another critical feature about both the politics of worth and what we can learn about it from VTC practice—what goes on in VTCs on a daily basis reflects not only their different rules and procedures (see Douds and Ahlin 2019) but their ongoing need to obtain buy-in for their work. Here, I draw on the concept of legitimacy, which, when applied to courts and the criminal legal system, usually refers to whether people believe in the authority of law and their duty to follow it (Gibson, Caldeira, and Baird 1998).

For readers unfamiliar with treatment courts, a court needing to legitimate itself may seem surprising. Judges in criminal courts do not hold events to showcase the work that they do. Criminal court budgets are determined by legislative bodies that may question a particular court's practices, but criminal courts are guaranteed by the Constitution. Budgets may be cut, but the courts won't disappear. Treatment courts, and VTCs in particular, are in a different category because there is no constitutional right to them. The result is that VTCs must continually assert their legitimacy to policymakers, funders, social service providers, criminal legal agencies, and even participants.

But add veteran and stir to the drug treatment court model also poses problems. One of the most salient aspects of the common narrative is that participants suffer from trauma (Piehowski 2022); treating people who have been traumatized from military service differently than those who have not served is a widely popular political position in the US (Liebert 2022). Yet, trauma is a mental health diagnosis, which is why VTCs are designed to model both drug courts and mental health courts. This makes them more malleable than drug treatment courts, which helps explain their popularity as well as the challenges that courts face in defining and realizing their goals (Rowen 2017). Despite the close connection between mental health and substance use disorders, mental health courts often take a different and less punitive approach than drug treatment courts, the latter of which more readily assume that a person's behavior can change with punishment (Gordon 2018). VTCs are able to shapeshift in ways other treatment courts cannot, but such shapeshifting can affect their legitimacy as fair criminal legal organizations (Casey 2004; Gallagher and Ashford 2021).

Beyond its utility to explain whether people think policymakers should expend resources on VTCs or participants should obey VTC mandates, the concept of legitimacy explains how these courts make choices in relation to their various resources (Loader and Sparks 2013). The politics of worth is not static; acquiring and maintaining value requires active engagement. The courts must prioritize external legitimacy with funders and policymakers; that is, those who provide the necessary financial and policy support but who do not work within the courts. Perhaps more importantly for their day-to-day functioning, the courts also must prioritize internal legitimacy among the treatment court team and the treatment providers they rely on. In order to realize their goals of changing individual behavior, VTCs must make participants want to comply.

These dynamics characterize all VTCs, but their salience and valence differ depending on locale. The result is that any study of VTCs that flattens differences leaves important gaps in understanding how and why they function as they do.

This argument about legitimacy builds from long-standing research showing that problem-solving courts share certain features but are distinctly malleable in their practices because they need financial resources to thrive (Berman and Feinblatt 2001; Zozula 2019). Treatment courts may follow a national model, explained further in chapter 2, but also differ according to factors such as individual judges' personalities and the availability of local social services (Boldt 1998; Wolff, Fabrikant, and Belenko 2011; Castellano and Scott 2017). The study of these variations in VTCs provides important insights even for those familiar with the variations of other problem-solving courts. This is because examining how these courts, predicated on their participants' worth, assert their legitimacy provides additional insights into the disconnect between the common narrative and daily court practices, as well as the limits of law to "solve" entrenched social and political "problems."

THE SEARCH FOR LEGITIMACY

The seeming irrelevance of military experience in most regular VTC hearings is in deep contrast with the more explicit, often public, efforts to prove—that is, legitimate—VTCs to local stakeholders. Since treatment courts are not a constitutional given—thus not an automatic line item in a municipality's budget—courts need to maintain financial support in numerous ways. Treatment courts require extra funding because of the resource-intensive nature of case management, and funders may restrict who the courts can help (Hummer et al. 2024). The people who monitor participants' compliance with court-mandated treatments must be paid. Further, many courts have a paid coordinator to manage other aspects of the court, ironically such as its need for ongoing funding. Treatment courts must also seek resources from the community to help participants access services. If a participant is unable to stay sober on their own, for example, courts often seek residential treatment. If there are no beds available, then the participant is either going to be living in the community anyway or going to jail.

In these ways, treatment courts are, by definition, only as successful in helping a participant as their funding and access to local social services allows.

VTCs are unique in this regard, and important to understanding the different dimensions of social inequality in the US. Eligibility to Veterans Administration benefits mitigates concerns about access to social services as a general matter. However, an individual's access to VA benefits is critical in VTC operations, and variation between, and the court's knowledge about, individual VA health services within a given locale impacts VTC practices.

Further, VTCs, like all treatment courts, must seek legitimacy with the criminal and legal agencies they rely on. Public defenders, for example, may not like a treatment court if it means that defendants must comply with onerous requirements. Prosecutors may not like a treatment court if they think people who commit serious crimes can enter a treatment court to avoid other forms of punishment. Again, the common narrative helps ameliorate this tension because criminal legal actors who prioritize retributive outcomes may view criminal legal defendants who served in the military as less deserving of punishment.

Finally, the VTCs must legitimate themselves to participants. A veteran charged with a crime or with a criminal conviction could simply stay in the regular criminal legal system, facing a judge or jury to decide their guilt and their sentence (if not yet convicted) or go to jail or regular probation (if convicted). If a defendant lives in a location with multiple treatment court options, they may choose one—such as a mental health treatment court that does not require regular drug testing—over another—such as a drug court that does. Studies of other treatment courts reveal how judges selectively apply, blend, and transform elements from both therapeutic and legal settings in ways that contribute to dominant cultural scripts (Kaye 2013), and how judges blend discrete court roles such as parole officer and case manager (Castellano 2017). These studies require us to redirect attention from the judges who decide their own approach within the institutional constraints of a treatment court (Castellano 2017, 417) to the narrow definitions of problems they can oversee and interventions they can use (Leon and Shdaimah 2021). Treatment courts are necessarily hybrid, using different logics of punishment and rehabilitation (Baker 2013), dynamically managing risk (Talesh 2007), and using praise and shame as performance (Singh 2018).

The common narrative along with add-veteran-and-stir suggests that military culture is also central to the courts' legitimacy with participants (Russell 2009). In many ways, military culture is in the background—e.g., mentor recruitment and engagement, staffing decisions, and out-of-court interactions between participants—more than in the foreground of VTC hearings. However, my observations over a decade suggest the military culture in treatment courts relates more to resources that come from the fact that they serve veterans, not necessarily from camaraderie, loyalty, duty, or other values commonly ascribed to military culture. Further, I saw many examples of court personnel explicitly rejecting the idea that they should mention military service, as many participants do not identify positively with their time in the military.

The efforts of VTC personnel to legitimate themselves to these various stakeholders, and the complexities therein, make sense given there is little information to suggest that VTCs are any more useful to veteran participants than other treatment court alternatives (Edwards et al. 2019; Tsai et al. 2016). Recidivism studies of VTC participants and graduates mirror findings from drug treatment courts, which show that there is nothing particularly useful about a treatment court just for veterans (Hartley and Baldwin 2019). VA studies on recidivism rates following VTC participation range widely, from 2.5 percent to 56 percent (McCall, Tsai, and Gordon 2018). Studies on VTC participants reveal that the majority of participants (upward of 90 percent) appreciate VTCs. However, these studies are specific to a court's features, such as having a judge who is a veteran (Herzog et al. 2019). Other studies underscore that not all people who are offered VTCs want it; those who decline may be frustrated with the demanding requirements and do not see the benefit of it (Moore 2022).

The three courts I studied throw another wrench into the recidivism data while opening a different line of inquiry. The data does not start or end in the same time period but provides a snapshot of differences between the courts, and the challenge of comparison. By January 2025, Northeast had graduated its 83 participants since opening a decade before and was still going strong with nearly two dozen participants still enrolled. Over the course of my observations, I saw only a handful of terminations. Snapshot data from West in August 2020 shows 222 graduates since opening in 2013, with 60 terminations (where the person just stopped showing up), 81 people choosing to leave, and 55 current participants. Our data from Southeast is even more challenging to compare. Over two years of observations from 2018–20, we saw 25 people graduate and seven participants terminated out of 76 total participants.

These data illustrate the different sizes of the three courts, which may initially appear as related to the size of the counties each serves. Northeast's court serves about one-fourth of the population that West serves, so its smaller numbers correlate. But Southeast serves three times the population of West, yet it serves significantly less people in its VTC. This is largely related to entry rules and requirements, as this book explains.

The more interesting data is the termination and graduation data. West has graduated many more people, but it has also terminated many more people. Rather than see this as a failure of the court, my observations suggest that this difference is also largely related to their entry criteria. And these entry criteria are directly related to their founding, and how they established and maintained legitimacy with the various stakeholders needed for success.

Through examining how each court establishes and maintain its legitimacy, the differences between individual VTCs—in their goals, strategies, and outcomes—is less surprising. Understanding the differences between locales and the different ways in which VTCs interact with their own stakeholders and participants requires close attention to *how* these courts legitimize themselves. From funders to social service providers to criminal legal actors and to participants themselves, VTCs must use different strategies, incentives, and institutional structures shaped by their locales. These local differences help make sense of the contradiction outlined above: the strikingly different ways that the VTCs in the Northeast, Southeast, and West operate. These differences show how local politics shape criminal legal organizations (Lynch 2011; Lynch and Omori 2014), with individual court unfolding in a "concrete social and material setting" (Kohler-Hausmann 2019, 99) and outcomes reflecting creative decision making in response to interorganizational constraints. As an even more practical matter, it means that a veteran choosing to use a VTC, a mentor choosing to volunteer, or a policymaker hoping to fund one, may end up with a very different type of court than they anticipated. And, their ability to succeed in the program, however that is defined, will also vary.

STUDYING THE PURPOSE AND PRACTICES OF VTCs

The methods appendix at the end of the book provides more details on my data and methods, while here I provide an overview. Like many studies of courts, most research on VTCs is either very broad or very deep, comparing all VTCs on limited, usually discrete factors such as presence or absence of a mentor program, criteria for entry, or explaining a single court in depth. Comparative case study ethnographic research helps bridge these differences; using this approach, I spent significant time in the courts and therefore evaluate what a typical and atypical interaction is like in court. Despite the hundreds of hours I spent observing courts, it is difficult to develop generalizable theories from case studies, just as it is difficult to know whether an observed pattern in a quantitative analysis of more VTCs holds for any particular VTC. Although case studies cannot provide insights into all the VTCs in the country, the long-term comparative case study method for this book, with its focus on court processes, can help readers who are unfamiliar with treatment courts to better understand what the experience is like, and how it may differ, for people who participate in one.

This study scales up from my initial research on Northeast, which is where I first contemplated the common narrative and its limits (Rowen 2020). That case study revealed the importance of local context to understand how these courts work. I selected the VTCs in Southeast and West as comparative cases by using existing VA research on VTC variation (see Flatley et al. 2017) and my preliminary research in Northeast, finding that court demographics, entry rules, legal outcomes, and mentor programs are central to these three courts' practices. For example, I wondered if the close community I observed in Northeast was a function of its more rural locale, which also connects to its more racially homogenous population. In seeking other courts to study, I wanted to find courts that were serving a different population, one with more racial heterogeneity and more representative of urban populations, with access to social services in urban settings, that many treatment courts serve. I also wanted to find courts that had different rules related to entry and different incentives for participation (e.g., different outcomes), as my initial observations suggested that court practices reflected who was allowed into the court and what the court could offer them.

Table 1.1 explains several of these salient differences between the courts (more of the differences are explored in the methods appendix).

One important thing to note about the different courts is that they do not provide generalizable insights into the regions where they are located. Even if they provide important insights into VTC variation, Southeast is not a typical city in the southeast region of the US, nor is West a typical city in the western US (if there is a typical city to characterize these vast regions). Each court had dynamics specific to it, which may hold across all courts within a given region (Douds et al. 2017).

TABLE 1.1. Court differences.

Region	Geographic Context	Treatment Protocol	Legal Outcomes	Entry Rules–VA	Entry Rules–Criminal Procedure
Southeast	Urban	14 months, five phases	Reduced charges	VA eligibility required	Only felonies, pre-plea only
West	Urban	Minimum six weeks (misdemeanor) or three months (felony)	Reduced charges, reduced sentences, expunged records	No VA eligibility required	Felonies and misdemeanors, pre- and post-plea
Northeast	Rural	18 months, five phases	Reduced sentences, no expunged records	No VA eligibility required	Crimes carrying less than five-year sentences, post-plea only

Source: Data collected and reported by author

This book draws largely on the observations of three VTCs over a six-year period, but also includes multiple other sources of data to understand how VTCs fit into the broader landscape of the criminal legal system and social services. The observations provide a significant amount of information about what goes on in each of these courtrooms, offering a unique long-term account of how these courts operate. The team-based courtroom observations occurred over a five-year period (2016 to 2021), with observations of approximately 77 sessions in Northeast, 97 sessions in Southeast, and 37 sessions in West, for an estimated total of 316.5 hours (average 90-minute session). The methods appendix details additional data that I collected from the courts as background information, including staffing meetings, mentor meetings, case reports, and administrative data on outcomes. The pandemic disrupted these observations but not the analysis, which I address more in the appendix.

The bulk of analysis focuses on court hearings, in part for consistency (i.e., I have the same data on hearings for all three courts, but different data on staffing meetings and participants demographics and charges for the different courts), but also because my primary goal was to understand what goes on in these courtrooms and why. To answer this question, court observations were not enough. Thus, I conducted 72 one-on-one interviews with approximately 55 people—I interviewed the members of each court team multiple times—between 2015 and 2022 and engaged in many more informal conversations with people I met over the years. I first focused on interviewing court staff, then conducted interviews with a snowball sampling approach as I learned who was instrumental in creating the VTC in each locale. I also engaged in additional observations at meetings related to substance abuse recovery held at a residential facility associated with the Northeast VTC. Similarly, I observed and interviewed incarcerated veterans at a specialized veterans pod at a jail in the Northeast region (not affiliated with the Northeast VTC) in order to better understand substance abuse, mental health, and criminal legal involvement among veterans.

A critical part of my data includes observations of three large national conferences for drug court professionals, organized by the previously named National Association for Drug Court Professionals—rebranded as All Rise in 2023 to indicate the organization's expansion into other treatment courts and criminal legal reforms focused on tackling substance abuse.[1] These national conferences provided me with a wealth of information about treatment court practices. They offer a separate "track" for VTCs, with information on how to better serve their specific participants. They also have a "mentor boot camp" in which people who plan to volunteer as mentors or mentor coordinators learn about their roles. I attended a range of sessions that discussed issues facing regular treatment courts, such as sanctions and incentives, as well as those faced by VTCs.

Finally, to understand how VTCs are presented to the public, I also collected 156 local media accounts from 2016 to 2018 about VTCs in these three regions. I also gathered relevant legislation on military personnel and relevant policy documents about the creation and implementation of the courts.

To analyze the data, I used a grounded theory approach to construct three different comprehensive codebooks (one each for interviews, media accounts, and observations) about VTC purpose and practices, with the codebook for observations evolving throughout the course of the research. What emerged from this analytic process is an empirically grounded analysis of how and why these three courts function differently from each other. Each has a different understanding not only of how to solve the problems of veterans involved in the criminal legal system but also of the nature of that problem. The analysis thus reveals a broader story about how the actors working in these courts legitimate their work to themselves, to their participants, and to their broader stakeholders.

OVERVIEW OF BOOK

Each chapter in this book provides a different entry point to understand the politics of worth as evidenced by VTCs. The book is designed for readers interested in veterans but unfamiliar with the criminal legal system, as well as for those familiar with treatment courts but interested in what these particular courts tell us about inequality. This means that certain chapters may be more or less beneficial depending on the reader's background knowledge and interests. For those familiar with treatment courts, for example, chapters 2 and 5 may be more descriptive than needed to understand the overall analysis. The book's chapters are designed to be beneficial for readers with diverse interests, using VTCs to examine larger patterns of inequality in the criminal legal system while also providing practical insights to those who want to know how these judicial organizations can help people who served.

This introductory chapter provides a theoretical overview and the book's main arguments, which are further developed in the following chapters. Chapter 2 provides insights into criminal legal procedures to explain how treatment courts, as a general matter, operate. As that chapter illustrates, the word *court* in "treatment court" has a different meaning than it does in the common parlance, and even law and court scholars may find it illuminating to learn how these distinct judicial organizations operate. The background on contemporary practices and theories of treatment courts is important for understanding what is unique, or not, about VTCs, as well as why the three courts examined in this book operate as they do.

Chapters 3 and 4 explain the material and ideological foundations, respectively, that have supported the creation and proliferation of VTCs. Chapter 3 focuses on how, in the United States, social and political beliefs about veterans as a uniquely deserving population manifest in material resources that form the (often overlooked) foundation for VTCs. Most accounts of VTCs don't consider the VA's vital role in the rapid expansion of VTCs. The underlying logic for the VA—that veterans deserve public benefits that other people do not—mirrors the underlying logic of VTCs. More specifically, it is the social services available through the VA that has enabled the rapid expansion of VTCs. These courts were able to start a separate docket in the criminal legal system just for veterans because there is a ready-made treatment provider to help them.

Chapter 4 moves beyond material accounts of VTCs to argue that these new treatment courts reflect a broader dynamic in US culture about veteran worth, not simply their deservingness. This chapter builds from observations of national meetings related to VTCs, media articles, and interviews with VTC personnel (including judges, clinicians, and mentors). It opens with an examination of popular media representations of the military and those who serve in it. It then turns to what people working in VTCs say about veterans in these courts. The chapter focuses on the dynamics of nexus, which suggest that participants in VTCs are in the criminal legal system *because of* their experiences in the military. Personnel recognize that the emphasis on this nexus—that military service and criminalized behavior are directly related—is not clear-cut. Despite recognizing its limits, these personnel still draw on the common narrative to legitimize the courts to themselves, to participants, and to other stakeholders. This finding animates the second part of the book: the need to assert their legitimacy is crucial to understanding what goes on in veterans treatment courts.

The following chapters turn away from the national story about the general rise of these courts to the specific creation and implementation of the Northeast, Southeast, and West VTCs. They highlight how a person using one of these three VTCs may go through the same legal process as the two other courts but find themselves in a completely different program because of where they are located. Chapter 5 explains the day-to-day practices in the three VTCs and shows how they reflect both existing criminal legal infrastructures and the local social service infrastructures that predate the court's existence. For example, although the West VTC had access to the VA and an excellent team of clinicians for treatments, half of its participants couldn't use the facility or be monitored by VA-affiliated clinicians because they were ineligible for VA benefits. Also, this court did not require sobriety in the same way Southeast did. Finally, there was very little by way of community in this court; participants flowed in and out, asking only the judge or clinicians what they needed to do but not staying to talk to each other. By contrast, the Northeast VTC fits the common narrative. Looking at these differences, the utility of a sociolegal approach to the study of treatment courts becomes clearer, as do the limitations of studying court outcomes related to recidivism or cost-benefit, both common treatment court analyses. Each court understands and implements their retributive and rehabilitative goals in different, and sometimes contradictory, ways, and they serve different populations.

Chapter 6 then explains why these courts are so different from each other. In analyzing the three distinct locales, the courts' creations, and their access to resources, it reveals that they must continually legitimize their existence. While all problem-solving courts must engage in legitimation strategies, there are distinct challenges for a criminal legal organization that works so closely with a well-established federal bureaucracy, and serves a population already seen as worthy.

Chapter 7 shows the complexities of these legitimation strategies by zooming in on how participants who struggled with the court responded to efforts to get them to comply. These dynamics illustrate the difference between a court designated to a group deemed worthy in addition to one deemed less responsible for their criminalized behaviors. While the conflicts that emerged are typical in any treatment court that subjects participants to intense surveillance, the chapter provides insights into how the common narrative shapes day-to-day court interactions. It focuses on how the logic of gratitude—that these courts were created to express thanks to the participants for their military service, and that the participants should in turn be grateful for the opportunity to use a specialized court—plays out in judicial organizations that try to generalize about individual participants' needs and experiences, offer them different levels of resources, and make them feel indebted.

The conclusion, chapter 8, returns to the overall question that asks what VTCs tell us about political and social inequality in the US, while also providing practical takeaways for those working in or hoping to start a VTC. VTCs provide a unique lens into inequalities in the US, and the opportunities and challenges of blending two dominant domestic institutions—the criminal legal system and the military. Veterans treatment courts are the ideal of a responsive law that seeks to ameliorate barriers faced by poor defendants, and to solve social problems with services rather than litigation (Nonet and Selznick 1978). VTCs are deeply American institutions, reflective of our commitment to using law to improve material and psychological well-being. As the quintessential "response to social needs and aspirations," these types of courts can also erode the legitimacy of the law by being too malleable (ibid., 14).

VTCs help reveal the outsized role that the military plays in US political and social life, while also fostering a narrative about veterans in the criminal legal system that papers over inequalities that may push a person to join the military, the harms experienced in the military, and the harms experienced after leaving the military. VTCs may be helpful to some participants, as all treatment courts are. They may also amplify preexisting inequality by, for example, replicating VA policies that distinguish between worthy and unworthy veterans. The fact that these courts are so popular, and that they have resources that other treatment courts do not, is emblematic of the resources that our country devotes to the military. This has long been true with the availability of public support for veteran services related to health, housing, and education. Now, by blending the military and criminal justice system, the latter benefits from the legitimacy offered by the former. This creates a new assemblage of punishment that further normalizes the use of criminal legal strategies to address broader social and political challenges, while also reproducing hierarchies based on beliefs about the value of the military.

On one level, this book is about military people in the criminal legal system who face trauma or who suffer from substance use or mental health disorders, but the analysis of VTCs also seeks to offer a more nuanced reflection and critique of how the US helps (or doesn't) people who struggle to find and keep employment and housing and/or to stay sober in an increasingly unequal society where basic necessities, such as affordable housing, and resources to help people advance, such as education, are out of reach for many people.

Two

TREATMENT COURT BASICS

As usual at the Southeast VTC, the judge was taking a while to enter the courtroom. Participants sat on the benches, chatting as they waited. I could hear a discussion about medical marijuana between a current court participant and someone contemplating joining. The latter veteran used medical marijuana for his PTSD and was worried that the court would make him stop. The current participant was positive that would happen; he told of a veteran who got kicked out of the program because of an argument with the judge about sobriety requirements that wouldn't allow for medical marijuana. He then mentioned how the court really does help, but that relapses into drug use were common: "Just go through the motions [answering questions in hearings and attending treatment appointments] and you will be all right. Just know you goin' be peeing nonstop for the next year. Best drink your water."

The new participant, an older man, was finally called up to the judge's podium, and he spoke respectfully and carefully with the judge, who used the opportunity to introduce in detail what the court offered new participants:

> Good afternoon and welcome. Welcome to our program. We saved you for last to get a general idea of what we do here. This is an alternative to [the] normal court system; it is a treatment court. It is not about the merits of your criminal charge—we are here to provide treatment, not punishment. We welcome you into our program. Some say they want it,

but you have to do work to be successful. You deserve this; we are here
for you. [Public defender] is your attorney and represents you, and there
is a state attorney rep who will announce your ultimate result in [your]
criminal case upon successful completion [of the program].

The assistant state attorney then explained:

> [You are] charged with aggravated battery, no priors. We will *nolle pros*
> or dismiss, I did want to bring to attention, there is [a] stay away order.
> The alleged victim is [a] girlfriend or ex-girlfriend, so [that] order is still
> in effect. She is pregnant, so she may readdress or modify, but for now
> no contact.

The judge said that they would talk about the criminal case, and that the participant would discuss those details with the public defender:

> This is about your treatment; I don't want any violations. Focus now, we
> are here to help you and ready to move forward. The program is broken
> into phases, and in the beginning it's close monitoring and frequent
> testing. You will be assigned [a] case manager. He will set up a schedule
> with contacts and meetings. . . . [T]he VA will prepare plan for treat-
> ment and treatment component. We are all one team, to best serve you,
> for tools we think you need.
>
> This is all science-based, evidence-based treatment. People much
> smarter than me and understand mental health and treatment tested the
> way. There are rewards and sanctions increased in strength throughout
> [the] program, from simple compliments to picking out [a] gift box. For
> sanctions, it could be [a] warning from court, or it could ultimate[ly]
> lead to time in custody. It is graduated. That is the overview and the sci-
> ence, think positive and you will have a case plan as to what is expected.

The new participant appeared uncertain and overwhelmed, particularly
concerning the information he had been given about using medical marijuana.
As this was the end of the scheduled court session, and it was now past 5 p.m.,
the judge rushed everyone out of the room. The man wandered away without
talking to anyone he was supposed to, neither his assigned public defender nor
the state attorney. His confusion was palpable.

CLEARING UP THE CONFUSION

Like this participant, readers interested in veterans' services or criminal legal reforms may be unfamiliar with what a treatment court is, and whether the judge's description accurately captures the experience and "evidence" about it. This chapter offers an overview of how treatment courts emerged in the 1980s from efforts to address the growing numbers of criminal defendants with substance use and mental health challenges, as well as to ensure judges' discretion in light of mandatory minimums and other punitive policies. Although they blend elements of mental health treatment courts, which tend to have more individualized treatment plans and a different approach to sanctions, VTCs draw largely from the adult drug treatment court model, which is why this book suggests that VTCs add veteran and stir. This is one reason why, on a day-to-day basis, these three VTCs display little military culture; except for celebration days such as graduations, they seem like regular adult drug treatment courts.

Next, the chapter discusses what happens when a veteran decides to join a veterans treatment court, information that would help this participant or anyone interested in these distinct judicial organizations. In addition, this more general overview is important because understanding the generalities of a VTC provides a foundation for understanding the specific variations and deviations in the three VTCs described in this book. In this overview, the chapter also explains the basics of criminal procedure, information that is not always part of required classes in law school. This means that some lawyers, let alone any potential participant, will not know the ins-and-outs of how a person navigates the criminal legal system after an arrest, and why someone might choose to join—or decline to join—a treatment court.

TREATMENT COURTS IN THE CRIMINAL LEGAL SYSTEM

As a starting point to unpack the puzzle of treatment courts, including VTCs, the first thing to know is that they are part of the criminal legal system. People unfamiliar with the legal system will be confused about the differences between criminal law and civil law. The former involves prosecution by the state while the latter involves a suit between two parties. In a criminal case, the punishment for being found guilty is deprivation of liberty—usually probation or jail time—along with a fine paid to the court. In a civil suit, a defendant found liable (or responsible) pays monetary compensation to the plaintiff but will never be incarcerated. Furthermore, in a criminal case, a defendant must be found guilty "beyond a reasonable doubt," whereas in a civil case the defendant can be found liable by a preponderance of evidence, meaning it is more likely than not that the person committed the wrong they are accused of.

Next, the US criminal legal system involves both federal and state laws. In the US, Congress passes federal laws while state legislatures pass state laws. This means that an arrested person may go to federal or state court, depending on the law they allegedly broke. This relates directly to jurisdiction, otherwise known as the authority of a particular court. Federal courts typically oversee crimes that are considered especially serious and that occur on federal property or across state lines, but Congress is limited in passing laws that criminalize certain behaviors.

The Constitution gives the federal government limited powers while it gives states more open power to pass laws on wide-ranging subjects that include health, crime, and education. This means most crimes in the US are tried in state courts, and thus most treatment courts manage state-level crimes. People charged with federal crimes—such as tax evasion or money laundering—typically cannot access treatment courts at all. In 2023, there was only one VTC for veterans found guilty of committing federal crimes, so this chapter, and the book, focus on state- level treatment courts.

People trying their luck in a treatment court rather than in the regular court system are usually facing incarceration; avoiding incarceration is their incentive to choose court-supervised treatment for many months, living out in the world, rather than possible time in prison. States have their own rules about which crimes are eligible for treatment court, but people in treatment court are often accused of or have already pled guilty to a felony carrying the threat of incarceration, as compared to misdemeanors that, with some exceptions, do not. Felonies are categorized by degree, so a more serious offense faces a more serious punishment. Most states have mandatory minimum predetermined sentences—without the option of a treatment court—if a person pleads or is found guilty of a particular felony.

Treatment courts are the brainchild of a criminal legal reform movement, which was instigated by judges and others concerned about the incarceration of people using illicit substances in the late 1980s and early 1990s (Nolan 2002). The movement for treatment courts within the criminal legal system emerged with less of a focus on justice (e.g., reforming the laws that criminalized substance use was not the priority) and more of a focus on the extraordinary inefficiencies of courts managing huge caseloads of people suffering from substance use disorders. Moreover, with the rise of mandatory minimums—which are legislative directives on how judges must sentence individuals convicted of crimes—judges were also looking for more ways to exert discretion over case outcomes (McCoy 2003; Burns and Peyrot 2008). Drug treatment courts emerged in 1989, followed by mental health treatment courts in 1994, and there are now over four thousand (including drug courts, mental health courts, veterans treatment courts, and juvenile treatment courts) throughout the country (National Treatment Court Resource Center 2022).

Given its origins and trajectory, the movement to create treatment courts occupies a unique political space. While concerned about efficiency, the movement sees the criminal legal system as essential to addressing the public health and public safety crises associated with substance use in the US. Many people who promote treatment courts are critical of "tough on crime" policies while equally concerned about harm reduction and defund/decarcerate policies and proposals that do not adequately consider that people with substance use and/and mental health disorders languish and suffer without proper treatment (Burns and Peyrot 2003). For these reformers, it is a necessary evil to leverage the criminal legal system to compel substance use and mental health treatment.

The movement also occupies an interesting space as a site of social scientific inquiry, with different academic fields approaching the proliferation of drug courts with inherent skepticism and others interested in outcomes. Scholars critique the extensive surveillance in the courts, which can create numerous hardships for participants (Nolan 2010; Tiger 2012; Kaye 2020), while others focus on whether and to what extent the courts meet their goals such as sobriety and lower recidivism and, relatedly, how these courts influence the overall legitimacy of the criminal legal system (Casey 2004). Still others point out the seemingly arbitrary distinction between drug treatment and mental health treatment courts, whereby a person suffering from both or either issue may end up in a treatment court based less on their needs and more on which court is available (Gordon 2019).

Importantly, the treatment court movement benefited from the new theoretical framework of therapeutic jurisprudence that began in the legal academy. Therapeutic jurisprudence suggests that law can be a "healing agent" if used in the right way (Winick and Wexler 2003). The framework and policy reform fit well together and are mutually reinforcing, despite their questionable assumptions about the relationship between punishment and underlying causes of crime (Johnston 2012). Treatment court proponents use therapeutic jurisprudence both to explain their goal and as a standard by which to measure the success of VTCs and other treatment courts (Wexler and Winick 1996). Together, the theoretical framework and intervention of drug courts expands the role of the criminal legal system in US society and instrumentalizes the law in a powerful way by suggesting that criminal punishment, or the threat of it, can provide practical benefits to people facing legal problems and trying to overcome substance use and mental health issues.

Despite millions of dollars of investment by the federal government over the past thirty years, my observations and other studies reveal that treatment courts still suffer from trying to do too much with too little, the result of severely underresourced social services for substance use and mental health treatment. Indicative of this dilemma, when I asked a clinician in West what would help their court, she immediately replied, "money": more money for treatments, incentives to participate, to help participants access education and other life necessities (clinician, West VTC, interview). A variety of estimates suggest that drug treatment courts require $2,000–10,000 per offender, with an average of $4,000 (see Bhati, Roman, and Chalfin 2008, 38). Although this is far cheaper than incarceration, which ranges from $37,000–307,000 per prisoner per year (Carson and Kluckow 2023), that cost to benefit isn't usually what policymakers and funders are thinking about when they decide to support a drug court. After all, they are not tasked with allocating funds to prisons or courts but rather where to siphon resources for an extra probation officer or court coordinator. As part of their goal to improve court practices and prove their effectiveness, All Rise has spent significant resources studying the benefits of adult treatment courts. The result is that there may be few criminal legal reforms studied as thoroughly, despite concerns about how these studies *measure* treatment court effectiveness. For example, studies rarely provide information on whether participants avoid rearrest or remain sober long term (Wilson, Mitchell, and MacKenzie 2006).

Although the scholarship on treatment courts can be contradictory, studies show that, for some participants, treatment courts can be more effective than regular criminal courts at reducing recidivism rates (Marlowe, Hardin, and Fox 2016). However, the numbers are not as impressive as some proponents would like them to be. First of all, the lower rates only apply to participants who complete the court requirements, not all who initially opt in to a court, let alone those who are not presented with the option. Data presented in a 2023 All Rise conference on the *Second Edition of Adult Drug Court Best Practice Standards* by nationally known drug treatment court researcher Doug Marlowe suggests that providing supervision and treatment through a drug treatment court will bring recidivism rates down by 10 percent for those who complete treatment; courts following the model, which include regular drug testing and stiff requirements, had a 13 percent reduction in recidivism over traditional courts.

Moreover, despite the reformist goals of its adherents, the treatment court movement has not impacted the high incarceration rates in the United States. One challenge for treatment courts is that many seek to only accept people identified as high risk for criminalized behavior and high need, meaning they have a serious substance use problem and they can't do treatment on their own. Marlowe explained at the conference that drug courts reduce recidivism by 28 percent but only if only high-risk and high- need people are in them.[1] However, this challenge of "correctly" identifying who is "high risk" and "high need" illustrates the dilemma for these courts when trying to tackle something as complex as substance use with something as blunt as the criminal legal system. If a participant in a treatment court for many months is terminated because they struggle with treatment court requirements, and are returned to the traditional court system, they may be under court supervision longer than their original jail sentence or potential jail sentence would have dictated (Marlowe, Hardin, and Fox 2016).

Further, treatment courts not only reflect but also may perpetuate racialized inequalities in the criminal legal system, an issue that is doubly complicated for VTCs because of the racialized disparities in access to VA treatment (discussed in chapter 3). There is the well- known "pipeline" problem for racialized minorities to get into any treatment court, as they are accused disproportionately of federal crimes such as drug trafficking or gun violations or more serious felonies that make them ineligible for treatment court (O'Hear 2009). Racialized minorities do not have the same success rates when in treatment courts, likely because a person's success is usually a function of their social capital (e.g., housing, having a job) upon entering the court. In a comprehensive study of how many people are arrested for drug offenses versus how many successfully get into drug treatment courts, Cheesman, Marlowe, and Genthon (2023) found a 5.3 percent success rate for Black arrestees versus 20 percent for white arrestees. Marlowe reflected on these findings at the All Rise conference: "We have failed as a field and should be deeply ashamed. If we have an Achilles heel where [reformers would say we should be] pushed aside, this [racial disparity] is it. The time has come to take it seriously."

Despite these well-documented inequalities, at All Rise conferences, treatment court professionals reveal both their deep commitment to these courts and the seemingly insurmountable challenges they face. Treatment court professionals continue to embrace new models, such as VTCs, that take the premise of court-mandated substance use and apply it to new populations.

WHEN A VETERAN IS ARRESTED

This background on treatment courts underscores what is unique, and not, about veterans treatment courts. While drug treatment court eligibility depends on charges and substance use disorder diagnoses, veterans treatment courts add veteran and stir. This means that to get into a VTC, a person has to qualify for a treatment court *and* qualify as a veteran according to that court's definition, which might reflect federal law, state law, or its own selection processes. Here, I outline the process through which a veteran might enter a VTC depending on its rules.

As a preliminary matter, from arrest to conviction, it is challenging to identify veterans—regardless of how we define them—within the criminal legal system and funnel them into treatment courts. Although it may seem simple to ask someone if they are a veteran, varying definitions and an individual's comfort level identifying as one make this question largely unhelpful. Many states treat qualifying veterans—typically defined by state law unless in a federal court—differently from other arrestees, with the goal of helping veterans avoid a criminal record or other punishment. Recent efforts to compare how many people in US jails and prisons self-identify as veterans versus how many served in the military reveal a staggering gap. At the 2023 All Rise conference (previously known as the National Association of Drug Court Professionals conference, as explained in chapter 1) panel "Use the VA Veterans Reentry Search Service (VRSS) System," researchers presented results from a VA study on identifying veterans in the Massachusetts criminal legal system. It found that of those who took the survey, 240 self-identified as veterans but 690 were identified by VRSS as having served. There is an ongoing effort to encourage law enforcement to ask prior, during, and after any arrest if the person served in the military, which is to help identify those who may benefit from the growing number of programs designed to divert veterans out of the criminal legal system.

In a criminal legal process in which a person might end up in a veterans treatment court, the initial event is an arrest by police, who bring the person to the police station for booking. After booking, the person may be detained in jail, or they might be released with information about where and when to appear in court. Whether detained or not, everyone arrested is assigned to a specific courtroom, typically in a courthouse with multiple courtrooms, in the county where they were arrested. There, during their arraignment, they learn what the criminal charges are and what their options are. In this arraignment, a prosecutor, usually an assistant district attorney (each state's district attorney, or DA, is in all but four states an elected official in charge of prosecutions within a given locale, and they hire and assign assistant DAs to cases) decides whether to bring charges, or they may drop charges prior to arraignment. This is known as nonprosecution, because the prosecutor diverts the person from the criminal legal system before arraignment to ensure that the accused does not have a criminal record for that specific charge. However, most people who are charged are also arraigned. If they do not have the money to hire a lawyer and face incarceration (as opposed to a fine, for example) if found guilty, they are assigned a public defender who is supposed to explain their options for pleading guilty or not guilty. In some states, an accused can also plead *nolo contendere*, or no contest, which means that the person accepts punishment but does not plead guilty; thus, the charge cannot be used against them in a future case.

A treatment court may be available to a veteran charged with a crime "pre-plea," meaning after arraignment but prior to conviction, or there may be another diversion option. After arraignment, the judge will either set bail or the requirements to remain free from jail for the duration of the criminal proceeding. If the judge determines that a person poses a flight risk or is a danger to the public, the judge may set bail at a very high dollar amount or deny bail altogether. This means that the accused stays in jail for the duration of their criminal proceeding.[2] A major criminal legal reform over the past decade is the elimination of cash bail, whereby courts cannot put people in jail awaiting trial simply because they cannot pay. Further, in some jurisdictions, veterans await-ing trial in jail are in "pods," where they live with other veterans in spaces that are usually more comfortable and with access to the special services available only to veterans.

Some states have specific laws about arraigning veterans for certain crimes, allowing veterans to be diverted from the criminal legal system prior to ar-raignment. In 2021, approximately 2 percent of prosecutors' offices offered a specific diversion for veteran criminal defendants (Council on Criminal Justice 2024). In these laws, qualifying as a veteran may require more than enlisting in the military. In Massachusetts, for example, a law known as the VALOR Act enables someone who served in the military to avoid charges if the person received an honorable discharge; it also requires that they have no previous convictions as an adult, no outstanding charges in the US, and that the crime they are charged with carries with it the potential for incarceration. What is interesting about the VALOR Act is that any person who qualifies as a veteran under state law and meets the criteria of the criminal charge is automatically di-verted from receiving punishment through the court system to get treatment at the VA. Although the act is easy to apply, a qualifying veteran may be required to engage with mental health, substance use, anger management, or other psy-chosocial treatment they are not interested in. Like a pre-plea treatment court (explained further below), the person will have their charges dropped—if they comply with their treatment or other probation requirements. The availability of laws such as these shape VTCs, as VTC participants will be those who do not qualify for diversion options such as the VALOR Act, usually because of a more serious charge, the participant's prior criminal record, and/or their dis-charge status.

After the arraignment, the prosecutor negotiates with the accused's defense attorney to bring a case to trial, to dismiss charges outright, or to offer another type of option. Dismissals and trials are rare in the US, so most veterans in the criminal legal system will end up with a different outcome. Such options include a continuance, which means that the case is not resolved and can be reopened if the accused commits another, usually related, crime. Some states have intermediate dispositions, such as no contest or continuance without a finding, which allow a person to admit guilt, to go on probation instead of to jail, and not have a record of a conviction unless they violate the terms of their probation. However, the crime may show up on a person's record if they are applying for certain items, such as the purchase of a firearm or for educational benefits such as scholarships. Another option is the *nolle prossequi* (often referred to as a *nolle pross*), or "decline to prosecute," which a prosecutor can file for any reason but often because of a lack of evidence or if the DA decides that the prosecution is not in the interests of justice. Accepting a continuance or other nonconviction option may affect a future case because these dispositions count as a first offense.

Overall, criminal convictions come through plea agreements or the rare jury trial. Even rarer is a bench trial (meaning the outcome is decided solely by a judge). Plea agreements, therefore, are the most common way for cases to resolve. While federal trials nearly always settle with a guilty plea (90 percent in 2018), large states, such as Pennsylvania, Texas, and New York, have trial rates of less than 3 percent (Smith and MacQueen 2017). The rest of the cases move through the criminal legal system through dismissal, continuance, diversion, or plea agreement. There is great concern among law scholars, policymakers, and others that plea deals are coercive, particularly for racialized minorities (American Bar Association 2023). Even though trials are rare, the risks associated with them are high, so people may decide to plea to a crime rather than face a trial. And if a person is held in jail while awaiting trial, they might plea just to be released.

After a finding of guilt, whether through a plea agreement or a trial, a defendant is immediately sentenced with either probation or incarceration. Just as there are diversion programs specific to veterans, veterans also have unique due process rights in criminal trials that can affect sentencing (Merriam 2014). As of 2023, twelve states passed laws that enable the jury or judge to consider veteran status in sentencing determinations (Council on Criminal Justice 2024). In *Porter v. McCollum* (2009), the Supreme Court held that a defense attorney's failure to assert a defendant's combat history as a mitigating factor during sentencing amounts to ineffective counsel. Still, if incarcerated, a veteran may serve the entire sentence or might be released early. If released early, the veteran may then be on probation for a set amount of time. Being on probation means that the veteran is still under court supervision and may be returned to jail if they violate the terms of probation. Those terms vary but can include restrictions on movement, often within the area of the court's jurisdiction. It can also include regular drug testing if a person's charge is related to drugs. Post-disposition VTCs are part of probation, meaning that a person in a post-disposition VTC may be sentenced to incarceration if they are unable to comply with the court's requirements.

ACCESS TO A VTC

For a veteran to avoid potential incarceration by joining a VTC, the VTC team must allow the veteran in. To allow a person into a VTC, the court's team must answer three questions: Does the person qualify as a veteran according to the rules of that particular court? Is the person deemed "treatable"? Does the criminal charge make the person ineligible for the treatment court?

Beginning with the third question and working backward, treatment courts have their own rules as to which charges make a person eligible or ineligible. The idea is that a treatment court is a benefit, and thus should not be offered to someone who is a public danger or whose alleged crime deserves greater punishment. There are debates over the types of charges that should be eligible for treatment courts, such as admitting veterans accused of crimes like domestic violence, involuntary manslaughter, or other violent crimes (Luna and Redlich 2021; De la Peña 2024). Proponents of treatment courts say that domestic violence, in particular, may indicate underlying psychological issues that treatment can help, while opponents suggest that people who commit domestic violence should face harsher punishment than meted out by treatment courts (Kravetz 2012). These divergent opinions reveal assumptions about the point of treatment courts: some crimes have underlying issues that treatment courts can help, while others do not, and some people deserve this criminal legal option, and some do not.

Overall, understanding the myriad rules is important for evaluating a treatment court because courts that take people accused of different crimes are dealing with different underlying issues, and all the variations in entry rules create complications not only for veterans deciding to join a court but for the defense attorneys or other advocates recommending a veteran to join one. Entry rules depend on both the state and the specific court, which in turn is governed by state law or municipal law, and a court's own practices and preferences. Eligibility criteria heavily depend on stipulations established by outside funding sources and bureaucratic requirements, but typically require the charge to be for a crime that is probation-eligible (Hummer et al. 2024). Once a potential participant applies for VTC programming, the entire VTC team determines whether the veteran is suitable for the treatment court, injecting subjectivity into the acceptance process and allowing the VTC to serve its local population better. There are multiple options regarding if and how a nexus between the offending behavior and military service is established, which team member can establish it, and its implications for VTC participation. One challenge in this decision making process is the lack of resources and services available to address uncommon offenses, such as arson (Hummer et al. 2024).

In addition to the type of charge, treatment courts do not accept people who may not benefit from the social services made accessible from that court. As a result, VTCs typically require a clinical assessment to decide if a person has a qualifying substance use or mental health disorder. In fact, being diagnosed with both substance use *and* mental health disorders may be required. The idea here is to avoid accepting participants who have types of psychological challenges, such as psychosis or sociopathy, which a treatment court does not have resources to address. The VTC model stems from drug treatment courts, so the idea is that people who need treatment for substance use or mental health issues but have trouble completing treatment could be compelled to completion by a VTC, whereas people who may not need treatment should not be in a treatment court. This matches the approach identified above of enrolling only those "high risk," meaning a participant struggles to follow rules and may commit a crime, and "high need," meaning a participant cannot control their use of harmful drugs. Limiting treatment court eligibility to high-risk and/or high-need people narrows access to these courts, but accurately assessing such risk and need is a challenge.

Emblematic of the add veteran and stir approach to treatment courts, eligibility in a VTC also relies on how the court defines veteran. As noted in chapter 1, at the federal level, veteran refers to a person's discharge status, which directly relates to their ability to access benefits from the Veterans Administration. However, VTCs can choose the discharge status they are willing to accept. Many VTCs accept people who are not veterans as defined by federal law, meaning they most likely have no access to VA healthcare benefits.[3] However, limiting VTCs to honorably discharged or generally discharged veterans is a way to make sure that participants have access to VA benefits. It is also a way to avoid concerns, as chapter 4 will show, that only people who are "deserving or worthy" have access to this criminal legal benefit. Also as noted, some states have laws that allow veterans to automatically enter other types of pretrial diversion, which typically lead to charges being dismissed.

Those ineligible for a VTC because of their discharge status may choose to join a drug treatment court or mental health treatment court, if available; those ineligible for any treatment court because of their clinical diagnosis or (alleged) crime will go through the regular criminal legal process. This regular process is always the background threat in a treatment court, as the idea behind treatment courts is that they are "voluntary." In a pre-plea court, the regular process means all the steps between arraignment and up to conviction and incarceration. In a post-disposition court, the alternative for the participant is to face sentencing without the probation option of a treatment court, which may include incarceration.

CONSIDERING A VTC

Just as VTCs can choose to enroll a veteran or not, a veteran in the criminal legal system has choices too. For a veteran who thinks that they may qualify for any type of treatment court, the first question is whether such a court is even available in the area where the person was arrested. According to 2024 data from the federal government, only 10–15 percent of veterans have access to a VTC in the jurisdiction where they live (Council on Criminal Justice 2024). Despite VTCs' proliferation to over six hundred courts across the US in just a decade, there are still few to none in many counties. As of 2024, six states did not have a VTC (ibid). Given that there are about four thousand treatment courts, over three thousand of which are adult drug treatment courts, a veteran that would qualify for a VTC may be able to qualify for a different treatment court.

If a VTC exists in the jurisdiction where a person is charged, the veteran must know if they qualify for it, discussed below, and whether they want to join one. In some jurisdictions, veterans must self-identify as veterans to be considered for VTC programming. As noted above, several jurisdictions put systems in place, such as relying on the Veterans Reentry Search Service or through direct outreach to jails by Veterans Justice Outreach services, to independently identify incarcerated veterans and inform them of their criminal legal options. Another approach to finding veterans who may qualify is outreach to prosecutors and defense attorneys in these jurisdictions, allowing them to recommend the court to their clients and then file the paperwork to join the court (Hummer et al. 2024).

I observed many eligible veterans deciding whether to join a VTC, which provided insights into their myriad concerns about choosing a VTC over the regular court process. These potential participants would come to a VTC court hearing and, often, speak with the judge at the end of the hearing. No one ever directly asked the judge, "What will I get out of it?" But each judge often tried to answer that unstated, obvious question while telling them what they must do if they decide to join the court. I saw similar discussions when the judge and established participant were discussing whether the person should continue in the VTC or return to the regular criminal legal system. These decisions reflect the trade-offs that come with choosing to submit to intensive supervision with the potential of receiving a criminal legal "benefit" of a clean(er) criminal record or termination of probation (see Douds and Hummer 2019).

The important questions for a veteran considering joining or leaving a VTC depend on whether the treatment court is pre-plea or post-disposition because, among other things, the type of court shapes the so-called benefit of the court. In the example at the start of this chapter, the new participant was entering a pre-plea court, where both outcomes and incentives are different from those in post-disposition courts. In the former, in addition to having the charges dropped, it may be possible for the person to have their arrest records expunged if they successfully graduate from the court program, pay all court fees (or have the fees cancelled), and wait the required amount of time following program completion without any new arrests or convictions.

A person usually joins a pre-plea treatment court after arraignment, and they always have the option of using the regular court system instead, and taking the chance that they will avoid conviction without having to submit themselves to the requirements of a treatment court. This option is not available in a post-disposition treatment court. Another difference is that the prosecutor (as opposed to a probation officer) is involved in a pre-plea court. Joining a pre-plea treatment court requires an agreement between a prosecutor and a defense attorney to allow a person to join a court and, potentially, to have their charges dismissed. The prosecutor holds a lot of power in a pre-plea court to decide whether a person will be allowed to forego the regular criminal legal process and join a treatment court.

The incentives in a post-disposition court differ. In post-disposition treatment courts, a person cannot join unless they have already been convicted, typically through a plea agreement, and they are on probation (that is, not in jail). Their probation officer (PO) monitors their compliance with the terms of probation and court requirements. Outcomes and incentives will be different depending on locale. In some states, a person may be able to get their conviction expunged if they join and graduate from a treatment court. In New Jersey, for example, drug court graduates can bypass mandatory waiting periods for expunging records. However, the Northeast VTC is a post-disposition court, and, due to state law, expungement is not typically an option.

As with the different benefits offered by pre-plea and post-disposition courts, termination from the program means different things too. If a person fails out of or chooses to leave a pre- plea court program, the defendant will be returned to a regular criminal court to face prosecution; if failing or leaving a post-disposition court, they face sentencing.

PRACTICES IN VTCs

While there is some standardization of practices among treatment courts, and strong efforts by those who promote drug treatment courts to standardize further, there is also wide variation across the thousands of treatment courts in the country. Chapters 5–7 focus on what is different among the three VTCs under analysis; here, I discuss the many similarities of treatment courts in general. In part, treatment courts are designed from a model developed over many decades and promoted by All Rise, the national organization dedicated to adult drug treatment described above. The drug treatment model adheres to ten components or principles, which are also critical to VTCs. They include:

- integration of alcohol/drug/mental health treatment with judicial proceeding,
- use of a nonadversarial approach,
- early identification and prompt placement of eligible participants,
- access to a continuum of treatment and rehabilitation services,
- frequent monitoring of participants for alcohol and drug abstinence,
- coordinated strategies that govern court responses,

- continuous judicial interaction with participants,

- program evaluation to measure goal achievement,

- continuous interdisciplinary education for participants, and

- forging partnerships among drug courts, public agencies, and community-based organizations.

Even if a VTC deviates from this model, judges and court personnel have been trained in it, often directly by All Rise teams or by attending annual All Rise conferences. And, given the emphasis on these ten principles, many advocates and scholars reify the ten principles as they evaluate treatment court efficacy.

In part, this fidelity to the All Rise principles is related to funding. Treatment courts receive funding from federal, state, and local grants, and grants can require attendance at the All Rise meetings. Court practitioners interested in setting up a VTC can apply to the Bureau of Justice Assistance (BJA) for a federal grant to help with start-up costs. Federal funding for VTCs has grown significantly over the past fifteen years, creating more opportunities for court personnel to create VTCs. The BJA granted over $22.8 million to 19 courts in 2024, up from $20.8 million to 25 courts in 2023, and $17.8 million to 20 courts in 2022. Other opportunities to fund the courts can come from state legislation allocations specific to treatment courts or discretionary spending. In some states, such as Ohio, the money comes from state agencies aimed at a drug and alcohol abuse prevention and is distributed through county boards (Fox and Wolf 2004). Some court practices reflect funding, as grants may be given under the condition that the court only accept veterans with honorable discharge papers, or those charged with nonviolent offenses. Federal funding for drug treatment courts has, in the past, restricted eligibility to those accused of nonviolent crimes, but that restriction does not exist for the 2024 VTC solicitation. Federal funding may have other restrictions, such as rules restricting marijuana use that may deviate from laxer state laws and, on the other hand, rules requiring the option of medication-assisted treatment (MAT), or the use of regulated drugs proven to help people with opioid addiction, in courts that may be resistant to these approaches.

Although funding may determine certain practices, such as eligibility requirements, most practices stem from court rules. These rules also vary, sometimes dictated by state legislation but also due to decisions made by treatment

court founders (Douds and Ahlin 2019). Treatment courts are typically over-
seen by a presiding judge, who works in collaboration with a treatment court
team. The staffing selection process varies by municipality. It may be that the
judge volunteers to supervise the court, or an assigned judge is relieved of other
job responsibilities to enable them to work in the treatment court. Some VTC
judges preside over multiple treatment courts, while others oversee only the
VTC and spend the rest of their time on regular court cases. Along with the
judge, there is typically a public defender, who, as necessary, may advocate for
or against a particular sanction related to a participant's compliance. As noted
above, treatment court teams also include either a prosecutor from the local
DA's office or a probation officer, depending on if the court is pre-plea or post-
disposition, respectively. In a pre-plea court, the assistant DA plays a crucial
role in agreeing to divert someone's case to a VTC.

Personnel who are not trained in law are also required. This includes clinicians helping participants access social services or directly providing those
services. As chapter 3 explains, someone at the Veterans Administration usually
provides this clinical role to VA-eligible participants, but the court must fund
a clinician for those who are not VA eligible. Other personnel may include
a court coordinator, but not all treatment courts have them due to a lack of
financial resources. Coordinators manage the documentation, organize the
funding, and oversee the general administration of the court.

INSIDE VTCs

For a person who had never been in a courtroom, a treatment court would
look similar to sets from movies. As in a traditional courtroom, the judge is
at the front and center in the room, the prosecution (or the probation officer)
sits or stands in front and to the left of the judge, and the defense attorney is
on the right. Although it appears similar to an adversarial hearing, treatment
court teams are supposed to work in a collaborative way, deciding as a team,
for example, what treatments are required, whether a person is in compliance,
or whether a person should be graduated, sanctioned, or terminated. The judge
still has the final decision on graduations, sanctions, and terminations (e.g.,
failure to graduate and sent back into the regular court system), but the treatment court model emphasizes the importance of group decision making on the
extent to which the participant is meeting court-mandated goals.

In a first hearing, the judge may explain what a participant must do to graduate. Courts may have unique requirements depending on the person's criminal charges while some requirements apply to all participants. For example, if a veteran participant has a place to live, they will not need help finding housing, whereas an unhoused participant will. Following the national adult drug treatment court model, VTCs often require people to go through phases—the Northeast and Southeast VTCs had five phases, with each advanced phase having fewer requirements than the previous one, whereas the West VTC had no universal set of phases, in part because of the wide range of people and charges they accepted. The intensity of the program decreases over time, based on the idea that the participant will stabilize over the course of their involvement in the court. The drug treatment court model requires frequent hearings and drug testing, particularly when a person first joins the court. The hearings may be weekly or biweekly, with some courts having more time between hearings. The schedule is based on the court's resources, such as if judges have other dockets and thus cannot spend as much time in the drug court.

The hearings are open to the public, and much of this book focuses on what goes on in those hearings. However, much of what affects a participant's move forward to a new phase or to graduation, or to sanction or termination, happens before each hearing. Court teams typically meet privately in what they call "staffing" to discuss how each participant scheduled to appear in court that day is doing. If the person is complying with court mandates, the discussion centers on whether they can advance to a new phase. With team permission, a lawyer representing a particular participant may join the meeting to discuss their client. These meetings are not generally open to observers; for example, I didn't attend a staffing meeting at the Northeast VTC. Although I do not draw on the confidential information disclosed in these meetings, I was a regular observer in the West VTC's staffing meetings and observed one staffing meeting at the Southeast VTC only because there were visitors from the VA present and the judge decided to let me join them to observe. Decisions are typically made during these meetings as opposed to during hearings, which are more about checking in with a participant and not about deciding compliance in real time. When questions about compliance or noncompliance are discussed, this is when these meetings reveal how different teams prioritize and compromise around legal and clinical questions about how to serve a particular participant.

Participants never attend these staffing meetings, and only hear about the outcomes in court. However, if there is a determination of sanctions, a defense attorney may challenge the judge during the hearing and get evidence from those meetings. Further, if the judge and team are not sure about whether a person is meeting requirements—a frequent occurrence at the West VTC, where it was difficult to maintain communication with some participants—a judge may use the hearing to make in-the-moment determinations about incentives, sanctions, and progression through the program.

WHAT DO PARTICIPANTS HAVE TO DO?

After a person is deemed eligible for any type of treatment court, they may be allowed to observe a hearing to decide whether they want to join. They are assigned to a specific courtroom at a designated day and time. If the person decides to join the court, they may need to sign an agreement that gives away certain due process rights. There are many conflicting court cases over what rights a participant in a treatment court can waive. However, several rights are clear.

Joining a pre-plea court requires waiving a right to a speedy trial; joining a post-disposition court requires a person to consent to warrantless and random searches. All participants agree that the court can require them to dress in a certain way, avoid certain people or places, and get a job. Concerns about whether or to what extent treatment courts can infringe on other due process rights have led to a growing number of protections specifically for drug court participants, such as the right to a hearing in which participants have legal representation and can challenge evidence if they face termination from the program.

Within these blanket due process protections, individual VTC requirements vary, as chapters 5 and 6 make clear, but there are also commonalities because VTCs are modeled on the drug court model of graduated phases. VTCs typically require participants to successfully pass each phase, but deciding when a person is ready to move to the next phase is complicated. Courts may have set amounts of time for each phase, but All Rise trainers in a panel on "Best Practices" at the conference in 2023 emphasized that decisions should not be time-based. According to these trainers, the phases are designed to help people the court decides are not "clinically stable" to become stable. This means losing cravings for drugs as well as symptoms such as anhedonia (that is, feeling no pleasure in life). Later phases focus on both short- and long-term behavioral changes with the goal not only to help the participant stop using drugs but also to gain a fuller life, including employment and housing stability. For example, in Phase 1, a participant may be required to come to weekly hearings, with that requirement becoming biweekly in the next phase, and finally needing to attend court on a monthly basis in later phases. They may be required to attend frequent, even daily, individual or group treatment sessions at first, then fewer sessions as they move through the phases. They may also be required to find stable housing to advance through the phases. Some phases have defined lengths of time, which may be shortened if the person appears to be complying with no problems.

Beyond court appearances, the requirements depend on what services the court deems necessary and what a participant can access. For example, if a person is dealing with a drug relapse, a court may decide that the participant needs residential treatment, which is when the participant is living at a residential facility for a set period of time while receiving treatment for substance use. Given the limited number of social service providers that offer residential treatment, participants may be held in jail until a bed in a residential facility becomes available.

A veteran's experience in court hearings will differ depending on whether they are simple check-ins or include a phase advancement. A person may receive an incentive when they move from one phase to the next, typically a gift card or some noncash item useful to the participant. Praise itself can be an incentive, as are reduced requirements with phase advancement. During most of my observations, when a person advanced through phases, the judge encouraged everyone in the room to applaud. In VTCs, a common incentive is the challenge coin, as mentioned in the opening vignette in chapter 1.

Sanctions, given for noncompliance, are designed to increase in severity if a person is not meeting court requirements. Sanctions may start with a verbal admonishment, then move toward the participant writing an essay on what is expected and what they did wrong, then more time- consuming court requirements such as community service. If a person continues to use drugs or otherwise not comply with requirements, the judge can order time in jail. Sanctions are among the most controversial part of any treatment court, as participants may spend significant time in jail if they do not comply with mandates, such as sobriety. At the 2023 conference, All Rise trainers in various panels discouraged the use of jail as sanctions, saying it should only be for extreme situations when there are no other options, and the person is a danger to themselves or others. In practice, participants may spend more time in jail than initially recommended if the court cannot immediately secure a bed in an in-patient facility.

When a person meets all the requirements of the court and passes each of the phases, they graduate. Graduations may include cake and other symbols of celebration; they can occur for individuals or groups scheduled to graduate on the same day. Sometimes the graduations are formal events with invited stakeholders, as this book's opening vignette shows, or they are more low-key celebrations that resemble a typical phase advancement. As noted earlier, only the judge determines whether a participant can graduate and receive the legal benefit they want—dropped charges or termination of probation. A participant who graduates may also then choose to stay longer in the treatment court program. If the court or a person decides that they do not want to continue with the program, they are sent back to take their chances in the regular criminal legal system. Returning to a pre-plea court, they will again face charges and go through the steps outlined above. In returning to a post-disposition court, they may serve the sentence that was suspended or shortened when entering the treatment court program.

ADD VETERAN AND STIR: THE INSTRUMENTALIZATION OF LAW

The practices described in this chapter have evolved over decades of research and advocacy for adult drug treatment courts. Both the research and the advocacy have been aimed at explaining the value—their cost savings and participant impact—of these courts to policymakers and others interested in criminal legal reforms. These efforts have staved off some criticism that treatment courts are ineffective at best and harmful at worst. Those critiques still circulate, of course, especially among social scientists, because of the intense surveillance that these courts require (see, e.g., Tiger 2012; Hannah-Moffat and Maurutto 2012; Kaye 2020).

One central challenge is that treatment courts are only as effective as the treatment programs and social service providers to which they have access—a fact that, as the next chapter reveals, makes VTCs particularly appealing because of better medical care for veterans than other populations. For example, at a 2023 All Rise conference session led by Marlowe on the major research findings over the last thirty years, he emphasized how a clinical team needs to constantly reassess whether a drug court participant is being asked to do tasks that they simply cannot do. People at the court level around me muttered to one another that they simply do not have the capacity to do what he was suggesting. He repeated that people should not call themselves a drug court if they do not meet with participants at least twice per month, and that clinicians "should find a new job" if they cannot tell the court team whether or not a participant is experiencing cravings—suggesting they are not clinically stable and therefore should not be asked to be sober or be punished. However, that suggestion requires personnel, services, and money that may be unavailable to the drug treatment courts.

These sessions reveal how people in treatment courts try to use the criminal legal system to make up for a deficit in social services through a sense of mission that is distinctly American in its faith in law; specifically, the criminal legal system will solve difficult problems (Nolan 2009). At All Rise conferences, most sessions focus on the day-to-day court practices and improvements that practitioners should make. However, the speakers rarely talk about the broader, structural challenges that make treatment courts so ineffective for so many people: it is challenging and very resource intensive to treat substance use and mental health disorders. Audience members frequently ask questions that include how limited their courts are because they do not have enough resources. They articulate an awareness that this is not an ideal situation, but there are no other ways for people with substance use and/or mental health disorders without significant personal financial resources to get the kind of support offered by the criminal legal system.

Finally, treatment courts are in an even more challenging political position with the ongoing and necessary efforts to reduce incarceration rates, particularly for crimes related to substance use. If people do not have to worry about incarceration for substance use–related crimes, they are not likely to submit themselves to the intensive supervision of a drug court for many months. The pandemic amplified calls for decarceration efforts, and in response treatment court participation dwindled in many jurisdictions (Rowen 2024). For those hoping to keep people out of the criminal legal system altogether, this situation is welcome. For those concerned that people are still suffering from substance use and mental health disorders, even more than they were before the pandemic, lower levels of treatment court participation is not something to cheer about.

All of these tensions also affect VTCs. However, as the next chapter illustrates, VTCs occupy a unique position in the treatment court movement because of their relationship with the most comprehensive social service provider in the country: the VA. Further, as chapter 4 details, and as chapter 1 introduced, VTCs are designed for veterans, who hold a unique political position as a group of people seen not only as deserving but worthy of public investment. This means that VTCs illustrate a distinct dynamic in the instrumentalization of law, using the criminal legal system to solve entrenched social and political problems, because of whom they serve.

Three

THE DESERVING VETERAN

During a fall 2020 hearing, a participant in the West VTC mentioned getting "a life upgrade." At a hearing the previous spring, he told the court he had never used opioids before coming to the city eleven years earlier. He suffered a traumatic brain injury while serving in the military, then struggled while in the military, and had been dishonorably discharged and thus had no access to VA benefits. By the time he came to the West VTC, he had been living on the street for years, was addicted to opioids, and using suboxone to get sober. In fall 2020, he left the residential facility he was staying in and was frustrated with how long it was going to take to get into a court-mandated therapy program with restrictions on his movement. Nevertheless, the court personnel were celebratory about his progress toward graduation.

Why? Their optimism about this "life upgrade" was a change in his discharge status, which would give him access to VA benefits. With the guidance of a local organization dedicated to helping veterans petition the VA for discharge upgrades, the participant had proven he had a service-connected disability. Although access did not resolve many of the challenges he faced as a person suffering for years from homelessness and substance abuse, VA eligibility opened a multitude of drug treatments and new options to find housing.

Even with some scholarly attention to the role of the VA in the proliferation of VTCs (Button 2017; Edwards et al. 2018), the agency typically remains in the background of stories about the rise of these courts. Understanding the role the VA plays in VTCs offers insights into not only how VTCs operate but what these courts tell us about broader inequalities in the US. This is, in part, because the VA can reproduce and entrench inequalities through their ability to deny services to people with "bad paper" discharges. Further, understanding the VA shines an important light on American political and social history and state development (Mettler 2012). Veterans have long received social services—particularly medical services—unavailable to those who never joined the military, and services for veterans often pave the way for services for civilians. Despite many problems with those services, as VA scholar Phillip Longman (2012) notes in his book's title, the VA is "the best care anywhere," at least in the United States.

In explaining the development of VTCs within the broader institutional history of the VA, this chapter advances three claims. First, the institutional history of the VA reveals how veterans have been socially and politically constructed as a uniquely deserving *and* worthy group of Americans. VTCs have proliferated because of the mutually reinforcing material and ideological infrastructure that supports veterans with benefits unavailable to other groups. VTCs were not immediately accepted by the VA, which illustrates how the agency's initial concerns about partnering with the criminal legal system gave way to practicalities; in particular, aiding the most vulnerable people who served now makes VTCs appealing to the VA, and serving justice-involved veterans has created a slew of new funding for VA personnel.

Second, understanding the VA's own challenges with providing benefits to struggling veterans provides insights into how the add veteran and stir to the drug treatment court model yields complications: VTCs can access the VA's many services but are also subject to its many constraints. VTCs therefore reproduce, and may entrench, the disparities created by VA policies. The very definition of veteran in federal law is tied to who qualifies for VA services, which is directly related to their discharge status. Understanding VA policies can help explain some of the puzzles outlined in chapter 1, including how VTCs serve many people who do not technically "count" as veterans.

Third, by bringing the VA squarely into the criminal legal system, VTCs foster a new assemblage of punishment that legitimizes both the criminal legal system and the military in US politics and society (Hannah-Moffat and Maurutto 2012). The VA continues to clarify the distinct role it can play in VTCs, reiterating the institutional boundaries between the criminal legal system and the VA (see, e.g., Finlay et al. 2019). However, there is little doubt that the VA's expansion into the criminal legal system is a novel development that shows just how pervasive that system has become in channeling social welfare in US society, with the VA relying on it to help identify and aid veterans.

Overall, this chapter reveals that VTCs would not be as popular nor function as they do without a dedicated federal bureaucracy that provides an array of social services to qualifying veterans in the criminal legal system. The VA offers more than just healthcare; it also provides vocational training, short-term and long-term housing, and many other services. This means VTCs have access to more resources than other types of treatment courts. Yet, the add veteran and stir approach of VTCs can also limit their flexibility in mandating treatments that the VA does not provide. Providing social welfare and now criminal legal benefits, the VA's history illustrates contradictions of military service, specifically the reasons people join the military, the resources they need upon leaving the military, and the damage that military service can do to those who enlist. More broadly, the history illustrates how publicly funded social services are a material manifestation of social hierarchies based on who the government deems worthy.

THE VA: MATERIAL FOUNDATIONS OF VTCs

The early history of veteran benefits reveals how those who joined the military have systematically received public welfare benefits unavailable to others. The legal origins of this selective welfare state begin with the Disability Pension Law in 1792, which states that Revolutionary War soldiers "shall be taken care of and provided for at the public expense." With the 1818 Pension Act, former service members became the first federally classified class of individuals below the poverty line (Resch 1982). After the Revolutionary War, officers received $240 annually, and privates received $96 (271). With their newfound social and political status, veterans could mobilize for more public benefits, shifting payments from an emphasis on status in the military toward status for simply joining the military.

The US volunteer army quickly became a conscript army by 1863, and nearly one third of all Northern men were conscripted. In his second inaugural address in 1865, Abraham Lincoln pledged to "care for him who shall have borne the battle for his widow and his orphan," a call that continues to shape current social welfare policies aimed at mothers and veterans (Skocpol 1995). The Civil War changed the policy of distinguishing service members based on their professional status to equalize benefits across rank. Further, to incentivize soldiers to join the Union Army, the federal government created a pension program for veterans even before the war's end (Linkler 2011, 15). Next, the 1873 Consolidation Act enabled service members who contracted illnesses after the Civil War to receive compensation. In this way, the government began to recognize its responsibility to veterans for illnesses that were unrelated, or seemingly unrelated, to their military service, and to establish policies for long-term care. After 1890, disability and old-age pensions were paid quarterly from the US Treasury to all applicants who could prove they had been Union soldiers, as well as to others as dependents of soldiers who had died during or after the war (16).

In light of their policy wins, veterans continued to actively use the law for material benefits. Their services entrenched a unique relationship between the military and citizenship in US society, whereby large parts of the federal budget were earmarked for people who served in the military. As veterans mobilized for more services, their efforts succeeded in changing popular culture, making support for veterans a way to express nationalist sentiment (more in chapter 4). Relatedly, beliefs about veterans also became tied to beliefs about the righteousness of a specific war and the choice that people made to fight in it (Adler 2000; Linkler 2011).

These beliefs about what veterans do in the service are related to beliefs about what led them to join the military. The government's decision to support veterans was based on the fact these men had no choice about joining the Union Army. And yet the politics of veterans benefits became contentious, like the concerns today that VTCs offer an unfair criminal legal benefit to veterans. At the turn of the twentieth century, fiscal conservatives looked to scale back benefits so as not to resemble European socialism (Linkler 2011, 19). In order to attract recruits as much as compensate them for their service, in the mid-1880s the government offered transferable land grants to servicemembers (Ridgway 2013). This controversial benefit attracted little public support or veteran interest, but Civil War veterans were still able to more easily acquire land than nonveterans (151). President Cleveland was staunchly against funding pensions, vetoing 228 pension bills, including one that would have aided all former servicemembers regardless of disability. President Harrison undid Cleveland's fiscal policy in 1888, prodded by soldiers upset about the ongoing efforts to deny them benefits (Linkler 2011). Succeeding presidential administrations grew the pensions for servicemembers so that by 1900 half of the entire federal budget went to these pensions, a sum greater than the entire German military budget (Ridgway 2013, 166). Eventually, President Theodore Roosevelt enacted a policy to allow all older service members to receive pensions rather than rely on medical disability, which greatly expanded the system because nearly all Civil War service members were over age sixty-five (Linkler 2011, 21). By 1915, the pension system cost more than $50 billion, more than the inflation-adjusted cost of the Civil War, and was a critical tool for politicians to appeal to aging veteran voters (Linkler 2011; Skocpol 1993, 115).

These growing material benefits and broader cultural beliefs about the value of military service were mutually reinforcing. From these early days, the federal agencies doling out benefits distinguished veterans as worthy or unworthy, with impacts that still reverberate all the way to today's VA and VTCs. Rather than basing service member benefits on a pension model, the approach to veteran benefits was remodeled on workers' compensation (Linker 2011, 29; Gordon 2018). Yet, that compensation was also not typical in that it was not based on the actual job but on a particular understanding of *job performance*, thus linking beliefs about veteran worth to their discharge status.[1] Receiving a dishonorable or less than honorable discharge (more below), registering as a conscientious objector, or bearing an injury that resulted from willful misconduct could bar benefits. In addition, the government struggled to help those with long-term medical issues. After World War I, for example, tuberculosis was rampant, and the government offered expanded veteran benefits as an efficient policy to address the disease while limiting care to service-related injuries (Stevens 2012). By 1919, the majority of veterans with medical benefits had long-term medical issues, not combat injuries. Notably, 3,800 had been diagnosed with neuropsychiatric conditions (Adler 2000, 96). As the benefit system grew to help more veterans with more types of injuries, the structure had to change to accommodate the 4.5 million soldiers who returned home at the end of World War I (Adler 2000; Linkler 2011).

In the early 1900s, leaders across the political spectrum supported benefits for veterans to pacify a group of people seen as more deserving—and more capable of using firearms—than others. Veteran benefits grew despite political opposition to socialism, largely because of concerns about veterans facing unemployment from the economic unrest in the early twentieth century. After World War I, politicians wanted to discourage veterans from joining the burgeoning socialist movement that was actively recruiting former servicemembers, so the government focused on helping them find jobs in the industries and places they worked prior to enlisting (Adler 2000; Jennings 2012). Reflective of broader inequalities in US social welfare spending, racialized inequalities in VA care became further entrenched. Sometimes, this was regardless of the federal agency's intentions. For example, even if the VA could support vocational training for all veterans, regardless of race, it could not force employers to hire racialized minorities (Keene 2012).

The cultural beliefs about the value of the military and concurrent material benefits grew as the US took on a greater role as a military power (Obinger, Peterson, and Starke 2018). Reformers in favor of expanded benefits for veterans made efforts to change the pension policies by glorifying war and linking it with masculinity, military service, and courage (Linkler 2011, 25). At the same time, the government wanted to be efficient in doling out benefits. In 1921, Congress merged all World War I veterans' programs—the Bureau of War Risk Insurance, the Public Health Service, and the Federal Bureau of Vocational Education—into the Veterans Bureau. Among the government's many goals in creating this behemoth organization, financial efficiency loomed large. The Bonus Army march on Washington, DC, in 1932, where tens of thousands of soldiers showed up to demand bonuses that they were promised for their service, revealed the political power that veterans could wield. Congress ultimately authorized the payments over presidential veto. Yet, previewing its later foray into the criminal legal arena, the Veterans Bureau sought to ensure that servicemembers were not wards of the state by creating policies aimed at helping veterans acquire skills for gainful employment.

After World War II, the most famous social welfare bill in US history, the "Servicemen's Readjustment Act of 1944," otherwise known as the G.I. Bill, was passed. Though simultaneously reflecting and reinforcing persistent racial inequalities in the country—by design, the bill was enacted through racially discriminatory state policies (Delmont 2022)—the educational benefits helped remake the US into a geopolitical powerhouse and cemented aid for veterans in federal policies. Writing in *Military Affairs* in 1945, Lawrence Kubie asserts: "No one will doubt that the medical care of veterans is a government responsibility. No one sees in this the specter of socialized medicine" (114). Emblematic of the growing connection between material resources and popular narratives about veteran worth, the G.I. Bill fully realized the idea that veterans deserve a multitude of benefits for joining the military.

Further, around the same time as the G.I. Bill was helping veterans returning from World War II, the concept of trauma emerged as a potent political construct (Fassin and Rechtman 2009). That construct is central to the common narrative that veterans have unique needs that a unique court focused on them can address. Accepting that military service was potentially traumatic, the VA expanded its services to veterans dealing with a wide range of psychological and physical challenges. Still, illustrating the politics of worth in this growing government agency, after World War II the government struggled to determine who should qualify for benefits. President Eisenhower, despite his military experience, wanted to limit benefits to those who had injuries from their service. The Bradley Commission, which he put together to determine benefits after the Korean War, emphasized that military service should be something that is part of citizenship rather than something that merits benefits simply for doing it (Boulton 2012). These midcentury debates contributed to policies that gave less and less funding to veteran services just as socioeconomic inequality in the US began to skyrocket, and the failed war in Vietnam left thousands of US veterans without either the material or social supports they needed.

SOCIAL SERVICES ARE NOT ENOUGH

In many ways, the creation of VTCs and their practices flow from the social and political fallout from the Vietnam War. Over several decades, the government shifted its approach of treating suffering Vietnam veterans as unworthy of public benefits to recognizing and responding to the various challenges they faced. By 1972, more than three hundred thousand veterans had physical or mental disabilities attributed to that war. Later, hundreds of thousands more registered for services related to post-traumatic stress disorder (PTSD) or Agent Orange exposure. They also suffered socially upon return as the war became increasingly unpopular in the US.

After Vietnam, the rise in and the visibility of the homeless veterans—stark signs that the war abroad contributed to domestic social inequalities—shifted political and social understandings of what the VA should provide. The growing acceptance of trauma as a medical condition contributed to the belief that an individual who was "broken" by their service needed to be made whole again, with the help of the government. In this politics of worth, people who had served should receive social welfare benefits unavailable to others with potentially similar medical issues but ostensibly different causes for them.

This politics of worth also reflects unequal social policies related to US military engagements abroad. Whereas the post–WWII G.I. Bill created numerous educational and vocational opportunities for returning veterans, there was no comparable support for those servicemembers returning from subsequent wars in Korea and Vietnam. Part of the challenge in passing new legislation for veteran benefits was the well-documented corruption arising from the G.I. Bill. In debates specifically about Korea vets, a 1966 bill died, prey to disputes over who "deserved" the benefits: those who enlisted or those who experienced combat? Without adequate provisions for those who suffered in fighting, military personnel returned with high need and little support (Boulton 2012).

This multitude of challenges facing returning Vietnam vets and the growth of the carceral state created a perfect storm for veterans to slide further into socially disadvantageous positions. Beginning in the 1980s, and in correspondence with the rise in homelessness when the US stopped investing in mental health residential facilities, the country experienced an exponential growth in incarceration rates. These rates largely correlate to Ronald Reagan's War on Drugs, manifesting in grossly disproportionate incarceration rates for communities of color. In the 1980s, racially minoritized veterans were particularly at risk of incarceration, but veterans as a whole were overrepresented in the prison system (Bronson et al. 2015; Holliday et al. 2023).

By the new millennium, the revolving door of incarceration, homelessness, and military service was clear enough that the federal government decided to act. Despite the VA's size and influence, over 80 percent of US military veterans do not use it as their primary source of healthcare; if not ineligible, many veterans have access to private healthcare through their employment. Veterans who rely on the VA tend to be younger, are more likely to be female, Black, non-Hispanic, and of lower socioeconomic status, and often have more severe mental and physical health problems relative to VA nonusers (Meffert et al. 2019). These populations tend to be more at risk for criminal legal involvement as well; veterans ineligible or not using VA healthcare are at even higher risk, and the VA wanted to help them.

For decades, veterans have been disproportionately represented among homeless populations, and being unhoused is directly correlated with high rates of criminal legal involvement and suicide (Tsai, Pietrzak, and Szymkowiak 2021). In 2001, the VA began to focus on identifying incarcerated veterans and addressing the challenges they face in accessing benefits while detained in jail or prison and upon reentry into society. In 2007, the VA created the Health Care for Reentry Program, designed to connect veterans leaving jails and prisons with social services. The goal was to offer preventative and restorative services, because the VA recognized that poverty and substance abuse were leading to veterans' criminal issues.

At the time, however, the VA was only working at the periphery of the criminal legal system. In part, this stems from the fact that the VA offers behavioral health services that the organization has wanted to distinguish from approaches designed to address risk factors for criminal legal involvement (Blonigen et al. 2017). Yet, as PTSD emerged as a formal mental health diagnosis in the 1980s, and the connections between military service, trauma, homelessness, and incarceration received more political attention, the VA turned toward new approaches to aiding veterans it had not been directly servicing.

THE VA EXPANDS INTO THE CRIMINAL LEGAL FIELD

The VA's creation of a specialized program for incarcerated veterans coincided with the emergence of the VTC movement. Many scholars and advocates point to Buffalo, New York, as the first VTC, an origins story that permeates understandings of VTCs. However, founded in 2008, the Buffalo VTC was not the first court to treat veterans as a unique group worthy of criminal legal support (Edwards et al. 2019). The first court to set up a special docket was in 2004 in Anchorage, Alaska (Smith 2012). Alaska has the highest number of veterans per capita due to the state's small population and the presence of military bases in the state. Thus, it is not surprising that a judge in Anchorage was the first to respond to what he believed to be a growing number of veterans with substance use and mental health challenges in the criminal legal system.

The origin of the Anchorage VTC illustrates the critical role that the VA played in facilitating this new specialized court. After proposing a special track for the growing number of veterans in the criminal legal system, the Anchorage court's founders had to wrestle with the challenge of creating a court that would require extra resources. A judge in the city's municipal court system volunteered to staff the court, but the district attorney's office refused to participate because it viewed the court as an unfunded mandate (Smith 2012, 97). The fact that the VA had services available helped legitimate the court to those worried about finances. The Anchorage VTC served only veterans accused of misdemeanors, so those accused of felonies could not access this benefit. The court did not last beyond its initial mandate, it did not document its practices, and it received little press coverage. As a result, it is often forgotten as being the first standalone veterans treatment court in the country (Edwards et al. 2019).

Five years after the Anchorage VTC started, Judge Robert Russell, from Buffalo, New York, set the VTC movement into real motion. Judge Russell was elected to the bench in 1991 after working as a federal prosecutor. He founded Buffalo's drug treatment court in 1995 as well as a mental health treatment court several years later. As he tells it, he became concerned about the number of veterans in his courts, but one experience, in particular, inspired him to think about creating a separate docket for veterans (Russell 2009). Jack O'Connor, a founding member of the Buffalo team and now a nationally known advocate for VTCs, explained to me what is by now a well-known account of how this court started:

> There was a Vietnam vet who came in mental health court, always mumbled and the judge would talk, he wouldn't look [the] judge in [the] face. [The j]udge asked if me and [the] coordinator would talk in the hallway. This man, a Vietnam vet, just wanted to talk to other vets, he trusted Vietnam vets.
>
> *(Jack O'Connor, interview)*

Judge Russell often retells this story (I heard it most recently in his presentation on VTCs at the 2023 All Rise meeting), noting that both this participant and Jack were Vietnam-era veterans. Although the participant was attending his therapy appointments, he did not appear to be engaged with them, and Judge Russell hoped that the vet speaking with Jack might help the participant in that regard. When Russell recounts the story in public forums such as All Rise meetings, he describes being "pleasantly surprised" that his strategy worked.

The story of this particular veteran is often recounted in interviews and trainings about the origins of VTCs, yet the role of the VA is less well known. When the Buffalo court began a special docket for veterans, there were no substance treatment options just for veterans. According to Jack, neither he nor Judge Russell knew if the VA would be interested in providing services to participants in Russell's drug treatment court. As luck would have it, Jack was a board member of the local VA hospital, and he and Russell asked the local VA to help this defendant access services there. Jack retells that, after three sessions, the defendant returned to court and said, "Judge, I'm going to do better." That is when Judge Russell decided to start a separate docket for veterans, to be held on Tuesday mornings. What was an ad hoc response to a single vet's need led to a national movement that has institutionalized VTCs in the national and local criminal legal landscape.

Through the dogged work of Judge Russell and his team, the Buffalo VTC became famous. Russell, now retired, is somewhat of a celebrity in the treatment court community. His lectures at the All Rise conferences are standing room only, and his warm smile and enthusiasm for VTCs is palpable. At the 2023 conference, his talk focused on "restoring hope" to veterans, speaking with deep passion and conviction about how VTCs help veterans.

Ironically, the respect now shown to the Buffalo VTC was hard-won; New York's trial court system did not initially support the effort, and neither did the VA agency. According to Jack:

> [The] VA was the worst provider, never answered questions or got back to us. I called the VA up; they wouldn't talk to us. We wanted a computer and a workroom in court, I went to the VA director, he laughed so hard I thought he'd pee in his pants. No federal agency is going to put a worker on a secure computer in a criminal court, it wasn't done before, and he wasn't going to do it.

The VA's initial resistance to working with VTCs may seem surprising given how actively engaged it is now. However, federal agencies are not nimble, and can take a long time to change course. For example, they are subject to both budgetary constraints and federal regulations, making it difficult for them to create new programs quickly. This is why it is surprising how quickly the agency's initial resistance turned into an, albeit cautious, embrace. In telling the origin story of VTCs, Judge Russell emphasizes the importance of having the VA involved in a local criminal court: "I want to tell you, that is major to send us one of your federal employees to come weekly to a local state court."[2]

Tenacity, of course, had to be matched by luck. A former colleague of Jack's,

Bill Feely, was then the VA deputy undersecretary in Washington, DC, under VA Secretary James Peake. Feely had been in his position just seven months. According to Jack, someone from the Buffalo veterans community called Bill to ask about the program. Bill said, "Put a worker in there [Russell's courtroom] and do it now." Jack explained:

> It all started under Bill Feely. . . . I don't think any other undersecretary would have approved [our request]. We got the VA to go to meetings, and the [Buffalo] court finally opened in January 2008. At the time, there was an advisory board at the VA. Judge Russell asked if they wanted to be mentors. All twelve volunteered.

Judge Russell also credits Peake for creating a temporary position within the VA to help with VTCs, and the following VA secretary, Eric Shinseki, for making the position permanent. This was, according to Jack, how the VA became involved with the criminal legal system.

Even with the VA supporting the Buffalo VTC, the court still had to gain acceptance from local criminal legal actors. According to Jack, "Judges hated it, cops hated it, thought we were giving veterans a get out of jail free card." This skepticism soon dissipated with national media attention. The first news article was by National Public Radio, which articulated the common narrative that the participants in the court experienced war, and implicitly suggested that those experiences are relevant to the court's decision making. The article told the story of a VTC participant who stated that their marijuana use, and the two pounds discovered in a police sweep, was related to PTSD and a medical discharge from the military. NPR made clear that the Buffalo VTC was working with the local VA, highlighting a partnership between these two disparate organizations and bringing legitimacy to this new court (Lewis 2008).

In creating a new judicial organization, Judge Russell had to seek legitimacy with more stakeholders than just the VA. Russell carefully grounded the VTC model on the well-established drug treatment court model that he was trained in. In another example of the add veteran and stir approach, Russell adopted the NADCP ten principles when defining the principles to guide his VTC (see chapter 2). He modified them only insofar as to emphasize that for substance use disorders, VTCs would seek treatment for both mental health and combat-related mental health disorders, not solely substance use treatment.

In this way, he helped create a hybrid form of the treatment court model that usually distinguishes mental health and substance use disorders. Adding veteran and stirring, Judge Russell emphasized the need to integrate the VA into these new adult drug treatment courts, as well as the importance of involving veteran peer mentors (Edwards et al. 2019).

Two years after the Buffalo court's founding, the *New York Times* published an editorial by a former-Marine-turned-state-court-judge, who explained how valuable this new court model was:

> Because the courts are reserved for veterans, they serve as a recognition of past service and an effective way to reawaken the service members' pride, discipline and courage, critical elements in helping many resolve their problems. It helps, too, that the veterans are in the program with one another, fostering a sense of camaraderie.
>
> *(Castille 2010)*

The op-ed also mentions that treatment can be provided by the VA and by community-based organizations, highlighting the material foundations that make VTCs so appealing.

These media articles stressed the common narrative about why VTCs are being created: to help veterans whose criminalized behaviors appear directly attributable to their military service. The narrative mollified concerns about a "get out of jail free card," the extra expenses associated with creating a new drug court, or that the law requires all criminal legal defendants to receive the same treatment (Jones 2014). Soon, judges around New York State were contacting Judge Russell to share their insights about the court. Jack suggested in our interview that the local police "changed their tune" after seeing the court's success, which he explained as including not only graduation from the court but also fewer veterans living on the street.

A NEW PUNISHMENT ASSEMBLAGE

The VA's integration into the criminal legal system through VTCs created a unique blend of social services and criminal courts, illustrating the interdependence of the criminal legal system and social welfare organizations (Hannah-Moffat and Maurutto 2012). What is notable is how quickly this assemblage gained political support through both the appeal of criminal legal reforms to address entrenched social and political problems and public support for veterans' benefits.

The VA's foray into the criminal legal system began with a glaring social and political problem: veteran homelessness. Despite decades of veteran homelessness, the agency's homeless program is relatively new. It developed, published, and began implementing its strategic plan only in 2010, in line with the federal government's efforts to combat homelessness. A year prior, in 2009, the Veterans Justice Office began as part of the VA's Homelessness Program, with the goal of diverting veterans from incarceration and into treatment before sentencing. The Government Accountability Office report on the VJO's origins and activities explains that "[a]ccording to a program official, VA has associated the VJO Program with 38 U.S.C. § 2023, and the language in 38 U.S.C. § 2022 is believed to be broad enough to authorize much of the program's operations" (GAO-16–393, VA's Veterans Justice Outreach Program, p. 6). This statute, 38 U.S.C. § 202, provides for the "coordination of services for veterans at risk for homelessness." In other words, the VA viewed the problem of homelessness as deeply intertwined with criminal legal involvement, choosing to direct resources toward VTCs as a way to mitigate homelessness. By 2019, there was a separate congressional statute authorizing direct funding for the VA to work in VTCs, the "Veterans Treatment Court Coordination Act."

The VJO's initial goal was to identify veterans in the criminal legal system as a way to help them access benefits. It wanted people who were service-connected—meaning with discharge papers that enabled them to access services—to use those services to break the cycle of homelessness and incarceration. Program employees are called veterans justice officers (VJOs), which metaphorically also blends criminal legal and military terminology. VJOs have social work and counseling backgrounds, and many responsibilities. VJOs focus on vets who have encounters with law enforcement, are incarcerated in local jails, are involved in VTCs, and on the reentry and/or probation needs of veterans exiting a VTC (Tsai et al. 2018). The Veterans Justice Office began with a focus on jails, where social workers or others with clinical training were to identify service-connected veterans.

But, by the early 2010s, VA staff were aware of the growing VTC movement and wanted to be active participants. The first Veterans Justice Office director,

Sean Clark, explained that the VA viewed itself as central to VTCs and advocated to be a part of the movement:

> It took a lot of careful explanation and messaging on our part to get across what can be a pretty complex message that we need to have a seat at the table for programs like veterans treatment court to be successful.
>
> *(Sean Clark, interview)*

With the establishment of VJOs and the growing number of VTCs, the add veteran and stir approach to drug treatment courts took hold. VTCs gained not only the political legitimacy that comes with providing social services to veterans but also the necessary resources. Drug court proponents, specifically the National Association of Drug Court Professionals (NADCP), the predecessor to All Rise, immediately seized on the opportunity to create more VTCs around the country.[3] In 2010, Justice for Vets emerged as a separate branch of the NADCP. By 2020, Justice for Vets had forty-five consultants available to help jurisdictions interested in creating VTCs. In all three VTCs discussed in this book, judges and court personnel mentioned receiving training from Justice for Vets, whether it was staff who came to their communities to provide information on VTC practices, or mentors learning about mentoring, or for all involved in founding or working in VTCs to attend All Rise conferences and learn from VTC presenters. The slogan for Justice for Vets includes "When Thank You Is Not Enough," tapping into the broader narrative that veterans are owed more than they receive, and that additional VTCs can help repay the debt.

The federal government offered broad support for these developments. President Obama expanded the VJO program as part of new federal programming. Both first lady Michelle Obama and second lady Jill Biden made veterans a policy priority, and VTCs were an innovative way to reach particularly vulnerable veterans. In 2010, the National Drug Court Institute (NDCI; which provides technical assistance to drug courts) and the Bureau of Justice Assistance (BJA; which administers federal funding for treatment courts) launched the Veterans Treatment Court Planning Initiative (VTCPI). This initiative funded, popularized, and standardized the growing number of VTCs. The pilot training program was conducted October 4–8, 2010, back in Buffalo, New York. This was a collaborative effort of several national organizations and VTC professionals.[4] The training consisted of presentations, group breakout sessions, and a visit to the Buffalo VTC to observe case discussions and hearings.

Given the institutional status of the VA as a federal agency, this new assemblage of punishment carries with it a distinct level of legitimacy and also creates enigmatic dynamics for local courts. In VTCs, courts must follow VA rules, not the other way around. Yet, funding for VTCs goes through the courts; the VA simply provides support in the form of a VJO and treatment services. One implication of this dynamic is that participants in VTCs who receive their benefits through the VA have more access to treatments and other benefits, such as housing, but they are also doubly disciplined by both the VA and the court. This enhanced partnership may explain an important research finding that VA-eligible participants in VTCs spend more time incarcerated than do their veteran counterparts in other types of treatment courts (Tsai et al. 2016). More effective case management also means more surveillance as VA case managers may be more successful in detecting noncompliance with court protocols. With VA resources, VTCs are unique in the panoply of problem-solving courts designed to bring social services into the criminal legal system; they may offer more treatment options and material incentives compared to other courts, and they may be more invasive.

MAINTAINING INSTITUTIONAL BOUNDARIES

The unique relationship between VTCs and the VA creates specific challenges for both the courts and VA health centers, as well as for the broader institutional structures in which they operate. In contrast to individual providers that a drug treatment court might rely on for substance use or mental health treatment, such as locally run community health centers, the VA is a rigid bureaucracy. Further, its institutional history and nature mean that the VA holds a level of authority and influence that judges may not be used to. For example, a VJO from the Southeast VTC explained these dynamics: "Courts have a lot of power, but we [the VA] are a federal, government institution, so they do not have a lot of power over us" (VJO, Southeast VTC, interview).

The VA insists on maintaining institutional boundaries so as not to compromise its own legitimacy with policymakers and patients who see it as a social service provider and not a criminal legal actor. In an interview, Sean Clark, the first national VJO director, explained his approach to walking the fine line between maintaining institutional independence and centering the VA in VTC planning and implementation:

> [The] VA needs to be a part of it [VTC]. But we are a guest, we need to be invited in, we need to build and maintain that relationship over time and we want to be sensitive to the fact that we as the VA are there as a treatment provider and we are not there as an arbiter of court operations or local criminal justice policy. We are there as a resource. We are there to enable them, we are not there as the setter of standards for these courts, we are not a criminal justice actor.
>
> *(Sean Clark, interview)*

To this end, VA researchers have collaborated with the Veterans Justice Office to put forth their understanding of the role that the VA should play in VTCs, which is to avoid legal recommendations in favor of simply a clinical role (Finlay et al. 2019). This is a boundary for any clinician in a treatment court, but it carries a distinct valence for clinicians employed by a bureaucracy with a complex web of internal clinical processes.

Further, although the VA specializes in care for veterans, individual VA health centers have mixed reputations that can affect the legitimacy of an individual VTC in the eyes of participants or those trying to help them, such as mentors. In recent years, the VA has avoided congressional efforts to privatize its services, in part based on concerns that its wait times and services were considered substandard. The few VA employees I spoke with did not mention this directly but instead alluded to concerns about maintaining the VA's reputation as the preferred treatment provider for VA participants. A VJO working with the Southeast VTC, which is served by a VA hospital with a mixed reputation in the community, explained:

> I think we obviously prefer that the veteran comes here as opposed to the community [providers]. Because they are veterans and that's who we are here to serve. That is also because some of the treatments that are here––as far as let's say post-traumatic stress disorder and military sexual trauma––we have experts in the field here whereas in the community, I'm not really sure what the trauma work is like or what kind of background the providers have. Here we get trainings all the time.
>
> *(VJO, Southeast VTC, interview)*

Even if the VA can provide better care than a local social service provider, there are numerous complexities that emerge when working with a federal bureaucracy. While all clinicians working in the criminal legal system have to balance competing objectives related to punishment and care, VJOs have a distinct dilemma of translating VA policies to the court system. VJOs are employed by the VA, so they must consider how their work on behalf of VTC participants affects other VA clients. The Southeast VJO explained: "It can't be one person is going to the program faster because he's in jail right now. Whenever we do a training or anything, I always say we can't expedite treatment" (VJO, Southeast VTC, interview).

Another VJO explained a common conflict for clinicians in treatment courts with regard to balancing what they see as a patient's best interest when the patient has violated court rules. This VJO contrasted being a reporter with being a therapist, saying that they may not "report" to the court because of the conflicts that could arise given their own ethical duties as therapists and their organizational duties as VA employees. Castellano (2011) discusses this challenge in regular treatment courts, where clinicians are "dual agents" serving different and sometimes contradictory goals. For VJOs, this dynamic is compounded by the VA's turgid employment regulations and treatment options, described further below. Since any treatment court is only as effective as the social services it can help participants access, establishing a good working relationship with the VA is extremely beneficial for a VTC (and increasing support for VTCs can mean more money for the VA). This dependency gives added power to the VJO in clarifying what the VTC can and should mandate for a participant accessing VA services.

Although there may be good reasons for the VA to actively support VTCs, that support should not be taken for granted. Despite its robust services, the VA is also resource-strapped compared with what it is asked to accomplish. This means that adding VTCs to its responsibilities is not a minor action. The VA regularly receives negative press for long waiting times, high turnover, and many job openings that are difficult to fill. VTC participants who access the VA require a significant amount of VA resources because VTCs often require weekly therapy and intensive outpatient or residential drug treatment. This means that VA buy-in is critical for a VTC, and that the VA pays attention to whether or to what extent its services are being utilized equitably among veterans as well as most impactfully. VTCs help VA locations meet their mission of providing care to veterans, including identifying people who may qualify for discharge upgrades, but the courts also increase the burdens on them.

These added burdens are being addressed by more funding for VJOs, which creates additional interdependence between the criminal legal system and the VA. In 2018, Congress passed the Veterans Treatment Court Improvement Act, which requires the Department of Veterans Affairs to hire at least fifty VJO specialists for the Veterans Justice Outreach Program. Per the law, each of these specialists must serve as part of a "justice team in a veterans treatment court or other veteran-focused court." A specialist hired under this bill must be placed at a VA medical center that complies with VA guidelines for specialist placement. The VJO specialist must work within a local criminal legal system, maintain an affiliation with one or more VTCs or other veteran-focused courts, and provide or establish a VA-approved plan in order to serve as part of a team focused on veterans in the criminal legal system. Although the Veterans Justice Office program was created independently of VTCs, this act illustrates how the program and VTCs have become more intertwined over the years. Funding for VJOs is now based on the presence of VTCs, just as the presence of a VTC is closely correlated with the proximity of a VA health center. In this way, VTCs have solidified a new assemblage of punishment.

ENABLING AND CONSTRAINING VTCs

The VA continues to play a central role in developing the VTC movement at the national level by enhancing the movement's legitimacy and contributing to knowledge about VTC effectiveness. The VA conducts comprehensive analysis of VTCs' abilities to help participants, though the agency is limited by the fact that they can only assess VTC effectiveness for VA-eligible participants. In addition to general dissemination of research, VA researchers are highly active at All Rise annual conferences, which bring together thousands of practitioners from around the country to discuss drug treatment courts.

Over the past decade, the conference has developed a specific track for VTCs, with presentations about up-to-date research on VTC practices as well as other programs dedicated to training mentors. VA personnel feature prominently on panels to discuss their research as well as strategies to better integrate the VA into local treatment courts. These national conference presentations make clear that the VA is deeply involved with the design and implementation of VTCs. At the 2023 All Rise meeting, for example, VA staff provided multiple trainings on how to address issues such as drunk driving, equity, and VA technology to better identify veterans who are involved in the criminal legal system. One notable presentation by a VA clinician and researcher focused on the importance of VTCs to help participants with less than honorable or general discharges to petition for benefits because they may be wrongly denied. In all of these talks, it was clear that the VA sees itself as critical to VTC practice because VTCs are working with veterans in need of social services.

The conference also provides insights into the problems that can arise from the close relationship between the VA and VTCs, including ongoing threats to the legitimacy of both the VA and the criminal legal system to support veterans in need. One common concern is that the agency cannot meet participants' needs because of VA policies that differ by locale. In a 2021 panel titled "VA Community Care Program: Mission Act," for example, an owner of a private rehabilitation center lamented publicly that most VTCs avoid using private treatment centers in favor of the VA. However, he noted, each VA medical center operates as an independent "fiefdom." To this, the crowd in the room nodded in agreement. He explained how the VAs in the two counties that his center serves are completely different, with one requesting his center's services and the other refusing to release a veteran to their care. He wanted to know:

> It seems inconsistent, and I'm trying to see, how a provider like me or you can gently push back without pissing someone off.
> *(conference participant, observation)*

This public complaint about the differences between VA medical centers reveals VTCs' ongoing need to figure out how to serve participants when there are VA constraints. VTCs must continuously negotiate to access the services that they mandate of their participants, particularly the resource-intensive inpatient treatments for participants dealing with severe substance abuse.

These examples suggest that the presence of a local VA is an enabler, allowing VTCs to rely on them for access to medical care that participants would be unable to attain elsewhere. This may help explain why VTCs are most likely to be created where there is a local VA health center (Easterly 2017). Yet the VA also constrains VTCs, as the agency's rules and the institutional logics behind those rules limit what VTCs can mandate. Further, although VJOs work in a regimented federal bureaucracy, they also must be fluent in the policies of their local VA healthcare center. In addition to knowing what treatments are available, those who do not work exclusively in VTCs must navigate their multiple responsibilities also toward veterans who are in jail or otherwise involved in the criminal legal system.

The complexities of VA healthcare rules can cause headaches for VTCs, as later chapters point out. While there are obvious conflicts between the logics of an organization focused on social services and the logics of an organization in the criminal legal system, the issue is even more complicated because the VA is a federal agency while VTCs are local. This flips the typical power dynamics between a court and a community healthcare provider with fewer resources but potentially less constraints than a federal agency.

For example, I observed frequent disagreements, particularly in West and Southeast VTCs, over VA requirements for inpatient treatment in which the participant stays overnight in a treatment facility. Even if the court team agreed that the participant would benefit from inpatient treatment, it had to follow the VA's policies related to graduated treatments. One clinician explained their concerns about inpatient treatment the following way:

> I have no control over the policies explicitly stated here, for example, that you need to start with the least restrictive level of care possible.
> *(clinician, Southeast VTC, interview)*

If a court mandates inpatient treatment that the VA will not provide, court clinicians must adapt to these constraints by either shifting their own requirements or using other community social service providers rather than the VA for inpatient treatment.

Furthermore, the power of the VA in providing treatment for VTCs means that the treatment court model designed to prioritize risk and need is subsumed by VA policies. For courts that require participants to have VA eligibility, access to the VA trumps risk and need. Moreover, the common narrative that VTCs are uniquely beneficial for all veterans because of their shared employment experience and the camaraderie that these courts offer goes against the growing effort to delineate people's treatment needs and criminogenic risks, and to funnel veterans who aren't high risk and high need out of the criminal legal system altogether.

THE ELEPHANT IN THE ROOM: DISCHARGE STATUS

As detailed so far in this book, the VA acts as a constraint on VTCs through its rules about which participants can access VA treatment. This affects VTCs on every level. For starters, requiring VA eligibility affects who a VTC can accept. VTCs increasingly recognize the dilemma of accepting only VA-eligible veterans, because this constraint leaves out people who may need drug use or mental health treatment the most. It also makes it impossible to measure the success of VTCs when there are such uneven levels of care depending on whether or not a participant has access to the VA.

Because of the VA's eligibility requirements, the add veteran and stir approach to drug treatment court makes VTCs vulnerable to a complex bureaucracy that reflects and reinforces the very social problems that VTCs are designed to address. VA eligibility is outside of the court's control: when a person transitions from active duty to veteran, they receive a discharge status related to the conditions under which they left the military—typically honorable, general, other than honorable, or less than honorable. Discharge status is complicated and highly relevant to the study of VTCs because the same challenges that make someone eligible for a treatment court—either substance use or mental health disorder or both—can lead to a less than honorable discharge. A less than honorable discharge can be for behavior that does not rise to the level of a court-martial but is still considered egregious. In the military, this can include illicit drug use, fights, and drunkenness (and during the era of Don't Ask, Don't Tell, engaging in same-sex relations) (Gordon 2018). There is also a shameful correlation between military sexual trauma and less than honorable discharge status (Thompson 2016; Nichter et al. 2022). Eligibility criteria for VA services are not static; federal laws have steadily expanded access for veterans, but discharge status still forms hierarchies among people who served.[5] The dilemmas caused by these discharge policies have received national attention, and there has been a national response. The first Trump administration, for example, passed a regulation enabling all former servicemembers to receive access to mental healthcare for one year after their service ended, regardless of their discharge status.

However, there are still hundreds of thousands of Americans who served but are ineligible for certain or all VA benefits. Veterans with General discharges do not receive education tuition benefits, and veterans with Other Than Honorable (OTH) discharges may not be able to access any VA benefits (38 C.F.R. § 3.12). An estimate from 2020 suggests that over 500,000 individuals who served in the military are not able to access VA benefits (Harvard Law School 2020). One result is that VTCs required to accept only participants with VA eligibility are inaccessible to those most in need of social services, which, in addition to harming a range of veterans, compounds the racialized disparities found in the criminal legal system because of the racialized disparities associated with unfavorable discharge statuses. Studies from both the Government Accountability Office and the Department of Defense show that racially minoritized servicemembers are more likely than their white counterparts to face investigations and disciplinary hearings that result in unfavorable discharge statuses (Cancelmo et al. 2025, 4). Black servicemembers are particularly affected by this disparity and are 1.5 times more likely to have an OTH discharge than their white counterparts (Connecticut Veterans Legal Center 2022). When the VA requires VTCs to accept only VA-eligible participants, it perpetuates explicit hierarchies among those deemed "worthy" of this criminal legal option.

Even if VTCs decide to accept participants who are not eligible for VA benefits, the differences between VA healthcare and other community options still create internal hierarchies. Disparities in the quality of care between facilities serving the West VTC, in particular, were striking. The judge lamented how much nicer it is for those in a VA residential facility where there is a view from the top of a building in a private room versus a bunk bed in a dark building at a non-VA facility. After years of watching their non-VA-eligible veterans struggle more than their VA-eligible veterans, the West VTC began to collect data on how VA access influences court outcomes (i.e., examining whether being VA eligible makes one more likely to graduate from the court) to hopefully access more court funding to improve options for all participants in their court.

These rules on VA eligibility serve as constraints on the courts in other ways. For one thing, someone in the courtroom must have specialized knowledge about the VA in order to know what a participant can access. This knowledge is not always available, even when a VJO is present (Foley and Rowen 2022). For example, to be eligible for benefits, a person must serve in the military for twenty-four continuous months, or the "full period" they were supposed to serve, but there are exceptions. A veteran may have access to VA-sponsored housing vouchers, for example, but not have access to VA healthcare because of their discharge status, length of service, or military branch.[6]

Having staff who know these requirements and exceptions would be helpful for potential participants considering joining a VTC because a person who
may appear ineligible for benefits might be able to access them. In addition,
the OTH discharge status, for example, is supposed to come with a written
comment from the Department of Defense as to whether the veteran should
have access to benefits. In a presentation at All Rise in 2023, "How to Reduce
Veteran Suicide by Helping Veterans with Other-Than-Honorable Discharges
to Obtain VA Services," VA researchers pointed out that the majority of these
discharge papers have no notation, meaning that thousands of veterans may be
eligible for benefits but don't know it.

This section illustrates the distinct opportunities and challenges that come
with the add veteran and stir approach to treatment courts. The VA has positioned itself as central to the VTC movement, but it has contributed to challenges related to whom the courts can and should serve, and how. Further, as I
show later in this book, courts must quickly establish trust with their local VAs
to help their participants, and courts that accept all veterans must also attend
to the challenges of helping those not eligible for VA benefits.

COMPOUNDING INEQUALITIES

The history of servicemembers' welfare benefits reveals the complex synergies
between the criminal legal system and the VA's massive federal bureaucracy.
Parting from the common narrative, this chapter suggests that what distinguishes VTCs is not necessarily the unique match between a group of people
who joined the military and a court that understands them; rather, it is access
to the best publicly funded social services in the country. Like VTCs, the existence of the VA reflects the unique treatment of US veterans, with beliefs about
veteran worth shaping the expansion of benefits, and the expansion of benefits
shaping beliefs about veteran worth.

The history of the VA also reveals how social services have been used as a
form of social control to manage people who return from the military who are
emotionally, socially, or politically disconnected. As the US engages in ever
more conflicts abroad, veterans have increasingly suffered with the fallout of
returning without the requisite level of social services. In these ways, the VA's
history illustrates broader inequalities in the US while also offering insights
into differences between treatment courts. Local VA health centers have dif-

ferent interpretations of rules about who can access benefits, which benefits they can access, and how those benefits are administered. Furthermore, individual VA medical centers have unique relationships with their communities; some have good reputations among veterans in the area while other centers are viewed with skepticism.

Regardless of the capacities of local VA health centers, the remarkable number and nature of VA services underscores how the United States has invested in those who join the military, deeming them more deserving of benefits that other social groups. VTCs are one more manifestation of this societal support for those who join the military. It is far easier to justify creating a VTC in a local jurisdiction when it does not require additional material resources. Moreover, in theory (and thus one selling point in creating VTCs), the availability of services through the VA makes it more likely that eligible veterans will succeed in accessing treatment and other necessary services. These veterans may receive payments for service-related disabilities, as well as have special access to home loans, education stipends, housing vouchers, and other public benefits that no other group can get. These benefits contribute to the common narrative that veterans can be rehabilitated through courts in ways that distinguish them from those who did not join the military.

By examining the origins of the VA within the origins of VTCs, this chapter illustrates the political and economic contingencies of VTCs, specifically the courts' legitimacy stemming from being associated with a federally recognized social category—veterans—as well as the VA's role in fostering the common narrative that veterans are uniquely deserving of US public benefits. At the same time, however, not all veterans are considered deserving: only those with certain discharge status can access benefits. The delineation of the status of honorable and of less than honorable discharge is a starting point to understand how societal notions of veteran "worth," not simply deservingness, shape VTC practices.

With their original goal to rehabilitate individuals with military service history, VTCs presented a unique opportunity for the VA to enter the criminal legal field. However, this new connection between the VA and local criminal legal system can entrench intersecting inequalities. The VA and its predecessor departments have always defined and reinforced the divide between so-called worthy and unworthy veterans, just as the unique benefits for veterans reinforce broader understandings about so-called worthy and unworthy members

of US society. Even courts waffle between celebrating the military and im-
plying there is something criminogenic about it. Those celebrating VTCs as
uniquely beneficial for a uniquely worthy group of people ignore how structural factors across America directly relate to the decision of someone to join
the military. Most people who join the military come from lower socioeconomic backgrounds than those who attend college and enlist in order to develop professional skills and/or help pay for college (Lutz 2008; Gade, Lakhani
and Kimmel 1991; Mankowksi et al. 2015). Enlisting is a "means to an end,"
with that end—professional stability and/or success—potentially unrealized
(Mankowski et al. 2015, 320).

Further, people who joined the military, the same people who ultimately
end up in VTCs, have similar struggles as those in the criminal legal system
who did not enlist (Culp et al. 2013). Yet, the differences between them include
the professional training and, depending on their discharge status, the material resources and social services that come with VA access. These statuses also
stratify individuals based on each person's ability to be effectively disciplined
by the military. Discharge status directly relates to the structural issues influ-
encing people to join the military in the first place, and the struggles they may
experience before serving, while serving, and after leaving service. Most explicitly, just as racialized inequalities are entrenched in the criminal legal system,
similar inequalities manifest in the military.

More generally, examining the origins of both the VA and the national
VTC movement illuminates the process through which this treatment court,
with its add veteran and stir approach to the drug treatment court model, facilitates the spread of the criminal legal system into US politics and society.
As Hannah-Moffat and Maurutto (2012) argue, "assemblages" involving community organizations illustrate the "co-existence and assorted combinations of
punishment, welfare, treatment and preventative practices that exist in local
penal fields" (202). This argument suggests that the entry of organizations
such as the VA or other medical providers into criminal legal settings does not
change the nature of punishment. Rather, it "reassemble[s] practices of welfare,
treatment and punishment and ha[s] given rise to new and disparate forms and
logics of punishment" (203). One illustration of disparate forms and logics is
that the presence of a VTC does not necessarily map onto a community's need;
counties that adopted VTCs between 2004 and 2014 were more likely to have a
local military base, a local VA hospital, greater VA compensation expenditures

per capita, and lower crime rates; additionally, they were likely to have a higher per capita income, a larger minority population, and a smaller veteran population than counties without a VTC (Button 2017).

Bringing the VA into partnership with courts lends legitimacy to VTCs and draws the VA more directly into the criminal legal field, with financial interdependence deepening as funding for VJOs increases. Penal logics related to efficiency, self-government, and individual responsibility align well within the VA, meaning that this combination of institutional fields enhances what Hannah-Moffat and Maurutto (2012) articulate as the "continued and intertwined emphasis on disciplinary strategies of change, dependency reduction, welfare provision and the treatment of pathologies" (212). In just one example of these intertwined institutional logics, the VA has been exploring how therapies designed to reduce criminal legal involvement, namely Moral Reconation Therapy (MRT), can be integrated into their behavioral health services that did not previously focus on criminal legal involvement (Blonigen et al. 2021). Another way to understand this assemblage is through the concept of "creep." Adams and Murray (2014) discuss "mission creep" when addressing the increasing role of the military in US foreign policy. Thinking of this new assemblage as "institution creep" focuses attention on the broader field-level changes that VTCs represent.

As the next chapter further illustrates, VTCs are built on a mutually reinforcing ideological and material foundation, supported by social service benefits that only (some) veterans can access. The VA and VTCs build up the broader narrative of veteran worth while providing additional legitimacy to criminal legal interventions that address entrenched social and political problems related to substance abuse, mental health issues, and poverty . . . and war.

Four

CREATING THE COMMON NARRATIVE

Ideological Foundations of VTCs

At a café on a busy street near the courthouse temporarily hosting all hearings for West's VTC, lawyers and case managers and police officers mingled over their late morning coffee. Personnel seemed relieved to see one another in a setting where they could relax and made small talk rather than address the heavy challenges they face daily. Across the street, the county's superior court was bustling. Prior to arriving at the café, the court coordinator and I had already had a busy morning. In the VTC courtroom we were observing, we heard a fight in another courtroom between detainees, and watched the security personnel in our courtroom run out to break it up. From another courtroom, we saw a woman yelling angrily, with her dog cowering nearby, that she had been told to go to the wrong courtroom. Court staff told her to retrieve the frightened animal. The court coordinator in charge of the city's veterans treatment court told the woman not to "take her anger out" on her dog.

The coordinator visibly relaxed in the café and started talking about that morning's VTC session. "That guy," the coordinator said, "if we could just help that guy, it would all be worth it."

"That guy" referred to a participant in the morning hearing, a young man who had served as a medic in the military but with an unclear discharge status—meaning uncertain VA benefits. The man was gentle and smiled deeply when he talked about how much he missed the military. He slurred his speech and appeared mentally impaired, which he explained in court was a result of a brain injury he received as a medic, and which had not been properly treated. The man asked to read a letter to the judge. In it, he said that he was ready to get the help he needed to graduate from the program. He explained that what he most needed was structure for his day: the kind of structure he had in the military. The judge asked in a variety of ways what kind of help that would be. The young man repeated that he needed a job. The judge, following the advice of the man's case manager, told him to go into residential treatment for drug use. It was not what this young man had in mind, but he acquiesced to the recommendation and thanked the judge, calling him "sir." The judge reminded him that he wasn't his military superior but that he was pleased to receive this kind of respect after delivering bad news.

This vignette illustrates two elements in the common narrative: (1) veterans are different from criminal legal defendants who did not serve in the military, and (2) VTCs are uniquely beneficial for veterans, primarily because of their ability to integrate "military culture" into their practices. Through illustrating how variation in VTC eligibility shapes access, a few VTC studies address the first element (Rodriguez 2024; Baldwin and Hartley 2022), while the second element lingers in the absence of research suggesting that VTCs are uniquely beneficial for veterans. Yet, the suggestion that veterans might be "undeserving" is taboo not only in applied VTC research communities but also in community groups where I have discussed this research, as many scholars view the query as denigrating the sacrifices that these military personnel made.

This notion that veterans are different than other criminal legal defendants relies on the narrative about the uniqueness of veterans with regard to why they are in the criminal legal system and how they behave in court. Usually, the common narrative is presented as a given truth, something that the audience— whether those interested in veteran issues, treatment courts, or policy making— should immediately understand. Some VTC proponents explain the narrative in a defensive way, suggesting that these treatment courts are not giving special treatment to veterans and that military service does not contribute to criminalized behaviors. A central way through which VTC judges and court personnel (e.g., clinicians) legitimate themselves to participants and others is by drawing on societal beliefs about veteran worth.

Building from previous chapters on how veteran benefits and beliefs about veteran worth mutually reinforce each other, this chapter explores how beliefs about those who join the military are rooted in societal beliefs about the value of military service and, by extension, the value of those who engage in it. There is a nuanced difference between VTCs being created because veterans deserve different treatment in the criminal legal system due to their service (regardless of what happened to them during their service) and VTCs being created because of the *quality* of people who join the military. This is what distinguishes veterans from other groups deemed deserving: giving them benefits is not about what they have done but who they are.

By trafficking in worth, VTCs reflect and produce beliefs about veterans in both social and political categories. At the same time, these beliefs may obfuscate what drives people to join the military in the first place and the material challenges facing those who struggle during their service and after their return home. Veterans have amassed political power as a group to receive social welfare benefits, as detailed in chapter 3; now, VTCs add a dimension to these benefits by reflecting and shaping societal beliefs about the relationship between participation in the military and responsibility for criminalized behaviors.

To make this argument, the chapter begins with an overview of how popular US media portray US veterans as a uniquely worthy group. It then draws on interviews with VTC personnel, media accounts, and court observations to illustrate how those working in VTCs make sense of these broader notions of veteran worth. I identify three facets of veteran worth—deservingness, affect, and nexus—to explain beliefs about what makes VTCs distinctively and uniquely capable of helping veterans.

Yet, whereas the popular narrative about VTCs is that veterans have unique needs that only a court for them can address, people working inside these courts have a more nuanced view. Their perspectives provide insights into the contradictions inherent in these courts and point to a crucial question: Are VTCs beneficial for veterans because of their emphasis on shared military culture; or is it how people think and feel about veterans that makes judges, lawyers, clinicians, and mentors, among others, want to work in these courts and make them successful?

Importantly, the emphasis on the relationship between military service and criminalized behaviors may be a convenient way to avoid a broader focus on inequality in the US and, relatedly, the need for professional opportunities and social services that would help people long before they were arrested for a crime. In these ways, VTCs reflect and contribute to cultural understandings of what it means to be a veteran, what it means to be a person worthy of social service, and what it means to be a person engaged in criminalized activities in a country that continues to rely on the criminal legal system to manage vulnerable populations.

VETERAN WORTH AND US CULTURE: THE WOUNDED WARRIOR

Support for veteran benefits, including criminal legal benefits, reflects the unique role that the military plays in American cultural life. Broader beliefs and representations about the military, and those who serve in it, make VTCs both legible and legitimate in US society. In newspaper accounts of VTCs, worth, trauma, and war are the most prevalent themes to explain the creation and implementation of VTCs. One also sees evidence of this military connection—rooted in an image of war as inherently noble and damaging—in American identity in sports, movies, TV shows, and news broadcasts. The result is a broader ideology that the military and the country are intrinsically connected and military service should be celebrated.

The construction of veterans as a worthy group, both capable of transcending class and racialized inequalities—while also entrenching them (Darda 2021)—occurs through multiple cultural practices within the US. The social and cultural construction of the veteran, through literature and film, has historically celebrated the veteran hero, a process that has allowed veterans to straddle the class, politically partisan, and even racialized divisions that have emerged in the last few decades' culture wars. In this politics of worth, the involvement of veterans in the criminal legal system—which is disproportionately people of color—is an aberration that must be fixed.

Veteran worth is socially constructed through numerous institutions. For example, while there appears to be no correlation between US political affiliation and interest in sports, there is a positive correlation in US support for sports and the military (Thorson and Serazio 2018). Following 9/11, the "sport–war nexus" solidified further (King 2008). The National Football League (NFL) has commemorated and memorialized 9/11 through rituals and ceremonies (Butterworth 2014; Fischer 2014), such as the NFL's "Salute to Service" campaign (Rugg 2016). A military manufacturer became the official sponsor of college football's Armed Forces Bowl game (Butterworth and Moskal 2009). At the Pro Football Hall of Fame, an exhibit called "Pro Football and the American Spirit" chronicled the NFL players who also performed military service, celebrating war and holding up these players as exemplars of American citizenship (Butterworth 2014). According to Silk (2013), linking the military and sports was a powerful tool used by the Bush administration that defined ways of being American in opposition to other ways of being (5).

Likewise, the so-called Hollywood War Machine celebrates the role of the military in US history and shapes popular understandings of American patriotism (Boggs and Pollard 2016). Bacevich (2013) argues that the start of the Vietnam War can be attributed to the militarism in which groups from politicians to soldiers to intellectuals to evangelicals promoted military power as an antidote to the societal challenges America was facing. Award-winning movies about white Vietnam War heroes helped normalize the wartime trauma and its aftereffects (Darda 2021). Superhero franchises produced by Marvel and DC Comics, such as Captain America, blend militarism with American identity, and production of such films increased after 9/11 (Buskaite 2021). Academy Award–winning movies like *Black Hawk Down* and *Saving Private Ryan* offer similar celebrations of the military (Klein 2005). Whereas earlier films emphasize patriotism based on love of country, these newer films emphasize patriotism based on loyalty to one's comrades and the ability to survive battle (Wetta and Novelli 2003). These films also support the myth of the "American hero" in search of an enemy (Suid 2002). This form of American militarism is also tied to Christian identities, which Barker, Hurwitz, and Nelson (2008) refer to as a kind of "messianic" militarism.

The news media both celebrate what veterans accomplish in combat and present them as unique for what they endure during combat. Broadcasts during the wars in Iraq and Afghanistan were a "somatic" experience, with cam footage shot from the helmets of American soldiers making the violence more real to American citizens (McSorley 2012). During the Gulf War, the US public was presented with a pleasant image of war, with military press briefings sharing impressive replays of American warplanes homing in on enemy targets with laser-guided "smart" bombs and "picture-perfect assaults" (Ebo 1995). News reports emphasized the relationship between American patriotism with an increase in sales of American flags and wearing yellow ribbons signifying support for the troops (Hallin and Gitlin 2010).

Many television shows make a similar connection between the value of military service and American identity. Shows such as *Homeland*, *The West Wing*, and *24* were wildly popular (and more so with the advent of streaming services) and reinforced dominant US narratives that vilified "bad guys" in the War on Terror (Holland 2011), often using Arabs as placeholder villains (Shaheen 2009; Holland 2012). The intersection between Hollywood and US military objectives is not coincidental; rather, it is the result of an active partnership in which the US military provides billions of dollars in equipment for filming with the caveat that filmmakers must either submit to censorship from the Pentagon or have their expensive props and sets taken away (Robb 2011).

In addition to film, video games play a prominent role in shaping the way that Americans engage with and understand the military, veterans, and war. Video games are particularly effective through their powerful visuals (Robinson and Schulzke 2016; Schulzke 2017). Games that simulate war do so with increasing accuracy. They owe their realism to their production by and for the military as part of a cybernetic weapons system for the US Air Force in the 1940s, during the Cold War, and for simulated battlefield networks in the 1980s (Crogan 2011). The "military shooter"–type games are the most profitable genre. Beginning with the US so-called Global War on Terror (GWOT), they experienced a significant boom in sales, and Payne (2016) suggests that these games contribute to the militarization of US society by creating a world in which the gamer is the hero at every level and by playing off American anxieties surrounding terrorism. This creates a simultaneous image of the American enemy alongside the image of the American (military) hero (Robinson 2012).

These representations are part of a wider cultural narrative about veteran worth that contributes to broad political support for veteran services. Although veteran social status has evolved—most notably from the Vietnam era, when being a veteran arguably became a less desirable social identity (Appy 2015)—beliefs about veteran worth reemerged in the wake of the GWOT. The draft that defined the Vietnam War ended in 1973; joining the US armed services is currently no longer compulsory, meaning that the decision to enlist is viewed by the public as voluntary and thus deserving of respect (Horton 2013). Beliefs about veteran deservingness manifest in a variety of ways, from individual special treatment at airports to massive spending in congressional budgets. As affirmative action for racialized minorities ends, hiring preferences for veterans continue because of the 1944 Veterans Preference Act that requires federal agencies to prioritize veterans in hiring and retention if there are layoffs. Importantly, this support for veterans crosses the growing partisan divides in the US. For example, in a March 2019 survey conducted by Pew Research of a representative sample of US adults, 72 percent (equal share of Republicans and Democrats) said that if they were making the federal budget, they would increase spending for veterans' benefits and services.

The foregoing examples reveal some of the mechanisms through which militarism manifests in US culture, and how ideas of veteran worth emerge from it. This cultural element, combined with social and political capital behind the VA, fosters a distinct hierarchy of worth when it comes to publicly funded social services. Coupled with the material support offered by the Veterans Administration and the expansion of the criminal legal system to manage social inequality in the US, the creation of VTCs makes sense. At the same time, there is a paradox between the positive images of heroism and military service and the idea that veterans in the criminal legal system are there *because* of their service.

One way to understand this paradox is through the idea of the "wounded warrior." Although the military is celebrated as part and parcel of American culture, there is also a pervasive belief that veterans are uniquely susceptible to substance use and mental health disorders because of their military service generally and combat experience specifically. The wounded warrior introduces the central feature of the common narrative: the supposed nexus between criminalized behavior and military service. Stories about the wounded, and deserving, warrior are central to the common narrative: veterans have unique needs that a specialized treatment court can address. This story is a critical part of VTC proponents' and practitioners' push to legitimize these courts, and themselves, to funders, policymakers, social service providers, and to the participants they hope will comply with court requirements.

CREATING THE COMMON NARRATIVE

The common narrative about veteran worth and VTCs' efficacy is actively constructed to establish and maintain the legitimacy of these courts. At events where VTC judges, staff, or trainers explain the court to other practitioners, such as lawyers or those interested in mentoring, I frequently heard the argument that VTCs offer a unique benefit for individuals who have a shared experience of being wounded in the military. The argument rests not only on notions of military-related trauma but also on the claim that VTC personnel understand the US military culture and that participants are better suited for these courts because of their experience with hierarchy and discipline. For example, every talk I attended at the All Rise conferences in 2020 and 2021, which has a separate "track" for VTCs in their broader conference on treatment courts, mentioned the ideal of veterans treatment courts as uniquely able to help criminalized individuals who were once in the military and who have substance use and mental health challenges.[1] They all repeatedly mentioned "camaraderie," "structure," and "authority" as being central to VTC success, because they create a cultural milieu in which these individuals thrive.

For example, at the 2020 conference panel on VTC "basics," hosted virtually because of the pandemic, Judge Russell and an All Rise–affiliated trainer for VTCs provided detailed insights into this pervasive narrative that VTCs uniquely understand and address military culture. The trainer described "core army values" of duty and loyalty and how they could be "leveraged" to get participants to comply. Leverage more broadly refers to practices, products, philosophies, and environments as vehicles that facilitate behavioral change (Fisher et al. 2007). This concept of leverage stems from public health efforts to improve racial disparities in health outcomes, and it has been adopted in VTCs based on the previously described commingled beliefs about veteran worth and what veterans experience in the military.

For VTCs, leveraging refers to how the courts can better encourage participants to follow their mandates related to behavioral reforms, which is the central goal of all treatment courts. The military seeks to create the ideal soldier who follows orders not simply because they are afraid of being chastised or materially harmed if they do not but who adopts the view of their superior, developing internal motivations rather than external, and becoming a disciplined individual. This logic maps onto and reinforces VTC logics that seek full buy-in from participants to follow court orders. The All Rise–affiliated trainer for VTCs, mentioned above, provided an interpretation of military values in relation to the court, speaking as if he were the court participant:

> *Loyalty*: I will comply with orders of the court, adhere to treatment directives, I ask you to stick by me in my challenges and struggles.

I have a *duty* to attend court sessions on time, I want to follow the rules of monitoring, you must hold me accountable, it's my nature to be held accountable.

I will *respect* you based on your position in authority (not because you are a nice person, have a nice smile, you have to prove yourself, I will respect you based on authority). Please don't refer to me in [a] derogatory manner as one of your cases, or as a defendant messed up; as soon as I perceive this is how you feel, you won't exist.

Selfless service: My involvement in the criminal justice system is burdensome to me, my family, employer. I have guilt; help me find meaning; I request redirection.

Honor: Don't generalize treatment and supervision, I have specific needs that need to be met from a strength-based approach. I was a pilot, JAG officer, rescue diver, medic. I was taught to say nothing that deceives others. This may not be the case now. Regaining my integrity may be [the] first step to [having a] family.

I need the court to hold me accountable, to question my choices in a consistent and respectful manner. Empower me to reset my moral compass, if I need it. I will need your support. Only I can do it.

Anyone who has studied treatment courts, been a participant in one, or worked in one, can immediately recognize how easily these military logics of authority, structure, and camaraderie map onto the disciplinary logics prevalent in treatment courts. Burns and Peyrot (2003) characterize these logics as "tough love," noting that the idea in treatment courts is to express care side by side with coercion. VTC advocates un-self-consciously talk about drawing on the disciplinary techniques of military culture to make VTC participants comply with the court. MacLeish (2020) refers to this approach as "coercive care" in VTCs that fosters the image of the veteran as "damaged" and "deserving." In the 2020 and 2021 All Rise conferences, the speakers repeatedly described framing participation in VTCs as the veterans' new "mission," how the mentor is a "battle buddy," and that veterans should understand that they earned access to a VTC as a "benefit" for the service they provided America.

Such comments suggest that drawing on military culture can be uniquely beneficial to VTC participants.

This notion of veteran exceptionalism, a variation on the "wounded warrior," has made its way into criminal law, with numerous jurisdictions allowing veterans to offer their experiences during military service as a mitigating factor in their criminal legal processes (Merriam 2014; Fagundes 2024). In a notable instance of how beliefs about veteran worth can influence court processes, a Tampa, Florida judge, himself a veteran who oversaw both regular criminal courts and the city's VTC, personally advocated for a veteran accused of aggravated assault. His advocacy, according to critics, blurred the line of judicial ethics, as he offered both a lenient sentence and tried to help the defendant access educational opportunities at the local university. The judge explained, "I'm advocating on behalf of each and every man and woman of this nation who face the same issues and demons that [this defendant] faces" (Borcheck 2015).

This contradiction between attributing criminogenic behavior to the military and suggesting that military culture can be salutary exposes cracks in the common narrative. These cracks reflect and contribute to inequalities that shape VTC practices. For example, the idea of military culture presents court participants as those who respect authority simply because it is authority. Yet, when talking with people working inside the courts, I often heard clinicians, judges, and others explain that many VTC participants struggled with authority, one explanation for why they have found themselves in the criminal legal system. In particular, those who were not honorably discharged likely struggled with authority in the military. The first-person statements, such as "It's in my nature to be held accountable," lump veterans together as a social group and overlook how these participants differ from one another. These accountability logics may be the espoused values of the military, but not all people who enlist actually embrace or even respond well to them. This is especially true for the people in VTCs who did not leave the military under honorable conditions and are unable to access VA benefits.

Echoing this articulation of the common narrative, at the 2021 All Rise conference presentation entitled "Who Am I Now? Identity Loss, the Transition from Military to Civilian Life, and How It Affects Your Courts," a VA psychiatrist presented on the loss of identity during the transition from military to civilian life, asking all attendees to close their eyes and imagine boot camp, combat, and return home. This is the same narrative of loss often found in newspaper articles about VTCs but does not necessarily map onto VTC entry requirements—which more often than not do not require combat. These efforts to leverage veteran identity illustrate how VTCs are predicated on societal beliefs about veteran worth that may flatten differences among veterans and are tied to assumptions about combat rather than the more mundane and common military employment experiences.

Interrogating these discursive strategies with long-standing insights from critical criminology, one sees how the notion of leveraging military culture puts the onus of responsibility on the individual for their challenges in the criminal justice system while also suggesting that the military was simultaneously, and contradictorily, a negative influence and the reason that the participant is even in the criminal legal system. Although distinct, the emphasis on military culture echoes the pervasive rhetoric within treatment courts about participants' power and control. For example, the message that a "moral compass" must be "reset" maps onto the "enforcing freedom" paradigm of drug treatment courts, that through coercion participants are able to return to a prior state free from addiction or mental health challenges (Kaye 2020). The argument that being "accountable" is in every participant's "nature" is a major assumption that may or may not be true for any individual. Regardless, this explanation of military values maps onto the disciplining techniques that are common in all treatment courts, and it suggests that veterans may be particularly pliable subjects who will more readily conform to court-mandated requirements.

These examples of the common narrative reveal the add veteran and stir approach to drug treatment courts. In adding veteran identity to the model, VTCs rely on logics related to criminal justice, rehabilitation, community accountability, and efficiency, while also integrating assumptions about what makes veterans different from other criminalized subpopulations (McPherson and Sauder 2013). These treatment court logics, in general, overlook factors related to the criminalization of poverty, substance abuse, and mental illness, which push people, especially racialized minorities, into the criminal legal system. For VTCs, these logics further sideline a more comprehensive understanding of why people enter the military at all—often for education and other professional opportunities and benefits (Bachman et al. 2000; Eighmey 2006)—and then exit to return to the communities that many sought to leave.

Further, the common narrative animating the VTC movement and practices is about insiders and outsiders—identities based on involvement with the military and the worth of those who chose such involvement. Such beliefs about the worth of particular individuals contribute to social stratification by individualizing successes and failures while also excusing individual behavior for structural factors. The common narrative is a distinct cultural practice, which can be an independent mechanism through which inequalities between different social groups emerge (Ridgeway 2014). As sociologist Lamont (2019) notes, this kind of stratification is culturally and materially determined, based on the belief that a certain type of success "does not depend primarily on the moral fortitude of exceptional individuals who have the strength to pull themselves up by their bootstraps, but on features of the environment––and the availability of narratives about possible selves (Markus and Nurius 1986) that resonate, inspire, and provide hope" (664). These cultural beliefs about which groups are "better" often translate directly into material advantages for some groups over others (Ridgeway 2014).

These dilemmas provide a starting point to understand how the common narrative that there is something distinct about veterans and VTCs' ability to help them reflects and reproduces inequalities. Rather than acknowledge the diversity of military experience among participants, these efforts to leverage military culture instead flatten distinctions and reproduce a narrative akin to the "wounded warrior" that does not map onto either VTC practices or how VTC judges and court staff think about those practices.

Looking in depth at how people who work in VTCs view participants and court practices reveals the contradictions directly related to the diverse groups with whom the courts seek legitimacy. VTC personnel and proponents use the common narrative to help the veterans in their community, with some seeing the value of VTCs as part of a broader criminal legal reform agenda. Through their understandings, we see how VTCs reflect, reproduce, and may entrench the social inequalities that define US society.

HOW DIFFERENT ARE VETERAN CRIMINAL DEFENDANTS?

Over the course of this research, it became clear that the argument about there being something unique about veterans was useful in understanding the proliferation of VTCs. Yet, a prominent theme from interviews is that experiences in the military do not necessarily make veterans different from other criminal legal defendants—an assessment consistent with research on veterans and nonveterans in jails; some research even suggests that military service may be protective against ending up in jail (Brooke and Gau 2018). This illustrates how the common narrative of these courts—that veterans are a distinct group and therefore need a distinct court—serves an important purpose in explaining their proliferation, but not their practices.

When asked what distinguishes veterans from other criminal legal defendants, court staff (e.g., district attorneys, clinicians, probation officers), judges, and proponents articulated three distinct themes, each revealing how they are part of the common narrative. The first theme is deservingness, which is different from worth, because it refers to what veterans should receive just for joining the military. The second has less to do with what veterans have done and more to do with what interviewees feel toward veterans. I label this as the affective dimension of worth. The third theme is nexus, or the reason the participants are in the criminal legal system at all. All themes overlap, and each opens up the challenge of distinguishing veterans from other criminal legal defendants, with court personnel aware that many of the features they describe as unique to veterans are also applicable to other groups. The role of the common narrative is vital in overcoming the challenge of distinguishing veterans from others in the criminal legal system; it is the core argument by the court to legitimate VTCs to its participants and stakeholders, despite the narrative's questionable accuracy. I next unpack the three themes.

Deservingness. The theme of deservingness focuses on what veterans did in their past and are therefore owed now, with the assumption that criminal legal benefits are necessary to remedy harms that can come with being in the service and returning to civilian life. This articulation of deservingness, though related, is distinct from worth because it is about what individuals have done rather than who they are. This belief about deservingness involves assumptions about why a person chose to join the military by focusing on the person's character that ignores possible economic factors (e.g., looking for college benefits). This theme, part of a broader belief about the heightened worth of those who choose to serve in the military, reinforces the status of insider versus outsider based solely on military service that may not be an accurate representation of why the participant signed up or what they did afterward.

The theme of deservingness was exemplified at a 2022 online presentation to a local bar association—lawyers who practice in the same city—near the Northeast VTC. The VTC's probation officer explained the court's goals: "We are trying to do something compassionate for veterans who have served our country."

The notion that offering a treatment court is "compassionate" reveals how practitioners explain veterans in the criminal legal system as uniquely deserving, and VTCs as uniquely helpful and not inherently punitive. Media accounts almost uniformly mention deservingness, with language focused on what the participants did in the past in the military. An article from the *San Francisco Chronicle*, just one example among many, noted that VTCs "ensure that more of those who served get the help they have earned" (Rubenstein 2019). The idea that veterans "earned" this criminal legal benefit is the essence of deservingness.

Yet, VTC practitioners—those who actually work in VTCs—use descriptions of deservingness that are coupled with the awareness that many participants did not experience combat, and some did not even finish boot camp. This means that beliefs about deservingness are not only about what happened to them in the military. Departing slightly from this account of deservingness based on military experience, some interviewees suggest that veterans are deserving simply for joining the military, not because of what they did in the military or what happened to them during their service. I first heard this from mentors in the Northeast VTC, who noted in a group interview that veterans signed up to do something "greater than themselves," and, as a result, they should get different treatment in the criminal legal system. A judge in the West VTC likewise acknowledged that that there are different participant experiences in the military, but that the court's approach is to treat all people who signed up in a similar way:

> The veteran population isn't monolithic. . . . Some spent a couple of months in boot camp and [got] out, others had tours of duty in Iraq. This is not the same set of circumstances, and I have no problem with

that. If you signed up, you should get as much help as we should give
you.

(judge, West VTC, interview)

Interviewees discussing deservingness frequently pointed out counterargu-
ments to those who think that veterans are getting undeserved special treatment through VTCs. These defensive explanations of VTCs arose in various
conversations but stuck out during one interview in the Southeast VTC with
an aide of a state legislator. The aide explained how the representative they
worked for was a veteran supporting the establishment of another VTC that
would receive local government funding. Even the legislator had to overcome
his impression that fellow veterans were receiving a "get out of jail free card."
This interview stayed with me because it was one of the first conversations in
which I heard that VTCs were not initially popular with policymakers. The
district attorney for Southeast VTC explained similar concerns about the "get
out of jail free card." The DA advocated for the VTC by calling on the well-
studied, though complex, relationship between treatment courts and recidivism, and that the courts were supporting public safety in addition to helping
this distinct population (DA, Southeast VTC, interview).

The most striking comment about VTCs' offering an unfair advantage
to some criminal defendants came from an assistant district attorney (ADA)
serving the West's VTC. This ADA was a former veteran and was assigned to
the court; he did not choose to be there, unlike many prosecutors working in
treatment courts:

> In veterans court we are making guidelines, saying that if you joined
> the National Guard and lasted one week, they are in. Think about that.
> They are now considered a veteran. I find that utterly repugnant.
>
> *(ADA, West VTC, interview)*

From his perspective, the court is treating individuals as deserving regardless of whether they have done something to deserve criminal legal benefits.
Though an outlier among personnel, most of whom celebrate the generous ad-
missions policies of VTCs, his comments nonetheless highlight the complexities of considering anyone who signed up to join the military as inherently
deserving of opportunities not allowed to others with the same legal issues but
without military experience.

Affect. The theme of affect reveals less about what proponents believe veterans deserve and more about how personnel feel about and around veterans. Explanations given by interviewees who work in VTCs about what makes veterans distinct from other criminal legal defendants frequently did not include what participants *did* in the military. Rather, they frequently articulated an emotional dimension to explain their work; in short, they like working with veterans.

Most notably, many of the people who expressed positive sentiment for VTC participants are not the typical criminal legal reformers who want to support criminal legal defendants. Many of the criminal legal personnel and VTC mentors in Northeast and Southeast, for example, are from social demographics (i.e., Republican) that typically embrace tough-on-crime policies. Their opinions, thus, illustrate why veterans are seen as distinctly worthy, yet also how distinguishing veterans from other criminal legal defendants perpetuates stereotypes about nonveterans in the criminal legal system. Comments included compliments about veterans on personal qualities that differentiate them from other criminal legal defendants. A probation officer in the Northeast VTC, for example, explained a preference to work with veterans because of how the vets approach the court mandates:

> These guys are pretty smart, and they're a lot wittier than a regular probationer, they have a higher education level. They all have good working skills. So, these guys know as soon as they violate, what they'll do is they'll get themselves into treatment or [local residential facility].
> *(probation officer, Northeast VTC, interview)*

This explanation that VTC participants work harder than others in drug treatment courts was common, though other interviewees noted that there is bimodal distribution in that some participants comply very well while others struggle. Most notable in these comments, however, was the care expressed by VTC judges and court staff for the participants, and how that care translated into the personal satisfaction of working with veterans. This probation officer said outright how much he likes working with the participants in his assigned courtroom.

Other interviewees also expressed that they like working with the veteran population because of the latter's attitude. A clinician reiterated the personal qualities that set veterans apart from other defendants or probationers: veterans are more compliant with the courts:

> Did the war make that population different? I don't know. There is less entitlement than with the public population, these guys don't feel that stuff should be handed to them. I worked in the jails, it was pretty difficult, with individuals saying more or less that [everything] is his fault, her fault. These guys take ownership, not all, but a good portion.
>
> *(clinician, Northeast VTC, interview)*

A court coordinator in the West VTC, soon after taking on the role, said in an interview:

> When our folks really commit, they do better than people in any other court pretty much. Like they're so engaged once they're engaged. And it's like also that military, you know, that this is what you do, you finish what you start. And there's this take on orders.
>
> *(court coordinator, West VTC, interview)*

Judges and staff in all three courts echoed this dimension of compliance that is usually ascribed to military culture, and their appreciation of it.

Media reports also compare veterans to other criminal legal defendants, often quoting court personnel in ways that underscore this belief that veterans are different than people who did not join the military. For example, a TV news station reporting on a new VTC in Sacramento, California, included Probation Officer Greg Turner making a similar statement: "This is actually the first time I actually liked everybody on my case load and respected everyone on my case load. . . . These guys are all American heroes" (CBS Sacramento 2015). An article in the *San Francisco Chronicle*, about a VTC in San Francisco, quoted a judge on how veterans treat authority in contrast with others in the criminal legal system: "They stood up straight, said 'Yes ma'am, no ma'am,' and there was no street talk. This was a different animal" (Nevius 2014).

Such generalizations about veterans as a group cross both racial and class boundaries ("street talk" implicates both race and class) and reveal how feelings about veterans shape beliefs about what VTCs offer to them. This affect both reflects and drives the argument that VTCs are uniquely beneficial for veterans, and that veterans are uniquely compliant in courts. Although the comments on camaraderie focus on the participants rather than the court personnel, some interviewees explained to my team how the chance to work with veterans was a welcome opportunity because of their personal connections to the military, highlighting how perceptions of worth, affect, and social proximity are intertwined. Although none of the judges in the three observed courts had any military service history, two had parents who were career military. Other VTC staff frequently brought up the ways in which their work felt like recognition for what their own loved ones experienced. For example, a clinician in the Northeast VTC explained their commitment to veterans by noting the value of military service and, by extension, their personal interest in working with veterans:

> I come from a military family background. I did not choose that path; I chose to go to school. I have some family members in West Point, a Vietnam veteran father. The military is a challenge every day, it keeps you focused. It's not the same, not monotonous, you are being challenged and that's great, challenged every day, solving a puzzle. I love hearing people's stories, not about the military but their family lives.
>
> *(clinician, Northeast VTC, interview)*

Worth helps make sense of these explanations, which are less about the unique nature of veterans' criminal offending, potentially caused by or related to their military service, and more about the feelings that criminal legal actors have for veterans.

Nexus. A central element of the common narrative is the assumption of a nexus between criminalized behavior and military service history. Nexus means that criminalized behavior is *because* of a veteran's military experience. This element is dominant in policy discussions about VTCs and how their entry criteria are decided (Piehowski 2022). Although VTC team members noted that some participants' legal troubles may be directly related to their service experiences, most also expressed skepticism about the relationship between military service and criminalized behavior.

The clinician in West, serving the highest need group of participants that I observed in all three courts, explained their participants the following way:

> I would say most have had childhood violence against them, transitional housing as a child, no parents, are of color, some sort of minority subsystem, LGBT, HIV positive. I have an interesting group of guys kicked for being LGBT; they get kicked out for personality dysfunction disorder as a line item.
>
> *(clinician, West VTC, interview)*

The clinician continued explaining that getting services for these participants was particularly difficult. Since many were kicked out for "behavioral outbursts," which leads to dishonorable discharges, they have to fight to upgrade their discharge status.

This contrast between the image of the noble warrior and the struggles VTC participants experience reflects the central contradiction in VTCs noted in other chapters: their simultaneous celebration of the military and attribution of criminalized behaviors to military service. It also reveals an additional dynamic of how this contradiction is exacerbated by the determination of veterans' benefits based on performance in the military and recognition that VTC participants present with similar challenges as those who are not able to access VTCs.

Among my interviewees, most of the concern about nexus reveals differing opinions about whether this nexus has more to do with the environmental factors that lead people into the military, what goes on in the military (not necessarily combat, but other socializing features), and what happens when they leave the military but do not receive adequate social or material support. The central logic of the nexus was summarized well by a judge:

> I think that I've always felt veterans got a short shrift, those in trouble may have issues springing from service, or exacerbated by their service.
> *(judge, Southeast VTC, interview)*

Nexus in the common narrative articulated here presupposes that veterans are struggling because of challenges related to the military, specifically combat, and that the court will help them "return" to a previous state. However, in an attempt to reconcile the common narrative with their personal observations, court personnel expanded the definition of nexus. A clinician from the Southeast VTC offered an understanding of nexus by pointing out how people who joined the military and then ended up in the criminal legal system fell from a position of security to one of insecurity, which they saw as different from other criminal legal defendants:

> These individuals were very useful, proud, had missions, and after that is gone, sleeping in the streets, begging for money and sometimes robbing so that they can try and forget by smoking crack. So how did you come from that to this, and the in-between is all foggy. They are different in that sense.
>
> *(clinician, Southeast VTC, interview)*

The judge who founded the West VTC defined the issues particularly facing Vietnam-era vets, whose struggles after the war are well documented:

> A large percentage of our population had never been in combat but rather had returned from the military, including the Vietnam era—and never been able to reintegrate into society. So, from that respect they didn't look any different from anybody that I saw in [regular courts]. They were homeless. They were drug addicted. They had mental health issues. They had alcohol dependency. They were involved in various petty crimes like burglaries. And so, in that respect, they didn't look any different from anybody else.
>
> *(judge, West VTC, interview)*

Echoing findings from VTC studies that show lower rates of combat-related trauma than the common narrative suggests (e.g., Tsai et al. 2016), court personnel from all three VTCs pointed out that few of the participants in their courts have combat trauma. Their insights about the relationship between military service and criminal legal behavior underscore contradictory opinions about how simply being in the military can be psychologically damaging. For example, court personnel also noted that the trauma experienced by VTC participants may not be that different from other criminal legal defendants:

> [W]hen you enter the service, when you get out, it changes you somehow. You are used to being told what to do, to being regimented, some people cannot handle that. (judge, Southeast VTC, interview)

The judge went on to reflect on how the trauma that is acknowledged in the veteran population may not be that distinct from the people in their courts who never joined the military, but it is not given the same weight:

> We see a lot of [hidden] trauma [in court], we don't see it [in society]. We understand that there could be trauma. For a grown-up in court, trauma is not necessarily considered. There may be some mitigation, but the more violent the crime, the less their traumas count, and we see traumatized victims all the time.

A veteran who helped create the Northeast VTC explained the dynamic factors facing veterans, having both trauma from the "first day" of boot camp as well as situations they return to after leaving the service:

It's as simple as first day of basic training, being screamed at, told you are worth less than, that sticks with you. That may be the case and I do not diminish that. That's not quite as common. I say this as enlisted at seventeen and from a happy household. The things that lead one to enlist and get out of a situation and leave can make one attracted to military. Those people may share traumatic history, criminal behavior and characteristics. They find structure, thrive, do one enlistment four or six years, and find none of the situations changed . . . [A] large number of participants [share] dual trauma, civilian and combat.

(staffer, Northeast VTC, interview)

Importantly, when asked to talk more about how VTC participants differ from other populations that they have worked with, most VTC staff and judges pivoted from "the military as a uniformly beneficial experience" to a more complex explanation of how military experiences affected participants. Their insights suggest that social pressures to conform in the military create hard-to-diagnose psychological challenges when service ends (Gala and True 2014). Interviewees acknowledged that participants struggle with substance use and mental health issues but suggested that this may have less to do with their military service histories than the common narrative suggests. Some said that the challenges they struggled with before joining the military intersected with the challenging attributes of military culture.

These sentiments echo my observations and interviews with veterans in a residential facility to support substance use disorders as well as those in a pretrial veterans' pod in a jail. Veterans often explained that they joined the military to get away from challenging family situations, and that they brought those challenges into the military. One interviewee from the jail pod mentioned attempting suicide multiple times before enlisting. He presumed those mental health challenges would preclude his enlistment, but at the time (post–9/11) the military was waiving many requirements. Another inmate explained that he was in and out of jail as a youth and went to the military to stop the cycle.

The tenuousness of nexus reveals the common narrative's contradiction about whether military service is something to be celebrated or concerned about. The lead mentor in the West VTC, for example, pointed out how the military culture contributes to aggression that makes it particularly difficult for men to have romantic and other relationships:

Veterans go through psychological issues themselves because they have issues working well with others, because people carry some of that military work ethic and they just start yelling at other workers when they are not supposed to. And also the culture of like––you can be overbearing––a misogynistic culture as well.

(mentor, West VTC, interview)

This mentor then described the specific problem of substance use, noting that normal behavior inside the military is not considered normal outside the military. Those who return to civilian life feel a level of alienation that, mixed with the casual use of alcohol in the military, contributes to criminalized behaviors:

I experienced a lot of drinking and debauchery with my own troops and so when you go home and kind of carries [*sic*] [this behavior] with you and I think it is the norm and a lot of these veterans that come home, they couldn't adjust to what is considered normal. What's that word? Being normal.

The tension between the military being both a noble pursuit and a harmful experience is evident in these explanations. Further, something pushed participants to join the military, and joining means eventually leaving. A clinician from the Northeast VTC explained that joining the military to avoid other trauma helps explain how being in the military can become a challenge that may lead to criminal legal involvement:

So just imagine you going in every day to work [in the military] with that [trauma] on top of you, having people yell at you every day, and you're not liking the job, people making you feel like trash every day. It's terrible.

(clinician, Northeast VTC, interview)

This comment suggests that just being in the military, without even seeing combat, can be detrimental to one's well-being. What is important about this suggestion is that it directly contradicts an idea I previously characterized as taboo, evident in a VA researcher's statement at a VA-convened meeting in 2022 on VTC research: "Do not suggest that the military is criminogenic." Given that research underscores the similar risk factors among veterans and nonveterans involved in the criminal legal system (Culp et al. 2013), the VA researcher's statement is accurate. However, whether or not military service is a causal factor in criminal legal involvement at the population level, people working in the criminal legal system take liberties to explain veteran's struggles as having something to do with military service.

Notably, some VTC team members mentioned that challenges do not arise from joining the military but leaving it:

> I'd hate to make a generalization, but I think that for most of the folks, they were struggling with something prior to the military, and maybe the military was a solution to their problems. For the folks that we see, that solution wasn't so effective, or it was effective until they decided to leave, chose to leave the military. For those folks who were successful for whatever period of time, two years, three years, and some folks longer, then they lost that structure and that support and went off the rails.
> *(clinician, Northeast VTC, interview)*

A probation officer from the same court relayed how these challenges from leaving are exacerbated by discharge papers that may not enable a person who served to access VA benefits. Such explanations of nexus illustrate how inequalities permeate the creation and implementation of VTCs. In line with scientific studies (Culp et al. 2013; Moses 2013; Stacer and Solinas-Saunders 2020), people working in VTCs also admit that the reality for many veterans in the criminal legal system is that their underlying mental health or substance abuse issues had nothing to do with any activities during their military service; rather, these issues may have pushed them to join the military and returned or got worse when they left it.

IS THERE A NEXUS?

Despite the common narrative that veterans need their own specialized court because of their distinct needs, many VTC personnel and advocates I spoke with suggested that veterans are much like the rest of the population: situational factors, not combat, make it more likely for them to suffer mental health disorders. Their insights echo Junger (2016), who puts forth a particularly compelling explanation about veteran suffering: being in the military gave individuals meaning that they cannot find as easily in civilian society, they suffer without meaning or purpose or a close-knit community, and they face the economic- and family-related stressors of reentry into civilian life. Yet, similar stressors affect those who never entered the military, including mental illness, substance abuse, and financial and relationship problems (Dao 2013).

What distinguishes veterans is not necessarily their experience in the military but their employment history—they are recognized socially and politically and entitled to far more public benefits than any other group, and those benefits make the creation of VTCs easier. Interestingly, my observations at All Rise conferences suggest that VTC advocates often assume that VTCs will help identify veterans in the criminal legal system eligible for VA benefits, and then connect them with those benefits. Part of this assumption reflects concerns that veterans in the criminal legal system may be eligible but not have access to their VA benefits. This stems from the important work that the VA's programs to help incarcerated veterans have done in connecting eligible veterans with benefits that they were not accessing (Finlay et al. 2016).

However, most participants in VTCs, just like veterans in prisons, are VA-connected (Brooke and Gau 2018). An estimated 74 percent of men veterans in state prisons and 77 percent in federal prisons received an honorable discharge or a general discharge under honorable conditions (Bureau of Justice Statistics 2021), making them eligible for VA benefits.

By pointing out the contradiction between who VTCs are imagined to serve—those in the criminal legal system because of combat-related trauma, eligible for but not accessing VA services—and the majority of whom they actually serve—many older veterans with severe substance abuse and related vulnerabilities, and who are VA-connected—and the criminal legal disconnect between veterans and civilians with similar histories, I *do not* suggest that, as a general or individual matter, there is no relationship between the military and criminal offending. Moreover, I do not seek to minimize the tragedy of suicide and other harms associated with military service or disparage any veteran as undeserving of the VTC system. Rather, my goal is to examine how people working in VTCs talk about veterans, unintentionally revealing how similar this population is to other populations in the non-VTC criminal legal system. Junger's analysis of veteran trauma, for example, points to the social need that all people have to be part of small groups with a clear sense of purpose and belonging (Junger 2016). The military can provide this type of meaning-making activity. VTCs are supposed to fill this gap after service is over.

Given the lack of a clear nexus between military service and criminalized behaviors, another way to understand veterans' criminal legal involvement is to consider that the same circumstances that push people to join the military may affect them upon return. That is, military service is not directly related to criminal legal behavior, at least at a population level (i.e., it may be directly related to an individual, but not across the millions of people who have served). Musheno and Ross (2008) document the relationship between pre- and post-military life in their study of reservists who were sent on repeated missions to Iraq and Afghanistan. In their typology of the different attitudes among reservists, they explain the "struggling reservists" as those with lower levels of education and with fewer job prospects upon return from deployment. They refer to these struggles as "homegrown" (8) to emphasize that deployment, on its own, is not the cause of their criminal legal behavior.

Another way to think about nexus is to understand the variety of factors that shape a person's propensity to engage in criminalized behaviors. There is a strong relationship between childhood trauma and criminal legal involvement among the veteran population, suggesting that the nexus between service experiences and illegal behavior is more tenuous than the common narrative suggests (Hartwell et al. 2014). While some studies suggest that the military can contribute to antisocial or deviant behavior (Brooke and Gau 2018; Akers and Sellers 2004), other studies suggest that the military can be beneficial to people who have already engaged in criminal legal behavior. These studies suggest that there is no difference between servicemembers and nonservicemembers when it comes to criminalized offending (Brooke and Gau 2018, citing Bouffard 2003; Bouffard and Laub 2004). Several studies point out that serving in the military can actually decrease one's likelihood of criminal legal involvement (Tsai et al. 2013; Brooke and Gau 2018).

There are well-documented connections between military service, alcohol use, and mental health challenges (Brown et al. 2013; Tsai et al. 2013). Mental health challenges and suicide among veterans are a national scourge, yet veteran suicide data obscures how military service affects mental health. Although veterans have much higher suicide rates than the general population (41 percent to 61 percent higher risk) (Kang et al. 2015), there is no statistical relationship between suicide and combat-related factors such as length of time deployed or frequency of deployment (Leard Mann, Powell, and Smith 2013). Despite the low percentage of contemporary veterans who have seen combat (approximately 10 percent), PTSD rates are higher than they have ever been among veterans (Junger 2016). One comprehensive study showed that deployment to Iraq or Afghanistan actually lowered the incidence of suicide, which may have to do with different criteria for accepting individuals into military service and deploying them (Kang et al. 2015). Other data reveals that the majority of veterans who commit suicide did not experience combat (US Department of Veterans Affairs 2022). Mental health disorders, including major-depressive and manic-depressive disorder and alcohol consumption, are the biggest predictors for suicide. Likewise, the majority of those who commit suicide are older, above age fifty, further illustrating how life events after service contribute to veteran suffering.

All of these studies point to the social and political challenges that drive people into the military and may make leaving the military harder. As the opioid crisis continues, as veterans return from wars in Afghanistan and Iraq, as Vietnam-era veterans age, and as the affordable housing crisis leaves vulnerable individuals without financial security to maintain their homes, it seems logical that veterans may struggle and find themselves in the criminal legal system. Further, as treatment courts proliferate to address the tragedy of substance use and mental health disorders (Nolan 2002; Tiger 2012; Kaye 2020), a treatment court dedicated to veterans is a logical expansion of the criminal legal system to address underlying social problems that require more institutions to address.

PUSHING NEXUS

Even if there is no clear nexus between military service and criminal legal behavior, VTC proponents rely on the idea of nexus to legitimize VTCs and to use VTCs to push broader social reforms. Their efforts have been bolstered by a growing recognition that trauma affects behavior, and the sincerely held belief that treatment courts can address underlying trauma and change behavior.

In relying on this facet of the common narrative, these courts privilege certain causes of trauma—military service—over others. The common narrative suggests that, since the government is implicated in that service, the government should compensate. A 2016 article in the *Fresno Bee*, a representative example of newspaper accounts of new VTCs, emphasized the government's responsibility to help veterans because it is that service that created veterans' criminal legal behaviors: "We owe it to our vets: We damaged them; we should work to put it right" (Kroeker 2016). This quote illustrates how nexus is central to the operationalization of VTCs, moving the onus of personal responsibility for a veteran's behavior and transferring that responsibility to the government.

This idea of nexus overlaps with the themes of deservingness and worth, outlined above. Those who work in VTCs articulated an expansive nexus to explain why veterans deserve specialized treatment in the criminal legal system, which reveals empathy for the myriad challenges facing those who serve in the military and return to civilian life. Their explanations suggest that the popular emphasis on combat, mental health, and criminal legal behaviors misses what makes military service challenging. As noted above, there is some acknowledgment that being in the military might contribute to criminal legal behaviors for reasons that have nothing to do with the common narrative's emphasis on combat trauma. However, VTC judges and staff avoid directly relating military service and criminogenic behavior because it could lead to stigma for the veteran community. They, as well as VTC participants and other veterans in the criminal legal system, shared stories with me about their military experience, particularly recent military experience. They not only talked about adverse childhood experiences but also how the availability of illicit substances and alcohol in the military, mixed with other elements of military culture, creates a perfect storm for those returning home and trying to reintegrate into civilian life.

I observed those who mobilized this idea of nexus becoming defensive when trying to dispel the notion that VTCs offer undeserved special treatment for veterans. For example, in spring 2022, at a meeting of a local bar association near the Northeast VTC, the discussion turned to changes in state legislative support for veterans. A state senator and a veteran himself (as mentioned earlier in this chapter) said the challenge is overcoming concerns that a criminal legal benefit is being offered to undeserving individuals—namely, those whose problematic behavior seems far removed from their military service history. The senator said his efforts to address these concerns resulted in changes in legislation, which received negative press after someone who had enlisted decades prior and never been deployed to a war zone was accused of domestic violence. To argue against this media coverage, the senator described to me in a later interview how challenges can emerge from joining the military, even if a person was never deployed, largely because there are so many struggles that can emerge with reintegration into civilian life.

This senator's comments underscore that the common narrative that veterans have unique needs *because* of their military service may be misleading and, instead, reveal that worth rather than deservingness animates calls for veterans to have distinct criminal legal benefits. The senator's insights, drawn from his own experiences in the military and reintegration, suggest that the common narrative's emphasis on combat trauma is somewhat beside the point when it comes to beliefs about why VTCs are needed. Still, the story provides ideas that politicians like him, and politically savvy court personnel, can draw on to legitimate a VTC's work.

An important implication of this finding is that decoupling criminal legal behaviors from military service, specifically combat, creates an opening for those interested in using VTCs to push broader criminal legal reforms. Complementing this concern about whether there is a nexus between what the participants experienced during their service—specifically combat—and their criminal legal involvement, some court personnel expressed that the approach within VTCs—specifically about the relationship between trauma and behavior—should be widely used throughout the criminal legal system. The West VTC judge explained that the issue of trauma, regardless of its source, is fundamental to VTCs:

> If a reason that we are providing treatment to people in a veteran's court is because they served in the military and that PTSD is the result of that experience, I argue that the PTSD of people growing up in certain neighborhoods in [this city] is even more pronounced for the following reasons. First, they are subjected to trauma at a very early age, which could include seeing a family member shot or having a family member shot and learning about it. In some cases, and again I am not generalizing, but in some cases, that I was involved with, they didn't have any family structure, whereas the people in the military have a structure in which to experience the trauma.
>
> *(judge, West VTC, interview)*

According to this judge, treating the same traumas differently (veterans in VTCs versus other people in the regular court system) exposes broad inequities and inequalities both in the criminal legal system as well as more broadly in society, and that VTCs can serve as a model court to address them. From this perspective, VTCs illustrate the need for criminal legal actors and policymakers to consider trauma more equitably, enabling other defendants in the court system to access social services, as participants can do in VTCs.

A public defender in Northeast made a similar observation, which he said was "heresy" in VTC circles because people say that this works because of something unique about veterans:

> We have a lot of people that barely have any military experience. It's my feeling that this whole concept, take away the veteran component, would still be a remarkably good way to deal with people, drug issues, mental issues, especially with mentors it would be remarkable.
>
> *(public defender, Northeast VTC, interview)*

In another example of how criminal legal reformers understand VTCs as a tool for broader reforms, a public defender in the Southeast VTC pointed out that many of the youth living in the city's urban center regularly hear the sound of sirens. He was concerned that the criminal legal system does not adequately consider the trauma that can cause but will consider the trauma of military combat. Even though this public defender was skeptical of treatment courts because they often put vulnerable people back into the legal system if they cannot comply with court requirements, he thought that VTCs were a great way to start to normalize trauma as a concept for any accused person. This public defender understood the limitations of the common narrative yet embraced it to meet broader goals.

Along the same lines, a judge in the West VTC explained that a similar logic of nexus for veterans—trauma leading to criminal legal behavior—could apply to other defendants:

> They [defendants in the traditional criminal legal system] didn't have health care or medical care or any kind of counseling with which to deal with the trauma, which was being inflicted upon them in child-hood, at a time when we know people are still evolving psychologically. It was repeated trauma. Untreated trauma. Unsupported.
>
> *(judge, West VTC, interview)*

For this judge, the de-responsibilizing logics—that is, taking the onus of responsibility away from participants' individual failings—of VTCs could easily apply to individuals who don't have the same level of social services support as the veterans. He went on to note:

> [Trauma is] a function of the environment in which they were, in that case, born into, as opposed to the environment to which they enlisted or were drafted depending on which era we are talking about.

A judge in the Southeast VTC, who also oversees mental health and drug treatment courts, expressed a similar idea about nexus: the common narrative that military service and criminal legal involvement are connected creates unfair distinctions between people:

> Just because somebody is not a vet doesn't mean that they shouldn't also be able to get the same benefit of a court that recognizes that you have a mental health issue, you have an addiction issue and that's what caused you––that was your primary reason for getting involved in the criminal justice system.
>
> *(judge, Southeast VTC, interview)*

These expansive explanations of nexus reveal the potential of VTCs to address broader inequalities while also undermining the argument that veterans have distinct needs that VTCs are uniquely able to address. These actors recognize that there is a tenuous connection between what happened to people during their military service and their involvement in the criminal legal system, but a growing appreciation of trauma in the criminal legal system helps their efforts to expand access to social services.

At the same time, to assert and maintain the common narrative, most VTC personnel reiterated that veterans are different than other criminal legal defendants, which implies that their trauma should be seen differently.

WHAT DISTINGUISHES VTCs: CAMARADERIE, STRUCTURE, OR DIGNITY?

In clarifying the common narrative, VTC judges and staff discussed not only what makes veterans different from other defendants but also what makes VTCs different from other courts. In particular, they mentioned camaraderie and structure as unique and beneficial features of VTCs. These explanations about what makes VTCs special rely on the notion that there is something special about veterans, and how military culture distinguishes VTCs from other courts. Again, careful observation of the courts, particularly their differences, suggests that those explanations help explain the proliferation of VTCs but not necessarily their day-to-day operations.

Jack O'Connor, the founding mentor coordinator for the VTC in Buffalo, New York, articulated the relationship between assumptions about veterans and assumptions about VTCs:

This is part of their makeup. They worked in a system built on structure, taught leadership, the expectation of competence, that their mission is for the common good, camaraderie. It's neat when you see a court full of veterans, the camaraderie.

(Jack O'Connor, interview)

He suggested that veterans in his Buffalo VTC immediately responded to the presence of other veterans, showing a willingness to share their stories and receive help from the court because other veterans were involved.

A clinician in the Southeast VTC also described veterans as being distinctly connected to one another through camaraderie in the courtroom:

They are very different, on Day 1 [they] pick up this silent brotherhood. I don't know if [it's] silent, as they mention it a lot, but how they click immediately [with] one with the other. Running in here, they introduce them[selves] and [do the hearing] ritual, how they['re] immediately, "You are army, navy," you can tell [it's] and different culture, talking to them.

(clinician, Southeast VTC, interview)

The emphasis on camaraderie—central to the idea of military culture—is well captured in the studies that focus on the important role that peer mentors play in VTCs (e.g., Jalain and Grossi 2020). In interviews and presentations, Judge Russell (see chapter 3) and other leaders in the VTC movement call these mentors the "special sauce" that makes VTCs uniquely beneficial for participants. At the All Rise conferences, there is a specialized track for people interested in becoming mentors. The emphasis on veteran worth is front and center in these meetings, articulated through discussions on why veterans deserve criminal legal benefits, and what makes them unique from those in the court system who were never in the military. At the 2021 conference, for example, the mentor session took place in a room crowded with attendees enthusiastically discussing their military histories and the courtrooms they serve. In the session titled "Bootcamp: Mentoring Lessons Learned from the Field," when speakers mentioned how little civilians understand or appreciate what veterans have been through, everyone nodded. Attendees mentioned their personal challenges with substance use and mental health disorders, and speakers articulated mentoring as a unique way to find community for themselves and others. One speaker introduced the role of the mentor as also being spokesperson for the court in their communities. He gave the following advice:

Go to social events, go to Rotary Clubs, social events. I have an elevator speech. I ask, "What you do?" They say, "Oh, what do you do?" I say, "I save lives." "Are you a doctor?" I say, "I am not, but I work with veterans in the criminal justice system, I work in treatment programs to get their lives back together so [they] can turn around and become [the] productive citizens they've always wanted to be, to get educational and business opportunities."

(presenter, All Rise conference)

These explanations about what makes veterans—and thus VTCs—unique start with the assumption that veterans are uniquely capable of behavioral change in part because other veterans are uniquely capable of helping them achieve those changes (Slattery et al. 2013; Ahlin and Douds 2020). Yet, my observations of VTCs find contradictions in these assumptions because the whole story about what veteran peers offer is more complicated. Although grateful for the extra support, court staff in all three VTC sites also expressed the challenge of having people who are not legally or clinically trained playing a central role in the court. Judges, probation officers, and clinicians reiterated the importance of veteran mentors playing a supportive role that is adjacent to both the legal and clinical teams. These findings are well articulated in research that discusses the lack of clarity about the role of peer mentors in VTCs, which can lead to conflicts with some mentors who see themselves as an enforcer of court rules or as a recovery support "sponsor" or simply as a friend (Douds, Ahlin, and Posteraro 2021).

In addition to discussing the camaraderie of being in a program with other veterans, over and again, VTC judges and courtroom staff frequently mentioned how veterans benefit from structure, revealing the implicit appeal of VTCs to those who believe that the criminal legal system can change behavior. The primary judge in the Southeast VTC mentioned to me in an interview the "science" of structure, emphasizing the "science-based approach" borrowed from the drug court literature. A clinician commented that veteran participants deal well with authority in jails:

The veterans that I would see in jail would function pretty well in jail. I think that maybe they are used to that level of structure.

(clinician, West VTC, interview)

A probation officer (PO) also noted that veterans respond better to structure than other types of treatment court participants:

They get it: this serves them well. When we provide a structured program, they get it. When there's authority, they get it. Not all, but the
majority of them.

(PO, Northeast VTC, interview)

These comments about structure promote beliefs that VTCs are effective
because many military veterans are alike, and that discipline in the criminal
legal system can be similar to discipline in the military. The same probation
officer quoted above explained to me how he sometimes feels like a translator
for other POs who do not understand the extent to which veterans benefit from
structure:

I have to sometimes put in, "Wait a minute. Hold on a minute. You
guys never served." I said, "This is what's happening. These guys don't
look for sorrow or for you to love [them]. They need someone that's
going to be there with a stern, clear, concise objective to them." Sometimes us feeling pity for them is why they're struggling. We've got to
get rid of that.

(PO, Northeast VTC, interview)

Clinicians in the West and Southeast VTCs explained similar concerns
that the judges in their courts were not strict enough with participants, giving
too much leeway when they didn't follow court rules, and that a more punitive
approach would be beneficial for participants.

Beyond reinforcing distinctions between those who served in the military
and those who didn't, this element of the common narrative—that VTCs provide the structure that veterans need—maps directly onto assumptions that
punishment, or the threat of it, is beneficial in treatment courts. The problem
is that substance use and mental health disorders are not so easily "treated"
through coercion (Tiger 2012). Kaye (2020) points out that the punishment
and rehabilitative logics behind drug treatment courts provide cover for the
fact that people medicate themselves, for example, in response to exploitative
labor practices and other social inequalities. It is well accepted that drug use in
the military is a coping strategy, so there is additional irony in emphasizing the
value of structure in making VTCs uniquely effective in helping veterans but
not nonveterans. I found personnel were comfortable in making assumptions
about veterans that they might not or don't make about other criminal legal
defendants. One clinician, for example, said that the threat of punishment is
uniquely beneficial for VTC participants:

They won't do it without an authority figure saying, "You've got to do this or I'm going to lock you up."

(clinician, Northeast VTC, interview)

In addition to reinforcing distinctions between veteran and nonveterans, these reflections on the importance of structure are important in understanding the central contradiction of VTCs: military service is both the cause of these participants' criminal legal behavior and a beneficial experience.

Further, when describing the benefits of structure, illustrations of internal court hierarchies and inequalities emerge and undermine the idea that all veterans are alike and all benefit from structure. A court coordinator explained that the differences between those who have VA benefits and those who do not shape how the participants respond to structure:

There's a bit of a caste system, you know, which is people who have VA benefits and those who don't. The service-connected ones are usually great at following rules, and the non-service-connected ones were mostly dishonorably discharged and are not as good at following rules per se.

(court coordinator, West VTC, interview)

This comment underscores the discussion in chapter 3, which is the ways in which VTCs depend on social services, particularly on the VA, and access to services differs not only by VTC locale but also by person. By this account, access to services also shapes how participants respond to the structure that VTCs offer.

These unique courtroom dynamics, which I explore further in later chapters, complicate the relationship between assumptions about what makes veterans distinct and what makes VTCs uniquely beneficial for them. Analyzing how VTC judges, court personnel, and proponents articulate the common narrative shows how it serves an important purpose in legitimizing the courts. At the same time, it also illustrates the courts' shaky ideological foundations.

INSTITUTIONALIZING A NEW TREATMENT COURT

VTCs are now a permanent feature of the US criminal legal landscape. In 2018, Congress passed the Veterans Treatment Court Improvement Act. The bill, supported by Democrats and Republicans and signed into law by then President Trump, authorized funding for an additional 50 Veterans Justice Officers to join the 314 then working at the VA. Still operating under the VA's homelessness program, this law illustrates the dedicated support that VTCs garnered over less than a decade.

Through its explanation of VTCs' ideological foundations to complement the material foundations offered by the VA, this chapter provides additional insights into the politics of worth. VTC judges and staff articulate a "sense of mission" and "distinctive competence" to realize their goals, two features that suggest VTCs have become institutionalized in the US criminal legal and social welfare landscape (Selznick 1957). Institutionalization requires a belief in the nature, rightness, and importance of an organization's responsibilities so that individuals become committed to what the organization does and how to sustain it. The findings here suggest that organizations with both material *and* ideological foundations can thrive regardless of evidence about their efficacy. The belief that veterans are worthy for simply having joined the military does important work in justifying and legitimizing VTCs, which themselves reinforce beliefs about veteran worth, which then reinforces the financial investment in VTCs.

Thinking of legitimacy as a political concept helps explain the proliferation of VTCs because it provides insights into how policymakers weigh competing demands and allocate resources (Loader and Sparks 2013). This chapter argues that VTCs are unique among treatment courts because they are dedicated to a legally recognized social group with a particular social status forged from decades of mobilization to realize social welfare benefits (Jones 2014; Skocpol 1995). This legitimacy, and therefore the financial and political support that the courts enjoy, are built from continuous advocacy that has contributed to broader cultural narratives about military service. The courts' legitimacy comes not only from the unique cultural space that the military occupies but also from the unique place of law in US culture, whereby courts are asked to solve complex human problems. These two cultural narratives—on the value of the criminal legal system and of the military—converge in VTCs, leading to an instrumentalization of law to aid a population deemed worthy of publicly funded resources.

To further understand the politics of worth, it is important to note what is missing from this chapter. VTCs present a structural argument for criminalized offending, only it's not the kind of structural argument that criminal legal reformers typically make. Despite the various ways in which VTCs celebrate military service, they also take the onus of responsibility for criminal legal behavior from other failed social and political institutions and place it on the military.[2] In addition, absent are any commentaries about criminalization itself, particularly how people with substance use disorders face criminal legal consequences for their addictions (Lynch 2012). Judges and court personnel recognize the many life reasons (and traumas) that lead people to join the military, and the struggles many have upon reintegration into civilian life. These challenges may have less to do with their military service and more to do with the difficulty of finding meaningful work and social supports both prior to and after their service (Junger 2016). Yet, these judges and personnel articulate the common narrative that military service is related to criminalized behavior to make sense of treating those who joined the military and are accused of illegal behaviors differently from people accused of those same behaviors but who did not choose to join the military.

By unpacking the common narrative about what makes veterans unique and what makes VTCs uniquely beneficial, we can better understand the inherent contradiction in how VTCs both celebrate military service and attribute criminal legal behaviors to it. The common narrative helps explain why these courts appeal to those needed to make them function (e.g., funders, social service providers), those interested in directly helping veterans (e.g., mentors), and those interested in broader criminal legal reforms (e.g., scholars, policymakers). The courts provide an opportunity to identify people who have served in the military and were found guilty of committing some crime. The courts help those struggling, especially with accessing social services from the VA (and elsewhere). And, for those interested in criminal legal reform more broadly, these courts normalize and center trauma as a means to understand and respond to criminalized behavior. This can help both veterans in VTCs and non-veterans in the regular criminal legal system.

This examination of the common narrative, or what is similar in VTCs, helps us to understand why VTCs have proliferated. However, as the second half of this book will show, VTCs are actually strikingly *dissimilar* in whom they serve and how they serve them.

Five

INSIDE THE COURTS

Operationalizing the VTC Concept

On a warm summer day in August 2017, a young veteran overcoming an opioid addiction, wearing a GPS monitor on his ankle due to a relapse, was called for his hearing at the Northeast VTC. Earlier that month, the participant and the judge argued over whether to remove the GPS monitor. The participant complained bitterly that the monitor made it difficult to find and maintain a job.

This day, the probation officer explained that the participant was doing well at the residential facility, working on becoming a mentor and facilitating support groups for the veterans staying there. The probation officer said that he would like the judge to remove the GPS.

The participant appeared happy and surprised, saying "I wasn't going to say nothing about it today." The judge replied, "See, you do all those good things so you don't have to say anything."

Referring to their earlier argument, the judge continued, "I want to tell everyone you wrote a thoughtful well written letter of apology for how you didn't keep your composure." The participant replied, "I was a jerk, it was a reaction. I should remember I was a Marine and should have tact and self-control. I was more disappointed with myself."

Across the country, on a crisp day in March 2020, a participant in West was treated with less sympathy from a judge who was, usually, as supportive and patient with participants as Northeast's judge. The participant was struggling to maintain contact with the court's clinicians, attend therapy, and meet other court requirements. The prosecutor at the time was often at odds with the court's clinicians and even the judge because, he argued, they would say that participants were complying with court orders even when they missed a requirement. The prosecutor started the hearing aggressively, telling the court to "not pretend" that this participant was in compliance. This opened a long exchange between the judge and the participant, which revealed the participant was living with severe mental health issues, and the judge's challenge in figuring out what his court could do to help.

For those who have spent time in treatment courts or reading about them, and the following exchanges may seem familiar. There is little difference between this scene than any other described by treatment court scholars studying how judges try to encourage compliance (e.g., Moore and Hirai 2014; Castellano 2017; Kaye 2020). The point of detailing these exchanges is twofold. One, they highlight the distinct lack of military culture I observed in West, compounding my initial query about the common narrative and its accuracy. More to the point of this chapter, this exchange illustrates the distinct challenges facing West as compared with the other two courts. West's participant population was the definition of high risk for recidivism and high need for social services, what treatment court proponents say is the group that courts should be accepting. However, the level of need and the court's difficulty meeting it undermined the common narrative that VTCs can be uniquely beneficial by adding veteran and stirring to the drug treatment court model. They also underscore the difficulty of generalizing about the veteran population and a court's ability to help them.

Strikingly, this participant's mental health challenges got in the way of the judge's attempts to understand what the court might do to support him:

Judge [to the prosecutor]: He needs a phone.
Participant: I have that, but there's been a major trademark breach, the monopoly game on the treatment that my family has rights to and Sony and I want that on record because the police don't do shit, I would like to be on the record if I lose it all today I understand everything that's going on

but I've been working hard and people have passed away and storage units have been broken into, other stuff has been going on. I'm at wit's end. I understand I'm not a full compliance, but I'm picking up the pieces to where I'm supposed to be with my brother passing away and family feud.

Judge: I understand you've been through a lot.

Participant: I'm working through it.

Judge: Has anyone ever recommended you take medications?

Participant: I'm not taking medications, if you're to add a toll booth in the Doritos, then you'd get a Ritas which is my mother, I have this anxiety issue.

Judge: You made it clear you don't want to take medications.

Participant: I medicate.

Judge: Just tell me why.

Participant: Why should I try to fill the pain with artificial medications when it's other people not doing their jobs, when inheritance gets stolen especially in this town, there's two of them here and other corrupt stuff and the police don't use shit and excuse my language. I don't be with Deborah here. I am being abused and everyone is trying to create badness. I've been a part of the industry since George Michael has written numerous pieces. I can back it up. At the end of day, justice needs to happen and I understand this is Veterans Justice Court, but when I say there's breach and there's a D3 I have rights to the internet. You don't have to believe me, I'll get a new lawyer and take it to the Supreme Court. At the end of the day, I'm just trying to make things work.

Judge: I'm trying to help make things work.

Participant: I can back it up, it's blackstreet, no diggity. Sorry I'm quoting music again, back in the day I wasn't mad but now I'm pretty pissed off they stole my baby goods and my company.

Judge: It's not that I don't want to hear it, I'm just having a difficult time understanding it. I'm not sure how much further we can get. If you want to do it your way, it's going to be difficult. (West VTC)

In this exchange, the judge tries to give the participant the opportunity to share his thoughts about medication rather than focus on the lack of compliance. West emphasized rehabilitation over punishment for people who continued to use illicit substances, one manifestation of its distinct culture focused on prioritizing psychosocial goals even if it meant the participants did not want to get the suggested help. The judge tried to encourage the participant to explain whether or to what extent he would comply so that no one was wasting their time.

Other exchanges between this same participant and the judge throughout the year were equally fraught, with the judge trying to make sense of the stories about the music industry, the food recently eaten, and sorrow over experiences in the city. One time, the participant expressed his frustration between his expectations for joining the court and what the court was asking of him:

> It was set only two years and I['d] get off of [this VTC] in six to nine months and it's been six to nine months. Just because I'm calling something out and trying to create a change, you can't go and say, "Oh, it'll be two more years." That's not justice. Don't mess with my freedom. I'm trying to get your shit together.
>
> *(West VTC)*

The participant's concerns reveal the dilemma that arises when the court prioritizes rehabilitation, as it can be at the expense of a clear and speedy criminal legal outcome. While this participant and judge worked harder to understand one another than was typical, exchanges exhibiting frustration, confusion, and genuine struggle were the norm in the West VTC. In fall 2020, when many participants were struggling with the pandemic and government shutdowns, there were even more challenging exchanges in the court about what participants were supposed to do to graduate from the program. Many hearings offered opportunities for the judge and court personnel to learn what a participant had been doing since their last appearance in court, but these exchanges did not resemble anything close to the common narrative of a court uniquely suited to help struggling veterans. Everyone was struggling.

Watching these exchanges, I tried to make sense of how different the West courtroom was from the Northeast or Southeast VTCs. In Northeast, I never saw anyone with similarly severe mental health challenges or expressing confusion over how long the program was supposed to last and how long it had already been. The Northeast VTC judge and court staff, unlike in the West VTC, didn't seem uncertain about what the participant's housing or medical status was, and seemed to know how a person was doing before they came to the judge's podium. There were rarely contentious exchanges between the judge and a participant, let alone exchanges that were adversarial.

Likewise, while I witnessed angry exchanges in the Southeast VTC, I never saw an exchange in which a participant was confused about reality. Nevertheless, that VTC had its own problems that often seemed even more challenging than what I witnessed at the West VTC. Most notably, when I first began observations at the Southeast VTC, I could not do so because the court was not accepting any new clients or even holding hearings for existing participants. The court's funder had blocked the court from continuing its work until it implemented a treatment plan meeting the funder's requirements.

What explains these striking differences in veterans treatment courts? Do these differences matter in the lives of participants? More broadly, what do they tell us about how the United States uses criminal law to solve complex and entrenched social and political problems?

To answer these questions, the second half of this book examines the three courts that I observed regularly over many years. My observations suggest that, while the common narrative may help legitimate the court to policy makers and funders, the court's day-to-day practices reveal the common narrative's fallacies. The add veteran and stir approach to other treatment courts produces widely different courts; this means that a veteran deciding to join one VTC may not know what they are committing to and may have a very different experience from a veteran participating in another VTC. The differences highlight that the idea of military culture in VTCs is subsumed by other aspects of a court community (Ulmer 1997), with courts understanding their goals and strategies in different, and often contradictory, ways.

The differences I observe here can be partly explained by the fact that adult drug treatment courts, of which VTCs are a subset, follow a particular model—the one promulgated by All Rise—but, like all criminal courtrooms, differ in relation to individual personalities and local contexts (Ostrom et al. 2007). Yet, as I observed them, I continually reflected on what the Veteran Administration's director of the Veterans Justice Office told me years prior: "VTCs are a concept, not a model." His comment was striking because the VTC in Buffalo, New York, was to be a type of model—which is distinct from a concept in that a model has a particular structure—and the common narrative suggests there is one. The model was supposedly based on the national drug treatment court but with dedicated veteran mentors and the support of the VA, with the aim of creating a distinct court to help veterans in legal trouble maintain sobriety and find housing and employment, among other court goals. Further, I frequently heard calls at All Rise to standardize VTCs so that the experience of being in one did not differ much depending on locale. I struggled to see how standardization was possible after getting to know these three courts over a decade.

Thinking of VTCs as a concept rather than a model reveals how the add veteran and stir approach draws on ideological and material foundations at the national level, but an individual court understands and implements the concept according to their own organizational priorities. In addition, understanding why they are so different reveals the distinct inequalities within both the criminal legal system and veterans' social services, and how these inequalities intersect within and between these different locales. In each court, the inequalities between participants may be amplified or diminished through court practices. Importantly, this showcases how these courts balance their rehabilitative goals through retributive practices in different ways. Serving veterans does not change these dynamics but introduces more complexities as the courts navigate veterans' social services and unequal access to them.

THREE DISTINCT ORGANIZATIONS

The rest of this chapter focuses on the differences between the three courts by first describing their hearings, which are the spaces where a VTC tries to create a feeling of community for the participants and those who work in the courts. Hearings usually occur weekly at designated times. Participants describe how they are doing, and the judge and court personnel offer resources. Participants are mandated to appear, though hearing frequency is based on the phase that the participant is in. In these hearings, the participant and court personnel each articulate their understanding of what is expected, and the judge engages in the unique art of encouraging compliance with court mandates. This is what Castellano (2017) calls "benchcraft," or the day-to-day creative work of judges in treatment courts.

While central to my analysis, differing benchcraft techniques are just one item in a list of contrasts among the three courts. Parsing the differences of these courts in their building of community shows how the same ideas, and even rules, can be applied in strikingly different ways. Drawing on the study of courts as organizations (Friedman 1975; Ulmer 1997), this chapter focuses on the people, their interactions with one another, and how a participant coming to court may experience the temporary community in each week's hearing. The analysis moves beyond studying outcomes—which are difficult if not impossible to compare across these three courts. My analysis focuses on the courts as social bodies, and as communities, each with distinct cultures that shape decision making (Eisenstein, Flemming, and Nardulli 1988). Culture, in this sense, is "the way things get done around here" (Ostrom et al. 2007) and is critical to understanding different court outcomes. Drawing attention to day-to-day practices is particularly useful to understanding VTCs because formal program requirements often matter less than priorities, norms, and practices, which can have significant impacts on both court participants and court staff (Gordon 2018). Each VTC used formal and informal processes to realize their goals, which were themselves defined in different ways.

Because each VTC has its own way of defining and realizing its goals, the differences between these courts complicate the narrative that VTCs are unique, and uniquely beneficial, because they incorporate military culture. Rather, my analysis reveals how difficult it is to identify what makes these courts similar aside from the presence of VJOs and the additional resources the VA brings, as well as the respectful treatment of participants—the material and ideological foundations identified in chapters 3 and 4. In so doing, it reveals how the add veteran and stir approach in VTCs creates an assemblage of punishment that links punitive logics from the criminal legal system to the rehabilitative logics of the VA, further entrenching the idea that there is something inherently worthy about military service and potentially salutary about criminal legal involvement. Additionally, the descriptions illustrate how different practices can amplify or diminish the inequalities that can predict treatment court success.

The following section describes, to the extent possible, a typical day in each of the courts. It opens with the Northeast VTC, which follows the model of a court with a robust community of court personnel and supporters to offer predictability for its participants. This community and predictability helps moderate the challenges that emerge from a court trying to help people with varying levels of support in the form of housing, employment, and other resources. The analysis follows with the Southeast VTC and then the West VTC, each of which deviates significantly from the model and struggles in different ways to foster a cohesive court community with predictability and support for its participants. While chapter 6 offers insights into why these courts are so different, the goal of this chapter is to show the challenge of comparing these three courts.

The descriptions suggest that the common narrative helps explain the creation of VTCs, but its absence in the courtrooms helps illustrate why add veteran and stir yields a complicated mixture, where the politics of worth in any given court have more to do with the court's founding, personnel, and access to resources than the fact that it serves veterans (chapter 6 explores this argument more fully). The observation that VTCs are a concept, not a model, reveals how much implementation of the concept matters for VTC participants and personnel.

Northeast VTC: A "Model" Court. The courthouse hosting the Northeast VTC was typically empty on Wednesday afternoons, making it easy to observe the different groups—participants, mentors, community members—that attended hearings. The courthouse was in the center of a small city, and the area had pretty plazas but empty parking garages, indicative of the industrial decline in the region. I often found a parking spot right in front of the courthouse, alongside a park that was also mostly empty. Getting to the courthouse using public transportation was not easy, though someone could take a bus if they lived along the route.

The VTC session started in the afternoon, almost always on time, and the ritual of entering did not change week to week. This regularity helped contribute to the feeling of community that the court successfully fostered, and a source of stability for participants. Such community and stability were espoused goals that the court was capable of realizing. Many days, participants who were living at the same residential facility would arrive together using shared transportation from the facility and chat outside the courthouse. In front of the courthouse, some would smoke cigarettes, others would eat a snack. Most were dressed in jeans and a clean shirt; some looked somber, and usually all looked sober. About ten minutes before court was set to begin, everyone passed through security at the front door and walked up stairs or rode the elevator to the second floor, which was the top floor of the building. More participants and observers arrived singly, some sitting alone while others mingled outside the courtroom. Everyone was typically in the hall and, together, waited for the courtroom to be opened. As they waited, people were mostly quiet though some whispered in groups. Judging from appearances, there were typically fewer racially minoritized defendants than the small city where the courthouse was located, but more than one would typically see in the surrounding towns that the court served.

Although the participants in the courtroom appeared to come from a variety of backgrounds and with different levels of access to stable housing and other resources, these starting points of inequality flattened out as we entered the hallway. Most notably, a group of well-dressed older men—the court's mentors—appeared shortly before 2 p.m. They arrived as a group, sometimes continuing conversations from their previous meeting, separate from the VTC staffing meeting mentioned below, to discuss how their individual mentees were doing. They each wore a pin with "VIP: Very Important Patriot" on it. There were usually five mentors, and they mostly showed up on a regular basis. One was African American, the rest were white; all were older and retired, and they were very dedicated volunteers. They had tried to recruit long-term female mentors over the years, but the mentors I regularly saw were these men. They walked around the courthouse with an air of pride. Unlike the two courtrooms described later in this chapter, the mentors did not spend a lot of time before, during, or after hearings speaking with the participants. Since these mentors regularly communicated with the participants outside of the hearings, they knew how their mentees were doing.

In addition to the feeling of community, there was also a feeling of predictability bordering on formality in this courtroom. Every week, a few minutes before or after 2 p.m., the security officer unlocked the courtroom. Entering was an orderly affair, and people were either silent or continuing their hallway conversations now in hushed voices. The security officer announced the judge, who entered from a doorway behind the bench. In the Northeast VTC, the bench, or the judge's place in the courtroom, was high above everyone else. Everyone stood to acknowledge the judge's entrance. The judge, wearing the traditional black robe, smiled warmly and welcomed the small crowd, expressing happiness to see the many participants, mentors, and staff in the courtroom. Everyone sat back down.

In the courtroom, the feeling of predictability continued as different parties populated the same spaces each week and stayed for the whole session. Clinicians and court members had already taken seats in the front row. As they did in all three courts that I observed, each team met in a meeting known as "staffing" before the hearing, which is why they were comfortably settled by the time the doors opened. If a participant was coming from the jail, which was a rare occurrence, the person, wearing an orange jumpsuit and handcuffed, also sat in the front row. Mentors typically spread out among the participants, though sometimes they sat in pairs together. They stood out due to their age—and the fact they were wearing military insignia. Participants also spread out, though also sometimes in pairs, and rarely talking above a whisper. The probation officer sat at the desk to the left and the defense attorney sat to the right, positioned as one might expect for trial. Of course, there was no trial.

Looking back at my many years of observations, the word conformity—or discipline—looms large as a way to make sense of how this VTC operationalized the VTC concept. For example, since almost everyone arrived at the same time, it was obvious when someone was late. People in the courtroom would turn to look, and participants walking in after the court started kept their heads low and slid into the nearest available bench. Like the stereotypical culture of the Northeast, this was not a courtroom where someone would want to stand out from the crowd.

The formalities continued with how each participants case was discussed. With everyone in place, the probation officer introduced, so to speak, each participant to the judge. The format was also predictable. The probation officer (PO) called the participants in alphabetical order, so participants knew when they were up next or close to being called. When their name was called, the participant walked up to the judge's podium. Their assigned mentor often followed, standing a few feet behind them. If someone did not know that this was a VTC, they might assume that the mentor was a defense attorney, given how the participant and the mentor were positioned in front of the judge.

The introduction provided an opportunity for everyone in the courtroom to familiarize themselves with the participant, humanizing each person and blunting judgments that might emerge from their different backgrounds and reasons for being in the courtroom. The PO introduced them by name, and then explained whether they passed their most recent drug test, their attendance at therapy sessions, their housing situation, any community service, or other goals achieved. The PO also included the participant's branch of the military, which was frequently the only military reference in the entire hearing. A typical introduction by the PO of someone doing well was:

[Participant] comes before you; he started Phase 1 on [date] and now he is in the second phase. He's from the United States Navy. [Participant] has continued to test negative on his Breathalyzers and also continues to be compliant with probation and also the veteran treatment program; and also, as I said before, he is in Phase 2 because of his positive work in the Veteran Treatment Court.

Fostering a feeling of equality among the participants, each introduction covered the basics of the participant's obligation to the court—drug testing, attending therapy appointments—and if the person was in compliance. Unlike in the other two courts, it was rare for more than one participant to be out of compliance, and it usually related to a failed drug test or not attending therapy as scheduled. Because most participants were in compliance, much of the hearing served as an opportunity to chat and hear about how each participant was doing.

Like these introductions, the rest of the courtroom sessions were usually predictable. Everyone knew that they would be in the courtroom for up to ninety minutes as the dozen or so participants spoke individually with the judge. Even if they did not participate in the staffing meeting before the hearing, everyone knew the basics of each participant simply by being in the courtroom on a regular basis. Participants often explained how helpful the court was, how caring their mentor was, and all the ways that they were trying to make healthy changes in their lives. Compared with accounts of other treatment courts (Tiger 2012; Moore and Hirai 2013; Kaye 2020), the main difference between this VTC and a treatment court not focused on veterans was the involvement of the mentors, the VA clinicians helping those VA eligible, and the overall feeling of community that emanated in daily hearings and public events.

Other factors also contributed to the feeling of predictability and community in the court. In contrast to the turnover in the other two courts, although participants changed over my six years of observations at the Northeast VTC, I saw the same staff. Except for one PO, who was a proud veteran, no other staff were veterans, but they were committed to helping the participants. The court had almost no turnover during the time I observed hearings—there was the same judge, PO, and defense attorney; the defense attorney was noteworthy because he was a volunteer. The one clinician who left was replaced by a social worker who had won public service awards in recognition of his dedication to veterans. These clinicians aided the participants who were not VA eligible. The other two clinicians worked for the Veterans Administration and, in our interviews, emphasized how much they believed in the court's ability to help participants.

Conversations between the judge and the participants were similarly predictable but were also informative, replete with expressions of pride and appreciation (deviations are explored in chapter 7). A typical conversation involved a few prompting questions from the judge, with detailed answers from the participants. Some more experienced participants explained in their hearings that they first felt reluctant to share, but later realized that the court was there to help them. Many times, the participants and the judge talked about what the mentors had done to support them, such as providing transportation to an appointment or other court obligation, or being available by phone when the participant wanted to talk.

In conversations that were more heated, the participants were typically able to explain what they were frustrated about and could come to an acceptable resolution with the judge. Often, their frustrations were not about the court directly but the places that the court asked them to stay for treatment. The predictability of these hearings was mirrored in the predictability of the treatment program. The Northeast VTC followed an eighteen-month model, with a set amount of time between the phases for people who were compliant. Those who were compliant for the entire program could move through the phases at a faster clip and graduate early, but most people joined the court expecting to go through well-defined phases. Again, consistent with the Buffalo, New York, model, based on the national drug court model, the Northeast VTC decreased its requirements as phases went on. In hearings, each phase advancement was treated as a major accomplishment. When someone moved between phases, the audience applauded, and the judge and assigned mentor expressed their pride.

My observations at the Northeast VTC suggested that participants sometimes felt frustrated with court requirements, but that the court also offered numerous resources. The availability of material resources complemented the human resources that helped smooth over court interactions. In particular, the mentors spent hours each week supporting their assigned mentees. It was clear during hearings that the participants often checked in with their mentors over the phone, as mentors took time explaining what the participants were doing. As noted above, the mentors met regularly before the court hearings to discuss together how their participants were doing. In these private meetings, they shared strategies with one another. Notably, after a few years of mentoring, they realized that participants would benefit from new clothes, particularly when they were looking for jobs, and they also needed other items that cost money. Part of the mentoring model is that mentors do not spend money on participants, so the Northeast VTC mentors started their own nonprofit to raise funds.

These different options for support moderated inequalities that define VTCs. Watching court hearings, it was rarely clear who had VA benefits and who did not, or how typical markers of inequality such as race played out in the courtroom. For example, even though participants without VA benefits had fewer treatment options, I only observed a few hearings where the court was struggling to find a treatment facility placement for a participant. And, even though there were different clinicians serving VA-eligible and -ineligible participants, the whole clinical team—VJO or no—appeared familiar with each participant.

I label this a model VTC because of the strong sense of community and how participants articulated their gratitude for what the court offered; occasional observations of this court would affirm the common narrative. Although the role of the military was far more nuanced than the common narrative suggests, those who suggest that VTCs are uniquely able to help participants because they draw on military culture might find support for their argument. There was little to no "leveraging military culture" as described in earlier chapters, at least with regard to overt references to duty, honor, or camaraderie. At the same time, the commitment of the mentors to helping the veterans, offering material support as well as care predicated on the idea that veterans are a worthy group of criminal legal defendants, distinguished this court both from the other two courts and from other treatment court programs discussed in scholarly literature. With this stronger sense of community and conformity—a "shared mission"—the court seemed better able to realize its goals of helping participants stay sober, access housing, gain employment, and other stabilizing resources. This is what VTC advocates hope to create. Yet, as chapter 6 illustrates, its creation was not happenstance. And, as the next two courts illustrate, this court should not be understood as the VTC norm even if it is a model.

Southeast VTC: Herding. I observed the Northeast VTC for a year before visiting the Southeast VTC for the first time. I expected a similar scene in the court, with participants sitting for the whole session, expressing gratitude to the judge and other court personnel, mentors circulating beforehand to check in with their mentees. My expectations quickly dissolved. I refer to this court as herding, as it often felt like the judge was trying to coax people who made it clear, either through their words or body language, that they did not want to be there and wanted to leave as quickly as possible. Military culture was mostly absent in this court, which borrowed heavily from the drug court model of co-erced sobriety, though the judge tried to convince the participants to comply by reiterating the common narrative that VTCs are uniquely beneficial for partic-ipants because court personnel understand military culture. Community and stability were espoused goals, but the court struggled to realize them.

Whereas the Northeast VTC was predictable, which helped foster a sense of community, this court was not. The courthouse where the Southeast VTC was located was in the center of a large city, surrounded by highways and hos-pitals, with little pedestrian traffic. Most of the buildings near the courthouse were filled with people working in the criminal legal system or the nearby hospital, coming and going between their offices or their appointments or their cars. Parking was always tough and expensive; and those who worked in the VTC complained about the tickets that they received when hearings went long. There was public transportation nearby, though it could be limited for those who lived throughout the sprawling city. In pre-hearing conversations, and even during conversations with the judge, these challenges shaped how some participants and even staff felt about coming to this court.

Inside Southeast's courthouse, the feeling was casual. After I passed through the security gates, I would often chat with the friendly guards. The courthouse was tall at eleven stories, but it was not particularly busy during the afternoon VTC sessions. I usually chose to go up to the courtroom using the escalators, which required me to round a corner on each floor. In addition to the court-rooms, each floor had private hallways at the end of the public hallways. On one floor, tucked away in one private hallway was the coordinator's office for the VTC, and nearby were offices for two VTC clinicians. Further down the private hall was the judge's office, with a large conference table where VTC staffing meetings were held.

I usually arrived right when the VTC session was scheduled to start. On my first visit, I was alone in the hallway, wondering if I had gotten the time wrong.

Slowly, participants arrived. People trickled into the courtroom, waiting for the hearing to begin, but never being sure when, except within the hour. I noticed that most of the participants appeared to be men of color, like most people in this racially diverse city. Unlike in Northeast, where it was rare to see someone who was not a participant, sometimes Southeast's participants had family with them, or someone who appeared to be a girlfriend. Participants were chatty with one another, often wondering when the court would start.

Those of us waiting to enter court experienced uncertainty from the time we arrived in the courtroom. Sometime after 2:00 p.m., or sometimes closer to 2:30 or 3:00 p.m., the VTC team, a multiracial group of men and women, arrived. Then the judge entered. The clinicians sat together to the left of the judge; the prosecutor and defense attorneys took their positions at the desks in front of the judge. Some participants came to court wearing orange jump-suits, indicating they were in jail. Because this was a larger courtroom than the Northeast VTC, the judge sat higher and farther away from us. Not only did we never know when court would begin, but those of us sitting through entire hearings never knew when they would end either, sometimes staring at the clock as it inched toward 5 p.m.

The feeling of uncertainty in the courtroom was exacerbated by personnel changes. In contrast to the Northeast VTC, which had little staff turnover over the six-year period I observed it, I often saw new people in the Southeast VTC. I observed two district attorneys over my six years in the Southeast VTC, while the public defender remained with the court until the end of my observations in 2022. The judge remained the same—the judge was the court's founder— and was dedicated to helping the people in this court. However, when I first observed the Southeast VTC in 2017, there was no dedicated VA clinician or treatment team coordinator. A few months later, both a veterans justice officer (VJO) and a court coordinator joined the team, and this clinician sat in the jury box along with the court's two social workers. One social worker remained the same, while the other changed every year or so. Personnel complained that the case manager's salary was so low that recruiting for the position was diffi- cult. One case manager described having sometimes to choose which meal of the day to eat because of all their expenses, including student loans for their academic degrees, which they needed to secure the job.

Mentors in the Southeast VTC also did not last long. On my early observations, I met a kind, white, older mentor who was very chatty. He walked between the rows to say hi to the participants, but he did not have a relationship with any of them outside the courtroom. Sometimes a new mentor joined him, also usually another older man. Southeast VTC mentors usually only observed, and they did not last long as volunteers. One day, one of these rotating mentors came over to our research team, and the coordinator asked how things were with his mentee. The mentor said that "he set him straight," telling him that he "doesn't know shit about the real world and jail would not be pleasant for him." He expressed pride in encouraging the participant "to put on a tie today," telling him that "he needs to look like he's going to church, if he is not leaving church." The mentor then talked about how his mother was murdered in front of him, and that he "got into real bad stuff, gangs and what not," so he knows about bad influences, and that is what his mentee is dealing with. "I told him if he ends up in jail, he's going to be someone's bitch. He won't be able to walk after what they do to him. And he's going be in there a long time. That is what really set him straight." When this mentor walked away, the court coordinator responded to our research team member's look of confusion about the exchange, saying the mentor "is just a crazy character."

While the Northeast VTC followed a clear script for each of its hearings, there was no similar routine in the Southeast VTC. Rather, the judge called the person to the podium and stated whether they were or were not in compliance. There was no mention of their military branch. There was no mentor standing nearby. Rather, the participant stood alone, directly below the judge's podium, with the prosecutor's desk to the left and the defense attorneys to the right. Occasionally, the prosecutor or a clinician provided additional information for the judge, giving context I rarely saw in the Northeast VTC because, I assumed, that information was covered in Northeast's staffing meetings.

After the Southeast VTC judge discussed compliance, conversations went in any number of directions. If there were no compliance issues, the judge and participant might engage in informal banter about clothing or appearances. These conversations were usually short, though the judge would reiterate the importance of following the court's mandates and ask the participant to share with the group about why it is good to comply. If the judge was scolding a participant for missing a drug test or therapy appointment, or even picking up a new charge, the conversation often took a long time. The judge would use the time to explain the value of the court, and how the participant needs to commit to the court's requirements. Nearly all participants walked out of the courtroom immediately after their own hearing.

As chapter 7 explains in more detail, hearings in Southeast were often heated. In Northeast, exchanges were typically polite and somewhat formal, to some extent reflecting cultural stereotypes. In Southeast, emotions flared. Sometimes the emotions were positive, with expressions of warmth and appreciation between the judge and the participants. More often, however, the emotions came out in adversarial exchanges, with the judge and participants expressing great frustration with one another.

During interviews, staff descriptions of the court's decision making matched the somewhat chaotic scenes my team and I observed. Staff often looked back and forth at one another as the hearings proceeded because they were unsure about how clients who were not in compliance were being managed. One clinician explained their frustration with the disconnect between what went on in staffing meetings and what went on in hearings. The clinician said that the purpose of the meetings is to agree on a plan, such as bringing in VJOs to discuss difficult cases, and that meetings should be where decisions are made on recommendations and best practices. The clinician continued:

> We decide on sanctions for infractions, the first, second, third, escalating, and then the judge makes different determination. This judge says, "I got it, I know what I'm going to say, tell him." Then the judge says, "Why are you doing this?" like [a] grand[parent]. No, no. We need authority, forcefulness. It doesn't have to be mean, that's not [the judge's] style, but with authority. That's what we rely on [the judge] for, and we don't get it.
>
> *(clinician, Southwest VTC, interview)*

The judge often repeated the benefit of this court just for veterans, but it was difficult to observe how this shared identity shaped experiences in the courtroom outside of the resources the court could leverage. In just a few weeks of observations at the Northeast VTC, I felt familiar with each participant, hearing about their families, their career goals, and their day-to-day routines. By contrast, I learned little about any participant at the Southeast VTC, particularly if the person was in compliance. The hearings lasted longer than in the Northeast VTC, and the judge spoke for the majority of the time. In just one data point for the different courtroom dynamics, after coding who spoke in each courtroom, we found that that the Southeast VTC judge spoke for 75 percent of the time compared with the Northeast VTC's judge who spoke for 20 percent. And, in contrast to the idea of leveraging military culture, in hearings at the Southeast VTC, the only references to the military occurred when discussing treatment options at the VA or when the judge told the participant that the court is based on evidence that veterans benefit from being in a treatment court program just for them.

This is why I characterize this court as herding: things always felt slightly but not totally out of control. And, despite the judge's insistence on the common narrative, that this court would be beneficial for participants if they would only comply, I struggled to decipher what made this a *veterans* treatment court apart from the presence of a dedicated representative from the VA who provided crucial stability to the courtroom participants when he was finally onboarded. This herding dynamic was particularly evident when the judge was sanctioning participants. At one session, two back-to-back participants were given sanctions with this "tough love" approach (Burns and Peyrot 2003), which rarely occurred in Northeast. That day, the Southeast judge assigned the first to community service to make up for a drug relapse, saying that the community service would be good because having more obligations would keep him away from drugs. The judge told the second participant, who had been picked up by police on new charges, that his assigned GPS ankle monitor would remind him that the court is there to help him. While this participant did not fight having to wear a GPS monitor, perhaps because he came from jail already wearing it, I observed heated conversations from others when the court decided on monitoring participants with a GPS because they were not complying with court mandates. Still, the judge appeared very reluctant to terminate anyone's participation, regardless of how often they broke the requirements.

In addition to trying to convince people that sanctions were good for them, the court tried to incentivize participants with more explicit coercion than I witnessed in the other two courts. To this end, participants appeared on display for apparent good or bad behavior. Recognizing that people didn't like waiting until the end of a court session to be called up, halfway through our observations the court developed the "A" team." Participants on this team were called up as a group at the start of the day's hearing. The judge told them that they were compliant and to keep up the good work, and that the court looked forward to seeing them at their next hearing. This public display made the hearings more efficient by reducing the number of conversations that would have simply affirmed each person's behavior. While beneficial for the individuals who did not have to sit through hours of the hearing, this also contributed to the lack of cohesion in the courtroom community as participants left after they were called up.

On the flip side, sometimes the judge asked people who tested positive for drugs to sit in the jury box, separate from the group. This was the court's efforts to emphasize community and celebrate good behavior through shaming. Again, this kind of incentivizing is part and parcel of the therapeutic jurisprudence model in treatment courts, but coupled with the common narrative suggesting that VTCs are uniquely beneficial because they enhance the "evidence based" approaches of drug courts with military culture, this kind of shaming struck me as potentially more punitive than it might if meted out under a different premise.

The judge tried additional techniques to foster a sense of community, with an add veteran and stir approach having little to do with "military culture." In one hearing, for example, the judge commented that participants might benefit from sharing journals or pictures to better understand "where they came from." It was unclear if the goal was for the court to better understand the participants or for the participants to better understand themselves, and several clinicians looked wide-eyed at the suggestion. The clinicians were well aware that many participants expressed frustration inside and outside court hearings about the court's numerous requirements. Sitting in the courtroom prior to and after hearings, the participants often vented with one another about their frustration in being there at all. Sometimes they became agitated waiting for the judge to enter, muttering comments such as "Come on, Judge."

The flailing mentor program was part of the herding quality in this court and revealed the extra pressures that the common narrative can put on a VTC that struggles to create a community defined by veteran identity. A VTC that does not have the peer mentorship that supposedly makes these courts different and more beneficial for veteran participants is add veteran and stir without the camaraderie that helps creates community. The Northeast VTC demonstrated the benefits of having a dedicated group of mentors, while the Southeast VTC had continual issues creating a mentor program. There was no dedicated mentor from the beginning who could gather a cohesive group of like-minded people. The one dedicated veteran who came every week to the Southeast VTC tried to connect with the participants and recruit other mentors. He told me that he frequently met other veterans who expressed interest in mentoring, and they even came to court a few times, but they usually disappeared a short while later. He remained frustrated, once sending an email to the volunteers he had found and lost, wondering if it was something that he was doing wrong. The problems were myriad: it was difficult to stay motivated when the court was not easy to access depending on where volunteers lived, court hearings started late and went late, and the participants did not seem that motivated or connected to the court. Overall, with little sense of community in the court in general and little emphasis on military identity in particular, it was understandably challenging for the lead/sole mentor to recruit others for more than a few hearings. Then, after this committed veteran underwent surgery during the pandemic, he did not return and did not communicate his whereabouts to the court.

While the Northeast VTC modeled the common narrative that VTCs are unique judicial organizations predicated on the camaraderie that comes from a shared military culture (and, I suggest, the social service resources that veterans can access), the Southeast VTC did not have this kind of camaraderie. The issues were not about material resources—Southeast did not struggle in the same way as West, described below, to help its participants access needed resources. Rather, the hearings in Southeast reveal the need for VTCs to establish their legitimacy early on with participants, staff, and other stakeholders necessary to realize their goals. A court offering structure, authority, and camaraderie was clearly an issue for this VTC, and underscores the limits of the common narrative by showing that a court predicated on the idea of a shared military identity may not map onto the reality of how people who joined the military want to engage with a court.

West VTC: Triage. If the Southeast VTC hearings always felt just a little out of control, like watching a teacher trying to get the attention of restless students, the West VTC was more like observing an emergency room triage with its attempts to keep people who were on the margins of society from falling into the abyss. Describing how this court operated on a day-to-day basis, thus, is a challenge. What was the same throughout my years of observations at VTCs was the extraordinary level of need by participants, and the extraordinary care that the judge and court clinicians and judges displayed in the face of the hardships they were trying to address. Fostering a sense of community seemed out of reach for this court, which set its sights on helping individuals make smaller gains related to giving up a particular mind-altering substance, gaining housing, or otherwise leaving the court program with more stability—but not necessarily long-term stability—relative to when they joined.

Whereas Northeast typically had less than two dozen participants and Southeast had about twice that number, West served up to one hundred participants at certain points in our observations. For those concerned about inequalities in VTCs because some courts only accept VA-eligible veterans, this court reveals the trade-offs of a more inclusive approach. By trying to help as many people as they could and prioritizing rehabilitation and avoiding retribution, West spread its resources—more abundant than would be available to a criminal legal defendant in a different treatment court or in the regular criminal legal system—very thin.

This VTC served participants with criminal legal histories and challenges that I rarely observed in the other two courts. Both by design and by the demographics associated with its locale, this court served more people with daunting challenges; many of them were regularly arrested or on warrant status. The participants suffered from severe substance use and mental health disorders that left many without housing, and the surrounding real estate is some of the most expensive in the world. Both Southeast and West are among the most unequal cities in the country when it comes to the proportion of the city's population holding the majority of the wealth, and West is among the most racially unequal in this dimension (i.e., the median income of a white household in West is over $100,000 more than the median income of a Black household).

The West VTC's hearings were as unpredictable as the Southeast VTC, with a sense of frustration that had a different valence as the court team sought to maintain contact with people living in extreme precarity. The feeling of triage was more palpable during hearings in the city's main courthouse. Even though Southeast and West are comparable in size, their main courthouses felt completely different. For a time, the West VTC was located in a bustling municipal courthouse in the city's center. The building is around the same size as the courthouse for the Southeast VTC, but West was full of lawyers, defendants, court staff, and others moving throughout the building. Scenes in this courtroom resemble descriptions from the books *Misdemeanorland* (Kohler-Haussman 2019) and *Crook County* (Gonzalez Van Cleve 2016), with a predominantly racialized minority group of criminal legal defendants milling about with their predominantly white lawyers trying to provide guidance to the criminal legal process. Animals, armed guards, and others wandered the halls; this frenetic energy of the hallways also characterized the VTC hearings inside the courtroom. Participants came and went, clinicians followed them in and out, and there was even less sense of community than in Southeast.

After two years, the main courthouse became too busy to donate a courtroom to the VTC, which had to move to the community courthouse a few miles away. Still, the VTC continued to hold morning hearings at the downtown courthouse for participants who were in jail because, for security reasons, they could only be transported to that courthouse.

In afternoon hearings at the smaller courthouse, things were calmer. This courthouse was used for the city's community court system, which heard cases involving minor infractions related to loitering or other misdemeanors in the neighborhood. Despite the various benches and seats for courtroom personnel, space for a jury and desks delineating prosecution and defense, this felt less like a courtroom. It had a seat for the judge to sit above and away from the participants, but even from the perch the judge and staff were closer to the participants than in the main courthouse. In addition, the participants in the waiting area were closer to each other in just a few rows.

The suffering of the city's transient population was evident in the pocket of the city where the courthouse was located, and it permeated hearings in nuanced ways. There were few people coming in and out of the courthouse, and people working in the courthouse seemed relaxed. I often wondered what kinds of interactions the guards had with the many people on the streets nearby. People suffering from substance use and mental health crises frequently wandered into the courthouse looking for services or asking if they were in the right place. One day in the VTC there was a group of preteens sitting in the jury box, observing the hearing as part of their school activities. The judge explained that the group may see challenging things, but they will also see the important work of the judiciary. As the judge talked with a participant about severe mental health challenges and substance use in front of the visitors, I wondered about the message these teens were getting. With no reference to the participants' military experiences, I saw the VTC through the eyes of the youth, who likely could not distinguish these participants from the many people they saw struggling on the streets of their city.

In some ways, West felt more predictable than Southeast. It also felt much less formal. Whether at the large downtown courthouse or the small community courthouse, there were usually a handful of participants already sitting in the courtroom by the time a hearing was to start. The court's assigned prosecutor sat to the left and, if there was one, the assigned public defender sat to the right, as one would expect in a traditional court. Whereas the other two VTCs had a dedicated public defense attorney, this court's public defender frequently changed. At one point during my team's observations, more than one court personnel commented to me that there hadn't been an assigned defense attorney for months. Participants also frequently had private defense attorneys representing them, because the city's public defenders often represented victims of the participants, and so they could not also represent the participant. The result was a feeling that the defendants were typically standing on their own in front of the judge, with only the help of the court's dedicated clinicians.

However, beyond the calm feeling when hearings started, each hearing was hard to predict and the overall hearings were rarely calm events. Everyone used the time in court to offer participants the chance to talk about the social services they needed. Like in Southeast, there was no clear order to who was going to be called up. In West, individuals were referred to as "lines" related to their criminal charge(s). In the other two courts, the judge frequently talked about phases, and there were frequent celebrations associated with someone advancing through a phase. In Northeast, especially, the phases were clearly defined in terms of how often the participant had to come to court and how long the phase would last. There were similar features in West, such as reduced requirements to come to court the further along a participant was in the program. However, when I asked a clinician about what was required to graduate, the answer brought more confusion:

> I don't understand it either. Once we get to a point of weeks of treatment, that is it. Domestic Violence [charged] folks they have fifty-two weeks or maybe we'll shoot for weeks of sobriety if someone has insights about addiction. Some people don't have a tentative end date until I think they will be safe in the community. Two people I have are about to be housed. We have a hold on them for thirty days and then let them graduate, make sure there is housing plan, stable income, and something else keep to them busy.
>
> *(clinician, West VTC, interview)*

Except for occasional court references to phase advancements and graduations, the overall program requirements were hard to make sense of because they were individualized. The requirements differed for those accused of crimes (and the type of crime), and depended on an individual's housing, substance abuse, mental health, or other need. Unlike in the other two courts, it appeared that many participants here were still using illicit substances without sanction. Case report files from 2018, for example, show a 100 percent service–connected former marine with an honorable discharge who was diagnosed with schizo-phrenia paranoid type and substance use disorder. He was facing charges of petty theft. That week, his drug testing showed him positive for opiates, co-caine, amphetamine, and cannabis, but the clinical note said, "Veteran should be praised for being in compliance the past two weeks, which is significant for him, and he should also be encouraged to work with providers to reduce the frequency/amount/variety of substance use."

As a clinician explained to me, forcing sobriety would not benefit their participants, so rather than enforce abstinence, this court took the approach of harm reduction. The judge and clinicians tried to keep participants from using particular drugs, such as methamphetamine or heroin, while being less concerned about drugs that may be less physically or psychologically harmful, such as marijuana. Sobriety appeared a central goal for both the Northeast and Southeast VTCs, but the West VTC was more concerned about stable housing, since many of the participants lacked it.

Even though the hearings felt unpredictable, there was a unique sense of community in this VTC. This court featured strong clinician commitment, and the amount of clinical support for those with VA benefits was striking. This added to inequalities within the court, but also helped address the striking inequalities in the community that the court was trying to address. Perhaps be-cause the prosecutor and defense attorneys were not that engaged, the clinicians in this court played a more central role in hearings than they did in the other two courts. Though there was turnover in the other roles, one VA clinician was there throughout my six years of observations; she and others showed care and empathy during their advocacy on behalf of participants during staffing meetings, and actively engaged with participants during hearings. This clini-cian engagement made the courtroom feel very different than Southeast's and Northeast's. The clinicians positioned themselves close to the defense attorney's side of the bench, and often did not sit. Clinicians sometimes checked in with a participant right before they were called up to the judge's podium, to confirm if they had attended court-ordered meetings. After a hearing, clinicians some-times followed the participant out of the courtroom to reiterate or clarify what was required of the participant to remain in compliance.

The clinicians' activity during the hearings stems from the high needs of its participants, and the court could not treat all participants equally. One reason that the clinicians were as active during hearings is that it was hard to maintain contact with them outside of hearings. The court boasted two and sometimes three VA clinicians for its VA-eligible participants—approximately half of the court's participants—and only one clinician for participants ineligible to use the VA's services. This non-VA position was funded through grants, making it a precarious role. There were three clinicians in this role over the course of my six years of observations, each one managing the same number of participants that the two or three VA clinicians split among themselves. At one point, the court could not accept participants who were not VA eligible because the sole clinician was overwhelmed with managing more than fifty participants. One clinician left the job during the pandemic to take on a better paying and more secure position, but returned, explaining to me that he liked the VTC's work better. In hearings, participants frequently referenced all the efforts he made to connect them to services. However, during a lapse in funding for this position, he once again left the court. When a new grant came through, the court hired a new clinician who had to rebuild that rapport. This unequal access to case manager support based on discharge papers illustrates how VTCs can replicate and compound inequalities that exist elsewhere.

Other courtroom dynamics added to the unpredictability and sense of pre-carity. The common narrative emphasizes the role of mentors in VTCs, yet both Southeast and West VTCs could not create a dedicated mentor cohort. In my early observations, I saw a few older Vietnam-era veterans working as mentors. Later, just before the pandemic, the court benefitted from a dedicated pair of younger mentors: veterans from the Global War on Terror. Even so, unlike in the Northeast VTC, these mentors rarely participated in the hearings, though the younger mentors frequently followed participants out of the courtroom to check in with them. The West VTC's mentorship model appeared more like that of the Southeast VTC and unlike at the Northeast VTC, where multiple mentors provided intensive support to their mentees. With few mentors and many participants, the West VTC's mentors had more superficial relationships with the participants, with check-ins occurring only during the court sessions. Still, these younger mentors were extremely dedicated, explaining to my team how much trauma they had witnessed and experienced in the war, and how much they wanted to help the participants they saw suffering from similar traumas. Yet, maintaining a strong mentor community proved challenging. As the lead mentor explained,

> I could see some on my team that are getting burnt out—they're work- ing with individuals who are very difficult but it's the best we can do. We invite them to all the services, to think of preventative measures. You can't save everybody, I am aware. But, at least we can try our best and put our effort in every day.
>
> *(mentor, West VTC, interview)*

I observed many changes over the years, adding to the feeling that this court was trying new approaches to help its vulnerable participants. During my early observations, the judge sat at the bench, sitting slightly higher than the others in the courtroom, just as the judges did in the other two courts. How- ever, by the end of our observations, the judge sat at a table with the rest of the court personnel, now looking up at the participants standing in front of him. The judge explained in our interviews that this adjustment was made to relate to the participants on more equal footing.

Interestingly, the effort to be informal also impeded a feeling of commu- nity. In West, there was neither an introduction when a participant was called to the podium nor a clear order as to who was called up next, in contrast to Northeast. Sometimes, the judge saw a particular participant enter and asked them up to the podium right away. Sometimes, the judge waited until the end to call up the people who were not in compliance, partly as a sanction but also to make the early part of the hearings more efficient because those in compli- ance could check in and then leave without a lengthy discussion.

The unpredictability in this court also emerged as the judge avoided general statements about the court's programming and tried to meet each participant where they were. Rather than project a forced narrative of community, the court focused on individuals as such. For people in compliance, the conversa- tions were quick. Unlike in the Southeast VTC, there were no lectures or long explanations about the value of the court. Over the years, I noticed this judge trying different techniques to encourage participants to comply, eventually (and repeatedly) asking the participant what *they* wanted to do. These prompts, which the judge used to encourage the participants to feel ownership in a process that was clearly disempowering, led to dynamic conversations, with some participants asking to be done as quickly as possible, and others listing their personal challenges, hopes, and goals. These conversations were varied in terms of intelligibility, with many people struggling to articulate a coherent plan for themselves rather than explaining why they were having such a hard time in general.

West also engaged in other practices that, through informality, showcased the team's individualized approach, using the VTC as a tool to help the participants with their various struggles. During hearings the judge frequently said "off the record" when having conversations about how a participant was doing, then "back on the record" to explain the participant's next steps through the program. I rarely saw such informalities or formalities in the other two courts; the contrast between the conversations about gritty details of life on the streets and "on the record" reminded me that I was in a courtroom rather than a social services office or even a therapy session.

After years of observation, it became evident that this court had a distinct understanding of what its goals were and how to achieve them. When talking with court staff, they proudly explained how their approach differed from neighboring VTCs that were stricter about sobriety or emphasized military identity more. For this team, creating an environment that was more "carrot" than "stick" was a priority.

A NOTE ON THE PANDEMIC

This chapter focuses on generalizations about the day-to-day in-person scenes observed at these courts before the pandemic, highlighting some examples of how inequalities manifested in court hearings and how the courts tried to foster a sense of community, predictability, stability and support for their participants. Whatever community dynamics did or did not exist before March 2020, they were amplified afterward, adding to the dilemma of flattening distinctions between VTCs.

Emblematic of its general organization, the Northeast VTC quickly pivoted to online court hearings. It maintained the structure and, to some extent, a feeling of community. Participants struggled but were housed. Court personnel recognized that they needed to adapt rules to better serve their participants. Even after participants were allowed to return in person, the court remained hybrid so as to better serve the participants. Watching the hearings, the same dynamics in the courtroom were present online. Usually, all of the participants were on the session and stayed online the whole time. Even when some participants called in from their jobs or their cars, the team tried to have substantive conversations with them. For a while, the team members (i.e., mentors, probation officer, judge, court reporter, probation officer, defense attorney, and clinicians) outnumbered the participants, illustrating how much support they were able to offer.

The Southeast VTC took a little longer to set up the online court hearings, and then had problems adjusting to in-person hearings when they were allowed to gather again. As with the physical sessions, its online hearings were not organized and went long. Technology was an ongoing issue, with dropped calls; plus some participants were difficult to hear. It was clear that participants were even less engaged with the court, and the judge and clinicians fought to keep them connected. Like in the Northeast VTC, these clinicians realized that, after meeting in-person was allowed, making participants come to the courthouse was an unnecessary burden. However, the judge, hoping to get more buy-in, asked the participants to return in person, and suggested even asking them to come to the courthouse more frequently than before the pandemic to keep participants engaged.

For the West VTC, most participants attended the online sessions but logged off as soon as they finished their individual hearing. The meetings were chaotic, with many technological challenges. There were also untold difficulties for personnel keeping track of the many participants who struggled with housing. The court experimented with a hybrid model as soon as everyone was allowed to once again meet in-person. According to the judge, it was critical to meet in the courtroom because so many of the participants were living on the streets and benefitted from being in the room. Even so, the judge also worried about making participants come to court, so it remained hybrid.

All three courts faced steep declines in participation during the pandemic as well as from decarceration efforts. The number of arrests dropped steeply, and courts across the country deferred all types of hearings. People accused of drug crimes, in particular, received reduced sentences because courts needed to reserve jail or prison space for more serious offenses. Without the threat of jail time, though, fewer people chose to join treatment courts more generally.

As with everything else that separates these three courts, they responded to participant declines differently. The Northeast VTC, while concerned about the pandemic's effects, had a steady stream of participants and did not need to change its program when it moved to online hearings. The Southeast VTC was already concerned about its declining numbers and worried that it might be shut down during the pandemic if it did not increase enrollment. According to court staff interviews, this concern led the court to be even more forgiving of noncompliant participants, because any terminations further reduced their numbers. The West VTC, too, struggled with declining numbers. However, with a previously bustling courtroom, the declining numbers gave the team more time to aid those participants seeking the court's help. Generally, all of the courts worried that the many people who could benefit from a VTC were not getting help.

THE VTC CONCEPT

The descriptions of these VTCs reveal how the common narrative—that VTCs are uniquely able to help participants because of their shared military culture and camaraderie that they engender—may be less common across VTCs than proponents hope. In so doing, the chapter reveals how VTC *as a concept* is implemented in three different locales. The idea of a VTC is powerful, built from strong ideological and material foundations. However, as part of the criminal legal system, these courts engage in similar "coercive care" that reflects distinct court cultures rather than a shared military culture (MacLeish 2020). Military culture may reveal itself under certain conditions, such as the presence of a dedicated mentor team, but that is not a given in any VTC. Further, because many veterans in the criminal legal system may not have positive associations with their military careers, court personnel may choose to avoid references to the military.

As a practical matter, the analysis shows the different ways that courts sought to create community and predictability for participants, and each court's struggles. While all courts operate according to local contexts, these differences undermine the common narrative that veterans are a distinct population that these courts are uniquely able to help. This is largely because the courts accept people with a range of military experiences and with different levels of access to VA care. However, more to the point, they have different understandings of what they are supposed to be doing to help the participants——e.g., keep them sober, get them social services, and/or help them establish new careers and stable housing?

Thinking of these courts as organizations that are hybridized in multiple ways (e.g., blending identities of veteran and someone with substance use or mental health disorder, the criminal legal system and the veterans welfare system), having distinct ways of balancing their organizational goals, helps make sense of all these differences. Yet, this framework is at odds with a common narrative that suggests VTCs have a distinct ability to help participants *because* they are VTCs. The differences between all three courts highlight how different VTCs implement the model of an adult drug treatment court, and explain the challenge of comparing courts that have implemented the model so differently. While the next chapter provides more insights into why these differences exist, this chapter shows the inherent balancing act that treatment courts must perform in order to understand not only how to meet their goals but also how to determine what their goals actually are.

The descriptions also show the value of analyzing treatment courts as judicial organizations, goal-oriented collectivities that must continually define their goals and develop strategies to realize them. The common narrative flattens differences between courts, justifying the creation of VTCs even where the court community may not be able to provide the help a participant seeks. The next chapter continues the discussion on what makes these VTCs so different from each other. Together, these two chapters reveal how VTCs simultaneously reflect and seek to aid their distinct local populations, further instrumentalizing law to rectify inequalities that pervade the criminal legal and social welfare landscape of the US.

Six

WHY ARE THE COURTS SO DIFFERENT?

*The Common Narrative Meets
the Politics of Worth*

On my first visit to the Southeast VTC, the warm February air and lush green-ery were a nice complement to the relaxed smiles and greetings from people I passed in the street. That feeling of relaxation dissipated as soon as I walked into the Southeast VTC's courtroom. Picking up following the aftermath of the court's closure because it was not in compliance with the federal grant that originally funded it, I could tell that the court personnel were still reeling. For three months, soon after the court opened, all court operations stopped. Par-ticipants at the Southeast VTC were mostly in the first (and most demanding phase) of the treatment program during this shutdown. Any new veterans who might have been eligible to join were turned away. According to people work-ing in the court, the VTC had been in disarray the year before, which was just after it opened. I was told that, prior to the shutdown, the judge had ordered participants to get treatments at the VA, but the VA only offered some of these mandated treatments, and only under certain circumstances. The local VA had recently hired a veterans justice officer (VJO) to work in the city's jails, but the local VJO was not working with the VTC when it first opened. Thus, there was no dedicated representative from the VA working in the court. The first court coordinator, according to court staff, did not have the requisite training for the job, and was no longer working at the court when I visited. The new court coordinator, who brought an intensity to her work that came from years as a drug treatment court coordinator, explained to me how important it was for the participants to have clear rules about sobriety and sanctions, which she was implementing.

The Southeast VTC's story is atypical in that I have never heard of any other treatment court shutting down because a funder tells them to. At the same time, the story is typical in that it reflects the idiosyncrasies of individual courts, with important effects on personnel and participants.

If VTCs are designed with the same goals in mind and from a national model (that is, the Buffalo, New York, court), why are they so different from one another? One way to make sense of these differences is to shift the analysis from the legalistic (i.e., rule-bound) features of the courts to examine their organizational features (Douds and Ahlin 2019; Hummer et al. 2024). My findings suggest that the different rules are important, but they offer limited insights into the experience of being in a VTC. Further, some of the rules reflect decisions outside of or within the VTC's control, and those decisions are also important because they illustrate how personnel understand the goal of a VTC and how to achieve it.

To this end, this chapter focuses on the contexts under which these three VTCs developed to make two claims: (1) the "success" of a VTC, which is difficult if not impossible to define, depends on its foundings, and (2) these courts are assemblages of their local criminal legal and social services, meaning the common narrative that VTCs are uniquely beneficial for veterans because they incorporate military culture obfuscates the importance of resources, human and material, that can make a VTC salutary and/or problematic.

Further, this analysis of VTCs' origins helps reveal the politics of worth by showing how each of the courts developed features in response to local opportunities and constraints, trying to establish legitimacy with the many local actors necessary for their creation and survival (Bitektine 2011; DiMaggio and Powell 1983). Existing studies reveal the difficulty of defining or measuring legitimacy and the processes that give rise to it (e.g., Gibson et al. 1998; Gibson and Nelson 2015). I take as a starting point that legitimation is a social process that requires resonance between organizational practices and broader societal beliefs (Johnson, Dowd, and Ridgeway 2006; Edelman and Suchman 1997).

At the same time, legitimation is also a political process. This analysis goes beyond procedural accounts of legitimacy (e.g., Tyler 1990) toward the study of legitimacy as a political concept, useful to "examine the impact of competing demands and allocations of powers and resources" (Loader and Sparks 2013).

As distinct judicial organizations working at the intersections of the criminal legal system, the VA, and other social welfare agencies, VTCs must focus on establishing, maintaining, and increasing their legitimacy to the various parties they depend on for their survival. Notably, this includes funders—whether the funding comes from a line item in the city or state budget or from a federal grant. Their need for funding does not dissipate after they first set up the court; personnel must continually look for ways to support themselves. The court must also establish and maintain support from within criminal legal bureaucracies, including prosecutors, defense attorneys, and probation officers. These parties must agree on who can participate in the treatment court. Courts particularly need the support of social service agencies to provide the court-ordered treatments. Finally, each VTC must get participants to buy into this court option.

To meet these extensive—and often contradicting—goals, all treatment courts develop "chameleon-like" strategies to appeal to different stakeholders (Peyrot 1991), displaying "organizational ambivalence" about their goals (Zozula 2019, 141). The benefit of this flexibility is that treatment courts can respond to local constraints and opportunities. One dilemma, evident in the vignette above, is that as the courts use flexibility to establish legitimacy with some groups, such as those that they rely on for financial and other material support, they may sacrifice legitimacy with other groups, such as their participants and/or staff. Politics involve trade-offs, and even a group deemed uniquely worthy of criminal legal and social service benefits may not receive those benefits because of the different ways that VTCs coordinate human or material resources.

FIRST ISSUE: LOCALE

After observing the Northeast, Southeast, and West VTCs, the simplest explanation I could think of for the courts' differences was where they were located. Locale creates a distinct set of opportunities and constraints for each VTC, as the descriptions in the previous chapter help illustrate. The opportunities and constraints are related to inequalities in each locale, such as racial demographics, access to affordable housing, and public investment in social services.

Locales have multiple dimensions, but one salient feature for the purpose of studying court communities is the population demographic. For example, the Northeast VTC is in a courthouse in a small city, surrounded by counties that are primarily rural and white. Although the participants changed on a regular basis, there were usually somewhere around twenty participants. In my earliest observations, six of these participants appeared African American, two appeared Hispanic, and the rest appeared white. While a seemingly small number of racialized minorities, particularly compared to the other two courts, this is a disproportionate number of people of color compared with the surrounding communities, which is approximately 73 percent white, 5 percent Black, and 16 percent Latino. The VTC team appeared to be all white, save for one probation officer who was Latino, which was reflective of the more racially homogenous nature of the region. Just as race structures so many dynamics in the criminal legal and social welfare fields, racialized minorities tend to view the criminal legal system as less legitimate than do their white counterparts (see, especially, Lerman and Weaver 2014; Western 2006). Thus, it may be easier to get buy-in for a treatment court from a less racially diverse population. And social cohesion in a courtroom may be easier to achieve when there is less racialized diversity.

By contrast, the West and Southeast VTCs are in urban centers with far more racialized minorities who have suffered more from the systemic racism in the criminal legal and social welfare fields. Although population where the West VTC is located is approximately 5 percent Black, the court's administrative records show the ratio of courtroom participants was over 40 percent Black, and an additional 20 percent were racialized minorities, predominantly classified as "Other," which includes a large proportion of Asian-Pacific Islander and mixed race. In the Southeast VTC, the ratio of racialized minorities to white participants was even more striking. Some days there were no white participants in the courtroom; other days there were just a few. Most participants appeared to be Black, Hispanic, or a mix of races. The city's Black population is around 14 percent, with an even smaller white (non-Hispanic) population than around the West VTC.

Race structured the courts in other ways as well. Unlike the areas of the Northeast and West VTCs, where there are stark socioeconomic differences between racial groups, in the Southeast VTC there is a robust middle class comprising racialized minorities. Many of the participants were racialized minorities, and so too were many of Southeast VTC's staff. In addition to the different ways that racial diversity can shape social cohesion in an organizational workgroup, given the grossly disproportionate rates of both poverty and criminal legal involvement among racialized minorities, particularly Black people, the racial composition of the courts also reflects the various forms of capital that defendants start with.

Locale matters in legal ways, too. Treatment court rules may be structured by state legislation, and/or by standardized practices across the state, and/or by individual court policies, and/or combinations of these and other federal, state, and local laws (see Douds and Ahlin 2019). Across the state where the Northeast VTC operates, for example, treatment courts are available only for criminal defendants who have pled guilty to charges that carry penalties of less than five years of incarceration. These entry rules are crucial to the differences between the Northeast VTC and the other two courts, as participants in the Northeast VTC had already pled guilty, and thus could not quit the treatment court without facing a prison sentence. As an assistant district attorney who helps oversee other treatment courts in the area told me, participants in this VTC had exhausted many other diversion options. This VTC's probation officer explained to me that requiring a guilty plea enhanced the court's "control" over participants, which he saw as beneficial for compliance. This approach to "control" reduced uncertainty that participants would not do as the court required; in short, participants knew they would go to prison if they did not comply. Thus, these participants, by virtue of already pleading guilty, had different incentives to stay in the program than the participants in the other two courts. The judge at the Northeast VTC had a set of carrots and sticks not available to the judges in the other locales: participants with no possibility of dropped charges, and guaranteed incarceration for those who could not or would not comply.

By contrast, the Southeast VTC was dealing with a different participant population by virtue of where the court is geographically. This is because of the demographics and also because of the laws around treatment courts. For one, the large city where the VTC is located is full of people who come for its mild climate. Many people in the city, including those who get arrested there, don't have the same kinds of family ties that bind people to Northeast. In the Southeast VTC hearings, participants frequently talked about living in other locales but getting arrested in the city. Such conversations were rarer in Northeast, though also common in West. This created challenges for participants who had to fulfill court requirements in a place where they did not reside.

Locale also mattered in terms of how much, or what kind of, political support existed for both public health services and criminal legal reforms such as VTCs. Interestingly, my findings show that locale is not a binary—a supportive or unsupportive community. In theory, VTCs are uniquely appealing to people across the political spectrum because they are a criminal legal reform that helps veterans. However, the VTCs I studied had to build support for this reform. For example, Northeast is in a predominantly liberal region in terms of support for criminal legal reform, but the VTC founders faced pushback from communities that, according to one early VTC leader in the state, saw potential participants as "just a criminal, served in military but just a criminal." One interviewee described concerns that VTC founders had to push back against the assumption that there were opening a drug clinic or methadone clinic, as communities "didn't want junkies walking around streets." However, reflective of the power of the common narrative, it was easier to get buy-in when the VTC was framed as "supporting the troops," something local policymakers were happy to mobilize around when creating the Northeast VTC. Furthermore, Northeast has a robust public health system and all residents, regardless of wealth, are able to access medical care.

Southeast's VTC also suffered from concerns about prioritizing defendants who may not be deserving; a local government official, a veteran himself, initially struggled to get support from the city council for opening a VTC because fellow councilmembers expressed concern that a VTC is an unfair "get out of jail free card," a theme explored in chapter 4. He and others explained that local politics were complicating their work. Various people working in veterans' services suggested that there is less overall support for veterans in Southeast because the city has fewer veterans per capita than do neighboring cities. A legislative aide for a local politician who championed creating a VTC in the city suggested that the municipal government initially balked at the idea of creating a specialized court for veterans. Other politicians had concerns related to the city's limited budget and the many needs of such diverse populations. This initial lack of legitimacy contrasts with the common narrative and suggests that there may be more ambivalence to treating veterans as a distinct, worthy group of criminal legal defendants than VTC proponents might assume.

However, Southeast was also shaped by the long history of treatment courts in the region, as well as residential facilities to help address homelessness. The city is full of lawyers, judges, case managers, and other personnel who train other criminal legal professionals across the country in the best practices in both drug treatment and mental health treatment courts. In our interviews, personnel from these other treatment courts were proud of what they accomplished in the city, particularly in how they had changed criminal legal practices in coordination with expanding social welfare services to help at-risk populations. They lauded the beneficial effect on both lower rates of arrest and homelessness compared with cities of comparable size across the country. In addition to being able to mobilize support for another treatment court, this commitment to the drug treatment court model meant that Southeast's VTC did not stir much in their add veteran and stir approach.

Like the other two courts, the politics shaping West VTC were driven by unique features of its locale. Most notably, West's VTC is in a region that is struggling more with the homelessness crisis than in any other area in the US. Rising housing costs, coupled with more temperate weather, make the area a hotspot for people without permanent places to live, a problem exacerbated by the upheaval caused by the pandemic, the opioid crisis, and other social ills. Until a 2024 Supreme Court decision, these cities were not allowed to issue criminal or civil penalties, such as tickets, for sleeping in public areas. Participants in the West VTC had immediate needs for housing and treatments for substance use and mental health, far more than participants in the other two sites. The West VTC is also in a state that allows both misdemeanors and felonies to be diverted to treatment court, so its participants had a range of charges, making considerations about public safety more challenging as the court grappled with incarcerating people picked up on new charges.

Although these different features affected each VTC, one would be hard-pressed to discern simply from these community-specific features what the design of its VTC might be. For example, although West's population appeared more at risk for homelessness, this fact does not by itself explain the court's challenges. A clinician from Northeast explained to me that most of their participants were also at high risk of homelessness, which the clinician said was different from other populations (i.e., nonveteran) they had worked with in the region. Rather than the specific challenges facing the populations, these courts' differences reflect how their founders mobilized available resources and established legitimacy with the many actors needed to succeed.

SECOND ISSUE: FOUNDINGS

While a court's locale no doubt shapes its functions, its origins are more important in fostering the kind of community that VTC proponents hope for. What I discovered over years of research is that the court's foundings set in motion a process that affected day-to-day operations for years. The foundings show the importance of the ideological and material support for VTCs at the national level but, more importantly, how individuals translated those foundations into resources at the local level. These foundings stories illustrate the politics of worth by revealing the important ways that each court had to establish and then maintain legitimacy with the various stakeholders necessary for success. As a social process that requires resonance between organizational practices and broader societal beliefs (Johnson, Dowd, and Ridgeway 2006; Edelman and Suchman 1997), legitimation strategies are key to illustrating how new judicial organizations emerge and define and realize their goals.

None of those who spearheaded the effort to create each VTC faced public pressure or explicit incentives to create a VTC. Rather, as they explained it, they had heard the common narrative that VTCs could be uniquely helpful to veterans, and they wanted to help what they perceived to be a vulnerable group of people who deserved more support. Although these court founders could not change many of the features in their specific locales, they did have some agency. Their decisions, in collaboration with their criminal legal and social service partners, put their courts on distinct trajectories that provide insights into the strikingly different organizations described in the previous chapter.

Northeast VTC. This court emerged after careful planning to find available resources and the dedicated personnel working within the local criminal legal system and social services. From the beginning, it established its legitimacy with necessary partners and its ability to maintain it with consistency (as chapter 5 details). This founding, particularly getting buy-in from the social services it needed, is exemplary in terms of establishing legitimacy with the different social service providers and criminal legal players necessary to create a court team; such an origin story may be assumed in the common narrative, but the other two courts' foundings suggest this may not be the norm.

Judges were the instigators of a new VTC in the other two places, but in the Northeast the idea emerged from the area's district attorney. This is an important feature of the Northeast VTC because prosecutors play a determinative role in deciding who should be punished after an arrest. Some DAs have gained reputations as being tough on crime; they are, after all, elected actors responsible for charging defendants and may have professional incentives to achieve high conviction rates. In conversations with VTC personnel, scholars, and advocates from across the country, I frequently heard complaints about prosecutors being tough gatekeepers on letting veterans join a VTC, preferring instead to have them go through the regular criminal legal system and face incarceration or other penalties for their alleged crimes.

The DA in the Northeast, who was elected on a progressive platform to reduce punitiveness and racialized bias in prosecution, wanted the opposite: to use his office to create options to divert people from the criminal legal system altogether, or at least from incarceration when possible. He was interested in the issue of veterans in the criminal legal system because of his prior legal work as a civilian on a military base abroad. He explained in our interview that he had noticed for years that many of the people suffering from homelessness in the more urban area that he served were veterans. The DA decided to start consulting about different options to help veterans in his jurisdiction, hoping to create an alternative pathway for veterans that would be effective. A judge in another part of the state spearheaded efforts to create a VTC soon after Buffalo's founding, and shared insights about what was needed. As one proponent from an early meeting explained to me, the DA understood the need to forge strong partnerships. According to him, the DA told them, "'We have to have people from here, there, mental health folks, and [the local residential facility] involved, probation involved.' He got this going." He explained how the DA looked to the first VTC in Buffalo, New York: "What we would do is meet once a week, basically creating the structure from the one that Buffalo originated." With support at the state level to expand VTCs into rural regions, the Northeast VTC benefitted from a preexisting and well-organized state infrastructure for treatment courts.

Rather than worry that the court might lose legitimacy with necessary stakeholders by admitting individuals who were deemed "dishonorable" by the military, Northeast decided to be inclusive. Even with the legal constraints from state policy (e.g., the Northeast VTC could not accept participants accused of more serious crimes—specifically crimes that carry more than five years of incarceration—or those accused of first-time offenses who had other diversion options), the VTC tried to be inclusive of a wide range of defendants. Unlike at the Southeast VTC, the founders of the Northeast VTC chose to include defendants who did not have VA benefits, opening the court to the many individuals who were discharged less than honorably because of substance use. A few years after the court opened, a case manager explained to me that they could not think of a single former servicemember who wanted to be admitted into the court program but was not allowed in. Participants included even those who did not graduate from boot camp. The probation officer and a judge defended this decision when, a few years into the court's operation, some of the court's mentors questioned whether everyone in the program really "deserved" the court's benefits. According to a lawyer working for the state's court system to help develop VTCs, the population the courts were serving was not what he expected. He "pictured people like" him, Global War on Terror veterans, who were given "a hundred pills a day" for "no reason." Instead, he found the states' VTCs serving Vietnam veterans who had been struggling with substance use and mental health disorders for forty years, in the "revolving door of the criminal justice system." According to a VA researcher who studied veterans in the region, many had been in and out of the criminal legal system for years, with even longer histories of substance use than participants in other treatment courts.

After deciding to create a VTC in the region, the DA and his team had to find a judge willing to dedicate time, and a courthouse willing to offer space. Though not a veteran, the judge they found grew up with close family members in the military and expressed enthusiasm about the opportunity to oversee a VTC. With the courthouse's support, and with advocacy from the VTC founders and supporters to quell concerns that the VTC was going to bring addicts to the small city, the judge was able to open a regular courtroom once a week for the new VTC.

Learning from the Buffalo treatment team, and gaining insights from VTCs in nearby jurisdictions, the DA sought to create a mentor team that would help the VTC establish legitimacy with participants. The DA connected with a dedicated veteran advocate who founded the mentor program. This mentor immediately found other willing mentors, mainly vets from the Vietnam era, through his social network. They all drew on their veteran identity to create a strict program to monitor participants. These volunteers viewed "raising one's hand" to join the military as a worthy act, regardless of what one actually did in the military (Rowen 2020). When this founding mentor passed away from illness, the team he created celebrated the legacy he left during one of the court's graduation ceremonies. This sustained volunteer support, local social service partnerships, and political support at the community and state levels were, and remained, essential to this court's functionality, along with everyone's shared belief this unique court benefits people who are worthy of investment. The strong mentor community, in turn, enhanced the court's legitimacy to both participants and other stakeholders.

In addition to these human resources, this VTC was able to mobilize material resources in a particularly effective way. Having treatment and housing options for participants makes that court more appealing to people who may be skeptical about coercing substance use treatment through a court. In addition to available treatment options, funding is an impediment to starting any treatment court—funds are needed to pay the probation officer, clinicians, and/or court coordinator. The DA was able to leverage state funds reflecting the state's growing interest in creating more VTCs. Even before a 2012 state law that mandated identification of veterans prior to arraignment, criminal legal actors working in the local jails were identifying anyone with a history of military service and contacting the VA and other veteran service organizations to help. The state's governor at the time publicly supported the creation of more VTCs as part of a policy to expand veterans services. State-level court administrators secured additional state and federal money to create more VTCs. The new funds allowed for a full-time position for a veteran-cum-lawyer to expand legal services for veterans and offered training to teams looking to start a new court in their jurisdiction.

Most importantly, the Northeast VTC was able to draw on local resources that already existed for veterans, an important example of how the material foundations that support VTCs shape their local implementation. The Northeast VTC proponents collaborated early on with a robust service network in the area, specifically a residential facility for veterans facing homelessness. This residential facility was on the campus of the local VA health center, and it offered comprehensive services for its VA-eligible residents. This made a dramatic difference in ensuring that all the VTC participants were having a shared experience. In summer 2016, I visited the facility on a regular basis to learn more about the community of veterans living there. In the daily support group called Back to Basics, participants shared their experiences, fostering a community among people who were away from children, spouses, and family. Volunteers ran various programs, such as arts and movement, further supporting the idea of community.

This residential facility could implement many of the VTC's treatment requirements, creating stability and uniformity for the court's participants. It was in this residential facility that I witnessed the kind of camaraderie articulated by the common narrative, and that camaraderie traveled with many of its residents who were also in the VTC. Although it only offered temporary housing, the facility worked with other local agencies to help people find permanent housing, usually with VA support for those eligible for housing benefits. VTC staff regularly mentioned how critical this facility was to their court's success in participants staying sober, finding housing and employment, and meeting other court goals.

With this abundance of resources in place, the Northeast VTC could develop into a model court. However, the story is not simply one of available resources; Northeast's founding illustrates the importance of forging relationships with both social service providers and the criminal legal actors that work in the courts.

———

Southeast VTC. During my observations in the Southeast's VTC, two clinicians shared an office, and the wall above the desks was filled with pictures of participants on their graduation days. The court's longest-serving clinician pointed at some of the photos and relayed stories to me of participants' long journeys through the court. There was clear pride shining on her face and from the beaming graduates. Some participants signed pictures of them with expressions of care for this clinician. During one of my visits to the clinician, I came into the room as a participant talked with her about his personal life, both cycling in and out of English and Spanish. He gave her a heartfelt hug before leaving.

As this scene illustrates, the challenges in the Southeast VTC were not for lack of care or commitment. The team members of both Northeast and Southeast VTCs were equally dedicated, but the Southeast court continuously struggled to get buy-in from its participants and mentors, making the courtroom feel like a place where, with some exceptions, the veterans did not want to be. The issue was not material resources; since all participants had to be VA eligible, all could access the robust social services at the local VA (so large that it took up an entire city block and had a marketplace for lunch options). Rather, the founding elements that made the Northeast court function so well—involvement of the VA, a dedicated and coordinated team, a robust mentor program—were largely absent at the Southeast VTC.

Unlike the Northeast VTC, the Southeast VTC's founding occurred in fits and starts. As the broader VTC movement got going in different cities, leaders working in the Southeast's criminal legal system thought about opening a VTC. They did not have the same level of state coordination as in Northeast, but they had a lot of local expertise on treatment courts. Still, there was general agreement across criminal legal professionals that a VTC would be beneficial. A judge who worked in other treatment courts explained to me that helping veterans through a treatment court was especially appealing because of the VA's financial resources. This judge not only saw a VTC as a way to relieve veterans involved in the criminal legal system but also believed it would lighten the state's financial burden to help mentally ill veterans more generally. According to the city's chief public defender, giving a special court to veterans introduced a new understanding of trauma into the criminal legal system that, ideally, could be extended to other criminal defendants. The city's district attorney explained to me that they believed in the common narrative, and wanted to identify people whose criminal legal involvement may be related to their military service and, therefore, were deserving of VTC benefits. Another judge explained to me that having a VTC brought legitimacy to the area's local court system: "People like to say that they have a drug court. They like to say that they have a problem-solving court. They like to say that they have a vet court" (judge, Southeast VTC, interview).

In our interviews, these local leaders in the criminal legal system expressed surprise that a VTC did not open in the city until well after VTCs opened in smaller, neighboring cities. Rather than push for a court right away, the founders of the Southeast VTC decided a first step would be to show that veterans needed additional support in the criminal legal system. The city's DA helped with an informal effort to track veterans who were being arrested and put in detention, and to make sure that those who qualified for veteran benefits would get access to them.

When a funding opportunity arose, the city's district attorney and the judge in charge of the district courts circulated emails to all district judges, asking who might be interested to participate in training by the National Association of Drug Court Professionals (rebranded as All Rise in 2023). One district court judge who accepted described the motivation as not focused on veterans per se but rather in bringing something new to the district and to the work. The judge asked rhetorically in our interview: "Why do I do these things? Is it about me? To say that I did something?" (judge, Southeast VTC, interview).

The judge's initial decision to "do something" was to attend the national Justice for Vets training, as part of the NADCP. Attending this meeting was no easy feat; the judge explained that there was a year-long waitlist. The judge said, after finally attending, the training proved beneficial. Beyond simply learning about the Buffalo, New York, court model, it provided a blueprint for next steps to get funding from the Bureau of Justice Assistance. The Southeast VTC applied and received funding for a three-year period. The money was used to hire the court coordinator and case manager, who ensure that participants engage in the court-mandated treatments. The money also paid for additional training from Justice for Vets, and a few team members even flew to Buffalo to observe Judge Russell's court.

This court's good fortune in getting a federal grant, ironically, contributed to its challenges. In interviews, Southeast's main judge reflected that the VTC may have been started before it was ready. Because of the grant, the VTC had to be more rigid than the mental health treatment court they also oversaw. Another judge involved in the region's treatment courts lamented that the grant may have limited their ability to help those with the highest need.

The problems this founding grant presented were threefold. First, the founders didn't have institutional partnerships in place. Second, their entry rules limited access to veterans who could benefit the most (that is, those without access to VA benefits); and third, and the biggest challenge, was that the court began accepting participants before they had service agencies lined up, which participants needed to complete the required court programs. As a founding judge explained, "Getting everyone, at the beginning, to be on board with that wholly was [a challenge], you know, it's probably still an ongoing challenge" (judge, Southeast VTC, interview).

One might assume (as I initially did) that the Northeast VTC's ability to create a cohesive court community was related to having participants with less needs, so one might assume the Southeast VTC's challenges were because its participants had more needs. However, this was not the case. Though the federal grant enabled the court to hire staff, it also had, as noted, several limiting provisions. Initially, the court required participants to have access to VA benefits. Obviously, this restriction leaves out highly vulnerable veterans who are not eligible for VA benefits at all, or others who fall through the cracks because their discharge type entitles them to some VA benefits but not others. Discharge status and eligibility for benefits do not always align, and during our court observations there appeared at least one participant who should have been able to access benefits but who was considered ineligible.[1] According to several people involved in founding the court, the grant made the court less adaptable to the needs of the veterans in jail as well as in-person participants.

Both external rules and founders' choices shaped the court's ability to incentivize participants to join and comply. Like many of the other treatment courts in the area, the Southeast VTC team decided its court would be pre-plea, meaning it would be available to those accused of misdemeanors or felonies but, according to state law, with the caveat that the person had no more than two prior felony convictions (considered a habitual offender). In addition, at the time the court was created, state law defined veteran as including those servicemembers "discharged or released under honorable conditions," or who were later upgraded to that status. Later, in accordance with changes in state laws, the court considered accepting post-conviction participants who were on probation, as well as veterans who were discharged under conditions other than honorable. Under state law, the court was also supposed to select participants based on nexus, that is, having a service-related mental health or substance use issue.

These different rules dictated who the court could accept. People charged with misdemeanors are less likely to face jail or long probations, so they are also less likely to opt-in to a treatment program. Additionally, because the court was pre-plea, some veterans prefer to just take their chances through the regular criminal legal system, where they have the possibility of avoiding a conviction or getting a sentence less demanding than the treatment court. All this means that the Southeast VTC ended up accepting participants who were charged with more serious crimes, including aggravated assault and battery, than Northeast, that all participants had access to the VA, and that participants could opt out without a certain criminal legal penalty waiting for them.

These early challenges and choices, coupled with the long history of drug treatment courts in the region, set the Southeast VTC on a distinct trajectory from other VTCs. After it temporarily closed and reopened with a new court coordinator who brought significant experience in drug treatment courts, the court decided to closely adhere to established drug treatment court rules rather than develop a different approach. This coordinator was emphatic about "evidenced-based best practices" that the court must follow, but not all team members agreed with this approach. For example, a year after this change in coordinators, a Southeast VTC clinician explained to me that the court's modeling after a drug court did not serve participants who suffered more from mental health disorders than substance use disorders:

> There are just really heavy court requirements that I think are a little aggressive personally. It's just so much. Like if the focus is on treatment, that's what they should be doing, but I think a lot of the guys are consumed with like the calls, the drug tests. And you know some of the guys don't even have drug charges, but it's just how the grant is written so everyone is subject to it.
>
> *(clinician, Southeast VTC, interview)*

From this clinician's perspective, the court struggled to get buy-in because it treated all participants, each of whom had a different life history, as having the same problems. Beyond the rules, the court also faced challenges because of how it developed, or didn't, relationships with necessary partners. While the Northeast VTC benefitted from a close working relationship with a residential facility that served homeless veterans, the Southeast VTC was significantly hindered because it did not have a working relationship with the VA when it was founded. Doctors at VAs must agree to court requirements, such as drug testing. Court personnel must work closely with VA providers and understand the VA's labyrinthine processes for which participants could access residential treatment. Although the local VA health center did have a Veterans Justice Officer assigned to veterans in jails, the Southeast VTC did not start with a dedicated VJO available to help them liaise with the VA; and neither the staff nor the judges had prior experience working with the VA. From the start, court personnel were perplexed on how basic VA practices related to treatments, and also how participant access worked. All these issues facing the court suggested a lack of legitimacy with the VA, in turn contributing to uncertainty for participants.

Although the common narrative presumes a partnership between the VA and a local VTC, the story of the Southeast VTC's founding reveals that this relationship isn't automatic. Rather, it must be built. The Southeast VTC ran into immediate problems, ordering participants into treatments that were either unavailable at the VA or only available under specific circumstances. A case manager explained the court's challenges in the following way:

> When I started a year ago, the communication with VA was trying to reach out to the Pentagon, everything is top secret, clearance for this and that, it was always like so difficult.
> *(case manager, Southeast VTC, pers. comm.)*

Years later, this VTC still struggled to determine who was even eligible for services. The case manager described the frustration and the "resentment" that grew by not having a working relationship set up with the VA. The communication challenges went both ways, however, with staff at the VA explaining to me that they were left out of initial court planning. This is one reason that led to the decrease in the court's legitimacy with the VA and increase of uncertainty for participants who didn't know what they needed to do to comply with the court-ordered mandates. On top of these issues, the local VA health center has a mixed reputation. Several clinicians explained to me that many veterans who are eligible for benefits prefer to get their healthcare elsewhere, presenting yet another problem for participants when the court mandates VA providers. Many of these problems were resolved when the court hired a dedicated VJO, who worked closely with the court and local VA to improve communication. Even so, the court continued to struggle.

The Southeast VTC's founding underscores the social processes behind legitimation. Even with the common narrative inspiring the creation of the VTC, operationalizing a VTC requires relationship building to ensure that any individual VTC has the supports it needs.

––––––

West VTC. The striking differences in the three VTCs show how add veteran and stir to the treatment court model creates something unique, not standardized. The Southeast and Northeast VTCs each created their court based on the Buffalo, New York, model while also drawing from regional practices. The West VTC's model is specific to its city's community courts system from which its VTC emerged. These community treatment courts typically do not adhere to the drug court model of graduated sanctions or ten principles, though they do follow a nearly identical approach of collaboration between criminal legal actors and social services. These community treatment courts are designed to partner with social services that can fulfill the specific needs of participants, usually by providing access to treatment related to "quality of life" crimes rooted in poverty, such as loitering (Fagan and Malkin 2003).

Creating a VTC based on the community treatment court model was, in part, a matter of political opportunities and of resources. According to West's founding judge, he had worked in the city for a year and heard about VTCs "popping up" in neighboring cities, making the absence of one in his court system confusing, telling me:

> When I came to the court, I had just seen [a VTC], and so one of my very first questions upon becoming a judge was, "Why didn't we have one?" The response from the then head of our [court system] was, "Well, there is not a sufficiently large enough veterans population to justify the court." To which I said, "Has anybody counted?"
>
> *(founding judge, West VTC, interview)*

The judge inquired about how to identify veterans being arrested or already in jail. He was aware of a local and well-established nonprofit dedicated to helping struggling veterans. It was working in jails with similar goals to his, and the VA had also recently begun focusing on this vulnerable population at the national level. He soon learned that the head of the VA hospital in his city was interested in starting a VTC. This was 2010, and the challenge for both the VA and the judge was that the city was undergoing a financial crisis, much like other cities at the time. From the judge's perspective, holding off on creating the court would have been a missed opportunity:

> To not have a veterans treatment court, when we had the support, this enthusiastic support from the Veterans Administration, which meant we had a whole panoply of resources available to people—would actually have been uneconomic and an unfortunate decision.
>
> *(founding judge, West VTC, interview)*

Despite general positive beliefs across the United States about veteran worth, the politics were thornier at the local level. The judge explained that those promoting the court first had "to demonstrate that the population was sufficient, that their resources were available and that it would be an appropriate thing to do." Second, the judge had to convince others that the veterans would not being treated in a way that was unfair to other groups. Fortunately, the judge didn't receive too much pushback to create a treatment court just for veterans. However, given budget constraints at the time, he had to rely on existing judicial infrastructure rather than create a standalone courtroom, unlike the Northeast and Southeast VTCs. The judge turned to the city's community treatment court programs to help him create a program for veterans. The director of the city's community courts agreed with the idea of adding a new calendar (aka sessions) just for veterans, and the court coordinator created a veteran-specific session in the community court. This means that there was not a dedicated residential facility just for vets as there was in Northeast, but a robust network of social service providers that already served the other community court participants.

For about eighteen months, the VTC operated exclusively within the community treatment courts system, meaning it served a geographically defined population in a courtroom far from the city's main courthouse. According to the court coordinator, this design was limiting, as the only people whom the court could help were those residing in the geographically defined area, and who were charged with misdemeanors and not felonies. The coordinator and others working in the court wanted to do more. After a year, the judge in charge of the city's trial courts suggested expanding the VTC to a standalone treatment court, with hearings for people carrying more serious charges and also not confined to the community courthouse. With this expansion, the site of VTC hearings moved to the city's main courthouse, and then it moved back to the community courthouse, except for those who were in custody—a euphemism for jail—when the main courthouse ran out of space.

I initially assumed that funding shaped the West VTC's expansive inclusion criteria and harm reduction approach that did not emphasize sobriety and graduated sanctions, but I learned that it received the same federal grant from the Bureau of Justice Administration that Southeast did. However, it did not start with that funding. According to the first court coordinator, there was no funding for the "original pilot project" of the extra session within the community courts program. Participants eligible for VA services had case management from the VA, while those who did not were supported by a case worker helping all participants in the community courts. Even with state legislation that suggested criminal legal benefits for veterans should be restricted to those whose criminal legal problems are related to their experiences in the military, the legal definition of nexus, this court actively expanded criteria for inclusion. It also deviated from the national drug court model that requires sobriety. Those creating the court said that such a requirement would be impractical, and even counterproductive, if they wanted to help as many veterans as possible. Finally, the court also developed its own interpretation of state law that, like Southeast's governing legislation, required a nexus between the person's service and their mental health or substance use issues.

In our interviews over the years, the court coordinator described feeling a sense of pride during meetings with other VTC coordinators from both nearby and faraway cities who had very different practices. The coordinator thought their court, because of its inclusive criteria, was fundamentally different than the others: the only requirement, with some limitations on charges considered more violent and serious, is that a participant wants to be in "some kind of treatment." The coordinator explained that eligibility for the court expanded over the years, to the point of having "four or five people in on attempted murder right now." As explained in chapter 5, the court did not have a set sequence of phases for all participants, instead adapting its requirements to each individual depending on their housing, substance use, and mental health treatment needs. Some people accused of misdemeanors could be out of the court program within a few months, with those accused of felonies typically must stay longer. The court did not demand sobriety—marijuana, for example, is legal in the state and many participants used it—but often required that participants refrain from using drugs that were particularly harmful for them, such as meth or heroin. Clinicians frequently told me that they wanted to make sure that people had "stabilized" before graduation, and that stabilization did not have the same meaning for each person.

The court's founding, moving from the community court system to a citywide court system, meant that the team had to shift and expand over the years. Unlike the Northeast VTC, which put together a team of dedicated individuals, the team at the West VTC was in constant flux. During my five years of observation, I saw more turnover in this court than in the other two, which posed numerous challenges for day-to-day court functioning. The reasons for this turnover were, in part, structural, rooted in the different ways that the various players in the criminal legal system are assigned roles. For example, judges in West rotate in and out of treatment courts and other assignments. Though West VTC's founding judge was dedicated to the court and stayed with it for several years, it took two years of flux for another dedicated judge to be permanently assigned to the court.

The court also had to work with the District Attorney's office and the Public Defender's office to have assigned prosecutors and defense attorneys. The defense attorneys, in particular, had complicated relationships with the court. Various VTC defense attorneys I talked to over the years explained that their office has a general skepticism of treatment courts due to concerns that participants are under months or years of intense surveillance, and they do not always receive the criminal legal benefit they seek. However, the most challenging issue for this court was the initial prosecutor, who did not choose to be a VTC prosecutor. In hearings, this prosecutor often expressed concern that the court was too lenient with participants, and even disparaged participants during hearings. During one observation in early 2020, the prosecutor referred to a participant as "recalcitrant garbage." After the hearing, a case worker tried to explain away this behavior as the prosecutor "probably feeling a lot of pressure; [A]DAs in the city are currently being fired because they are at will," referring to the fact that a newly elected district attorney can terminate prosecutors who worked for the previous district attorney. The case worker mentioned that prosecutors in the past used the VTC as a temporary assignment to launch their careers, but that the assigned prosecutor in West VTC had been stuck there for years.

In our interview, the prosecutor explained to me that he was assigned to be the DA in this court almost as a demotion. He was skeptical of it, concerned that it was "paternalistic" and did not require participants to "face the consequences of their actions." This prosecutor stopped working at the VTC in 2020, which multiple staff expressed relief about. The timing coincided with the COVID-19 shutdown, meaning the court's practices were in tremendous flux. In fall 2020, when I asked the judge about the biggest change due to pandemic, he said it was the change in prosecutors, not the shutdown.

Mentors were also in flux. Having started as a new calendar within the community court, West did not have the same involvement of veteran mentors from the beginning as, for example, Northeast did. The city did have a robust set of supports for veterans without VA benefits, with one organization playing a prominent role in helping to identify and support these veterans. That organization was working in the city's jails even before the VTC became involved. During my early observations, a staff member from that organization played a prominent role in the VTC, but ended up having conflicts with the treatment court team and stopped participating.

The court's origins shaped its practices in other ways. Since this court originated in the community courts system, its ethos was inclusivity rather than exclusivity. This court had more than three times the number of participants than the Northeast VTC, but it did not boast three times the number of case managers. Although the court had a close and highly effective working relationship with the VA, half of its participants were not eligible for VA benefits. More participants mean more case management, and accepting people who are not eligible for VA benefits means that the assigned case manager must find funding from sources other than the VA. While the Southeast VTC faced major challenges with getting participants care at the VA, the West VTC's major challenge involved supporting the participants who were not eligible for VA benefits. A temporary solution for the Southeast VTC was to stop accepting any participant until it reorganized itself. Meanwhile, the West VTC temporarily stopped accepting people who were not eligible for VA benefits because the case manager was so overworked.

In many ways, this court's founding and the locale's features are more difficult to disentangle than the other two courts. For example, throughout my six years of observations, finding the funding for the case manager serving VA-ineligible veterans was a problem. Adding a participant who couldn't access the VA meant relying on public agencies that several interviewees referred to as "dysfunctional." According to court staff, agencies such as the local Department of Public Health did not want to put its resources into case manager positions, and it was nearly impossible to get grants for a case manager. Three times over the course of my observations, from 2015 through 2023, the court was under threat of losing this case manager because of funding issues. As explained in the previous chapter, for a few months at the end of 2022, there was no funding for the position. This lapse in available funds led this experienced, caring case manager to find another job. And these destabilizing events had direct consequences for the participants. During one of my observations in

March 2023, a participant on the verge of being terminated from the program refused to work with the new case manager.

Whether the challenges were purely related to resources, or whether there may have been some way to get stable funding for a case manager, West faced ongoing challenges stemming from its community court founding. With its severely high-risk and high-need population and expansive inclusion criteria, fostering a community similar to the one found at the Northeast VTC proved impossible. Instead, the West VTC settled for seemingly modest goals: getting participants off the most dangerous drugs, finding them housing, and hoping that they would choose to take care of themselves without a court demanding that they do so under the threat of punishment. Still, in light of the challenges its participants faced, this was an ambitious goal.

While common narrative suggests that veteran worth demands a specialized court that considers their military culture in its operation, West VTC's personnel did not bother with that pretense. Rather, they intentionally avoided talking about the military in the courtroom, with some explaining to me that many of their participants do not think fondly on their military years. Interestingly, and further complicating the common narrative, Northeast's judge relayed a similar concern and practice. But West's VTC, by including anyone who served in the military and with less regard for the types of crimes they are charged with, had many participants with tenuous attachments to their military service. In some ways, this approach takes the common narrative to an extreme, working from a belief that a VTC can help anyone who participated in the military in some way.

By serving people truly high risk for recidivism and high need for services, with less regard for the nature of their military service, West's reveals the opportunities and challenges of trying to serve as many people who participated in the military as possible. In addition, its different starting points in terms of population and goals underscore how evaluating this court along the lines of recidivism or other typical measures of "success" can give a false impression. This court had many more participants who were unable to complete the program than the other two courts, but my observations suggest that this is because the court was willing to take a risk on many more people in need.

VTCs IN CONTEXT

With the broader goal of understanding what VTCs tell us about inequality in the United States and how we use law to solve entrenched social and political problems, this chapter focuses on the operationalization of the VTC concept in three distinct locales. In so doing, it illustrates the limits of the common narrative that VTCs, by their nature, are uniquely able to help veterans in the criminal legal system. VTCs are not a new criminal legal technology uniquely suited to help veterans. They build from existing criminal legal and social service infrastructure in a given locale. As a result, they have strikingly different goals and strategies that reflect, among other influences, the specific steps of their founding, the resources available to them, and how individuals working in them were able to harness those resources and build the relationships needed to create the kind of community proponents hope for.

This chapter also reveals how treatment courts develop day-to-day practices based on their need to establish and maintain their legitimacy across diverse stakeholders. As Ashforth and Gibbs (1990) explain, a legitimate organization is one that accords with social norms, values, and expectations, pursuing socially acceptable goals in a socially acceptable manner (177). VTCs carry with them the legitimacy of the military and criminal legal system as defining institutions of US society. At the same time, this analysis of the founding of the three VTCs shows that "socially acceptable goals and manner" are locally defined. Each VTC must respond to its distinct social and political contexts.

These different locales are dealing with different dimensions of inequality in the US, and the VTCs gain legitimacy in addressing these different dimensions. Although many of these problems are beyond the VTCs' control, these origins stories show where and how they have agency. For example, inequalities in Northeast were minimized because of the availability of a residential facility, but access to that facility was not a given. The team worked from the beginning to integrate the facility into the program. Southeast, by contrast, did not immediately develop strong relationships with the service provider it needed—the VA—and that created challenges for the court. West, despite the team's efforts, evolved from serving individuals suffering from long-term, chronic homelessness and substance use, and was limited in what it could do to help that problem.

These local origin stories also provide insights into why VTCs are difficult to compare. These three courts not only have different approaches to what they do and who they serve but also about what they are *supposed* to do. Treatment courts are designed to be hybrid—a blend of justice and rehabilitation. VTCs, however, are even more complex because they blend two types of treatment courts (i.e., drug court and mental health court) and "add" in the common narrative that there is something special about veterans that requires different treatment. The origin stories show the different holes in that narrative. Each court decides who it counts as a veteran and what counts as help. Each court analyzed in this chapter addressed these complex questions differently. The Northeast VTC elected to be liberal in its admission policies but made sure that participants first pled guilty in order to receive the court's treatment benefits. The Southeast VTC implemented the national drug court model: get and keep participants sober and help them back into the workforce. The West VTC sought to keep their highly vulnerable population alive, get them as many social services as possible, and minimize the negative consequences of the criminal legal system.

VTCs are also complicated by a foundational contradiction: they are predicated on the deleterious effects of the military on participants while implicitly celebrating the military to establish the courts' legitimacy. These origin stories reveal how this contradiction shaped each court's founding, with those promoting VTCs as an to aid a group they saw as both uniquely vulnerable and uniquely resourced. These three courts drew on the common story, supported by both ideological and material resources, to establish their legitimacy with their own stakeholders to meet distinct goals and strategies. But, in each place, the courts had to rely on existing criminal legal and social service infrastructure. That means that the implementation of the courts leads to very different organizations, ones that not only have different approaches and different understandings of what they are supposed to be doing, but different levels of services available. One thing to note is that all three courts are in places with more social services than most jurisdictions across the country, and they still struggled to meet participant needs.

Overall, the findings reveal neither the common narrative nor the inevitability of a particular treatment court approach. Rather, they reveal how each organization is shaped by the choices of the person or team who started it. What they have in common is the ongoing reliance in the US on criminal law to address entrenched social and political problems related to substance abuse, mental health, poverty, and now militarism and war and the benefits of a nationally funded social welfare system for veterans. They are each shaped by their local institutional and organizational environments, the availability of social services and the functionality of the local court agencies. Within these constraints, they must each find creative solutions to aid the populations that they serve. Through this analysis, we see how a court predicated on the existence of a unique military culture struggles to address entrenched, deeply local social inequalities that create challenges for the vulnerable veterans who find themselves in a VTC program, and for those individuals hoping to help them.

Seven

CONFLICTED GRATITUDE

Sitting in Southeast on a pleasant December afternoon, I watched a VTC graduate come to the podium in a celebration of his graduation from the VTC program. After the prosecutor listed the benefits of having charged dropped and fees waived, the participant looked up at the judge and asked in earnest, "I have a comment/question––why are you so passionate and sincere about the veterans? You are incredible." The judge looked taken aback, deeply grateful for the rare acknowledgment of the judge's hard work to encourage participants to stick with the court's demands. The judge replied: "It makes me feel so good to see someone get well, doing this work as a judge in this division, you don't get that feeling often, you don't see a lot of positive things; and this is a whole team we are working with to help veterans." The participant replied with sincerity, "I thank them all."

This exchange illustrates what the court personnel, particularly the judge, hope to hear: the participant not only complies with the court's demands but also is grateful for the programming. Among my years of observations, it was one of the more explicit examples of a participant expressing appreciation for the court, and the kind of exchanges that kept the judge motivated through the many conflicts that arose in the courtroom.

This was an unusual exchange in Southeast, though I witnessed several similar exchanges in Northeast. Still, Northeast also had its share of conflicts, the details of which help illustrate the central contradiction in creating a court that simultaneously celebrates military service, blames that same service for a veteran's criminal legal involvement, and depends heavily on a federal bureaucracy with its own hierarchies of worth.

In just one example, early in its existence the Northeast VTC had issued a warrant for the arrest of a participant, a veteran in his late fifties, who had been honorably discharged from the army after two years of service. The reason for the warrant was that he missed his court appointment that day, not that he committed another crime. The police picked him up, and he rejoined the court a week later, explaining that he had been in a bike accident that left him temporarily unconscious. The judge reminded him that the requirements of the program were that he not use cocaine, for which he tested positive that day, or marijuana and alcohol, which he admitted using the week of the accident.

The participant was clearly struggling, and said that if he had died in that accident, "You wouldn't have to worry about me anymore." Then he told the court that his daughter informed him that she was pregnant, and he was going to be a grandfather, adding: "I guess there's something to live for." The judge told him it was time to place him in a residential facility, where he would have to reside full-time for one month and stay sober the entire time. A few months and a few warrants later, along with a few nights in jail, the participant was back in the VTC. The judge explained his supervision would be stepped up, requiring the participant to carry the Sobrietor. His mentor described it to him as a "blow tube" that detects alcohol on one's breath, but told the participant, "This is not punishment."

The participant, frustrated, said, "It is punishment."

His observation that this experience was punishment, while obvious, seemed a taboo in this courtroom that promoted the image of a cohesive community dedicated to help get participants social services. The narratives produced by the personnel and the participants, as in other treatment courts, typically minimize the fact that this is a criminal legal process. Instead, they framed the experience as an "opportunity" that "honors" the participants' military service. This participant did not view this "opportunity" as the court hoped he would.

By the summer, his anger boiled over. The probation officer introduced him at a July hearing, saying that he missed meetings, to which the participant shot back, "This is all wrong." He argued with the judge in a scene that was unusual for the Northeast VTC, where conversations were usually staid. When the probation officer said the participant was in Phase 1, typical for someone who was still using drugs and alcohol against the court's rules, the participant insisted he was in Phase 3. He complained that an earlier GPS monitor got him into trouble unfairly, which "must be obvious" since he was wearing a new one and was not having issues. Mostly, he argued about being forced to stay at the residential facility, angry that he was not allowed to come and go when he wanted and concerned that staying at the residential facility was interfering with his long-term housing options through the VA housing benefits known as HUD–VASH (Housing and Urban Development–Veterans Affairs Supportive Housing). He asked, with exasperation in his voice, "Are you [aware] that I might lose this apartment because of this? Did anybody tell you that yet?"

The judge calmly replied, "That's why we want you to be compliant with the program." The participant finally stopped arguing and went to use the Sobrietor, as he was supposed to do throughout each day. Nevertheless, by the end of the month, the participant was in another residential detox program, still unable to follow the court's mandates for sobriety.

This participant's dilemma between following the court's mandate and enjoying the benefits of VA-assisted housing illustrates a broader theoretical and practical dilemma in VTCs. VA-eligible participants in VTCs are subject to disciplining processes in (at least) two complex bureaucracies: courts and the VA. And, for those who are not eligible for VA benefits, they move lower in the hierarchy of court participants in terms of what resources they can access to move through the program.

While many of the participants are grateful for the court's support, exemplified by the first vignette, they understand they are being coerced to comply with requirements that interfere with their daily lives. Hence, the participant above emphasizing that "this is punishment." VTC participants understand and respond to the material and ideological foundations of VTCs in ways that reveal this unique judicial organization's precarious premise, and their pushback in the courtrooms provides important insights into the legitimacy trap of presenting participants with the idea that a VTC is a benefit when they experience it as a burden.

WHEN THANK YOU IS NOT ENOUGH

Anger over court requirements is a common hurdle for all treatment courts, which ask for months-long or years-long commitment by participants (see, e.g., Burns and Peyrot 2003; Tiger 2012; Kaye 2020; Shdaimah et al. 2023). However, this anger takes on a different meaning in a court model that literally advertises itself with the slogan: "When Thank You Is Not Enough"—which is from the Justice for Vets national training center. The common narrative that VTCs are a benefit for veterans—the legal manifestation of "thank you for your service"—carries a reciprocal expectation that court participants would, could, or should be grateful to be in the program. Another implication is that this gratitude will help them respond in a constructive way to court mandates.

For judges and VTC personnel, admission to the court is one form of thank you, and the opportunity to join the court can feel like a matter of life or death. All three courts discussed in this book have had participants who overdosed and died under their watch. And yet, knowing the challenges that participants face to comply with court mandates, they understand the anger expressed over the burden of daily or weekly therapy appointments, random drug tests, and coming to a courthouse that may be far away from where participants live.

VTC judges, personnel, and advocates all make efforts to explain their courts as an expression of gratitude, which reveals an important way in which they seek legitimacy among funders, participants, and policymakers. In all three courts, I observed moments in which participants similarly expressed gratitude like in the opening vignette, the kind of displays that advocates and treatment court practitioners celebrated in private and in public. Yet my years of observations also revealed the flipside to this gratitude. In the same court sessions, one participant might express gratitude while another would use highly charged language of resentment. For example, during the same hearing at the West VTC, one participant thanked the judge while another quit the court that day, telling the caseworker that the court was making him "dance like a slave."

Building from earlier chapters that underscore the mismatch between the common narrative and a VTC's day-to-day practices, this chapter draws on common courtroom conflicts to further examine the disconnect. In a court predicated on "thank you for your service," understanding the dynamics around gratitude provides a useful entrée to the underlying contradiction of using a criminal legal organization to address entrenched social and political problems related to poverty and substance abuse—as all treatment courts do— and militarism and war—as VTCs do. It also highlights how VTCs expressly mobilize veteran identity to create a specific narrative about how the participants can reform themselves (Sherman 2024).

The common narrative presumes that gratitude flows both ways between court and participants, which promotes cooperative behaviors between benefactors and beneficiaries (Cavanaugh 2010; McCall et al. 2019; McCullough et al. 2001). By offering a treatment court for veterans, VTC advocates and court personnel present themselves as the benefactors, and the participants as the beneficiaries. To do this, the judge and VTC team members may use identity-oriented language with the goals of providing a community and a sense of structure to transform identities and help people successfully progress through the program (Sherman 2024). And some research suggests that veteran identity increases participants' perceptions of the court as fair and legitimate (Gallagher and Ashford 2021).

Yet, the frequent expressions of anger and frustration toward the court, particularly in Southeast and West, highlight the contradiction of the court as an ostensible benefit that creates so many burdens for those it is seeking to help. Personnel explained in interviews that they often resist the initial pushback because the participant may eventually come to appreciate what the court is offering. And, of course, many participants do. At the same time, personnel also relayed that, because they believe in the transformative potential of VTCs, judges can be reluctant to terminate participants who simply do not want to be in the court.

I refer to these contradictions as conflicted gratitude (Rowen 2020). This conflict dynamic, which manifests in concerns over individuation, resources, and indebtedness, emerges from a premise that VTCs offer a distinct benefit to veterans specifically based on beliefs about the worth of military service, laid over the experience of VTCs as a burden, something both the court and participants are well aware of. Despite demanding compliance under the threat of punishment, VTCs stress its benevolence to participants and funders by suggesting that the court is itself an expression of veteran worth. What differentiates their experience of conflicted gratitude in a VTC from a criminal legal program not predicated on veteran identity is how the idea of "thank you for your service" permeates courtroom dynamics. Whether or not the words are said directly, or whether or not the personnel reference the services available to veterans (and, by implication, not others), gratitude structures courtroom expectations. Participants, many of whom have been in and out of criminal legal settings for years, make it clear that they see through this (mis)representation.

The conflicts witnessed were not evenly distributed across the three courts. Rather, they are reflective of who the court lets in, what the court mandates, and what the court offers in return. For this reason, conflicted gratitude is a useful lens to understand both the specific dynamics of individual courts and the broader politics of worth reflected in VTCs.

In the rest of this chapter, I first explain how gratitude relates to indebtedness. I then turn to the contrast between how VTC personnel try to "sell" the court as a benefit and how participants push back against them. In the analysis, we see that conflicted gratitude is a VTC feature, not a bug. At the same time, it appeared differently in the three courts, a function of how the judges and the participants relate to the common narrative that veterans are uniquely deserving, and VTCs are uniquely effective in helping them, the latter of which reflects the court's capacity to actually help its participants (the reasons for which are explored in the previous chapter). Through analyzing conflicted gratitude, we see the distinct ways that veteran identity is mobilized in VTCs, which has dimensions that are both ideological and material.

By looking at how gratitude and conflict manifest in the courts, the chapter further shows the challenges presented by the add veteran and stir approach to treatment courts that VTCs take, while also illustrating broader issues posed by the politics of worth. In designating veterans as a distinct category of criminal legal defendants, VTCs suggest that there are, at once, structural reasons for veterans' involvement in the criminal legal system while also emphasizing individual agency in overcoming their challenges, the kind of responsibilization that is the modus operandi of any treatment court (Kaye 2020). Conflicts help illustrate the ways in which these courts carry the baggage of inequalities evident in the drug treatment courts they modeled themselves on (Cheesman et al. 2023), as well as the inequalities within local criminal legal and social service organizations that distinguish between veterans and nonveterans, and worthy and unworthy veterans.

GRATITUDE AND INDEBTEDNESS

Gratitude is a natural extension of the common narrative that veterans are uniquely deserving and are amenable to the VTC process. The presumption is that if veterans see the court as an expression of gratitude for their service, they should want to comply. There are both conceptual and practical dilemmas with this presumption. For example, from the perspective of moral philosophy, a supposed benefit—the basis of gratitude—should not create an obligation (McConnell 2017). Following this line of reasoning, people should not be expected to express, or even feel, gratitude when being asked or expected to perform requirements. This is particularly true if they are being asked to give more than the benefit they initially receive, as they may simply want to discharge the duty rather than fulfill it (Manela 2016; Peng, Neliseen, and Zeelenberg 2018).

Further, coupled with their premise that there is something unique and distinct about military culture, with its emphasis on duty and loyalty (or conformity), mobilizing gratitude can be particularly coercive. Rather than foster an exchange where the expectations are clear, gratitude carries with it emotional dimensions, whereby a beneficiary must perform their worth by performing gratitude. These emotional logics animate VTC benchcraft strategies (Castellano 2017), whereby treatment court judges operate as both a "coach" and "leading actor in a therapeutic drama" designed to transform individual participants (Winick and Wexler 2003). To varying degrees, VTC team members reinforce the VTC "drama" predicated on the idea that a VTC is a material manifestation of the verbal "thank you" that veterans may hear from strangers on the street.

The mobilization of gratitude in a VTC is distinct from other treatment courts not only because of the "thank you for your service" tagline, but also due to the fact that part of the common narrative is that VTCs are more effective because they foster community among participants that is based on the camaraderie offered by the military. Some research from social psychology suggests that feelings of gratitude lead to a desire for social proximity (Ma, Tunney, and Ferguson 2017), or becoming close to the benefactor (Kubacka et al. 2011). Yet, other research reveals that feelings of social proximity must exist before feelings of gratitude (He et al. 2022), and communicating expectations of giving back can decrease positive feelings of gratitude and increase negative feelings of indebtedness (Watkins et al. 2006; Oishi et al. 2019) and resentment (Manela 2016).

It is also useful to reflect on the role of gratitude in treatment courts because compliance and conformity are closely related. Together, many participants and the personnel co-construct the common narrative that these courts are an important benefit beyond criminal legal outcomes and social services. However, like the "outcasts" vs. the "true believers" who perform compliance or lack thereof in treatment courts (Moore and Hirai 2014), those who do not conform and who reject this narrative can face an additional emotional burden. Feelings of indebtedness can bring guilt and shame, which are emotions that lead to social distance rather than proximity (Sznycer and Lukaszewski 2019). Blending the military element of camaraderie with treatment court logics creates a potent tool for compliance or the flipside of honor, the kind of dishonor that the participants may have felt if they struggled in the military. For courts that accept participants dishonorably discharged, this dynamic can be even more problematic.

Although this book is not focused on individual psychology, instead relying on observations to explain courtroom dynamics, these theories are useful to understand the conflicts in VTCs as many emerge in relation to which social services the participants can access. Obviously, when judges present the court as a benefit, they face the dilemma that most participants do not want to be in any court. And, ironically, those who reject the court end up asked to do more; they may be asked to attend court more often, have more supervision, and do more activities that affect their work, family, and leisure time. Further, the extra resources that VTCs have in comparison with other treatment courts mean that VTCs may be able to offer more social services, particularly VA services. However, in addition to themselves reflecting and creating hierarchies about veterans' worth, both VTCs and the VA services they access may have additional rules and restrictions as well as an enhanced ability to surveil.

This disconnect between the promise of VTCs and their reality can foster not only resentment but disenchantment in participants (Gallagher 2006), a feeling that arises when people respond negatively to the difference between the symbolic nature of the law and the reality of what it demands.

DYNAMICS OF CONFLICTED GRATITUDE

The three conflicted gratitude dynamics outlined below—individuation, resources, and indebtedness—help illustrate the nuanced relationship between the positive emotion of gratitude, which facilitates social proximity, and what Galvin (2004) refers to as the "perpetual feeling of obligation." Such coercive dynamics are typical in treatment courts, but in VTCs notions of veteran worth can make their way into the courtroom as a way for each party—judge and participant—to establish their own legitimacy and authority in the space. When participants push back, they are attempting to assert their agency as veterans in a court that presumes their gratitude. Thus, in contrast to scholars who suggest that mobilizing veteran identity is a useful way that VTCs transform lives for the better (Sherman 2024), these examples highlight the contested nature of such mobilization.

The following analysis shows that there are similar conflict dynamics across the three VTCs; namely, participants expressing expectations of the court based on it being designated for veterans. Yet, there are also conflict dynamics specific to individual court features. In part, expressions of frustration and anger on the part of participants reflect the basic structure of VTC hearings and a judge's personality. These, of course, differ by court. However, and more importantly, it is the availability of a court's resources, and the policies shaping who is allowed into the court, and what veterans must do to graduate, that differently affect the participants. In these conflicts, we see how each court fosters a unique hierarchy not only among who is allowed in or not but also among its own participants.

Group vs. Individuation

The dynamic of group vs. individuation is the contrast between how court personnel express the value of a VTC being created for veterans as a group, and participants' complaints that the court is treating them all the same. In each court, I witnessed conflicts between participants who asked to be treated as individuals, with their own criminal legal history and substance use behaviors and mental health needs, and the court's effort to construct a community based on shared experiences. Such conflicts carry a distinct meaning in a treatment court based on an employment experience. Rather than focusing on individuals with either substance use or mental health needs, or on people who have committed specific crimes, VTCs serve people with a wide range of histories and needs even if they all were once in the military. This means that participants may have very different challenges with substance use and mental health, as well as experiences in the military and the VA.

I witnessed the clearest example of this conflict dynamic on a summer afternoon in the Northeast VTC. One of the few women participants sat in the front row, handcuffed and wearing an orange jumpsuit. She had been in jail for over a month. She did not have eligibility to access the VA's services, and therefore had fewer options for inpatient support. She explained forcefully that jail was not helping her because she had only been to one meeting for Alcoholics Anonymous there. She asked to be released to her mother's home, to be with her young son and to recover from the recent death of her partner of seven years. The judge asked her to share more information about herself. The participant volunteered that her father had been in the Air Force, so she joined the Reserves. She met her son's father and got pregnant. Shortly after the birth of her son, she discovered heroin. Her partner had been using it; she was curious about whether she could use it without a needle, and she did. A few weeks shy of graduating with a degree in health services, she was kicked out of her program for too many absences.

When told she would remain detained until the court could find her a space in a residential facility, she yelled as I had never seen a participant do in the Northwest VTC, claiming: "You treat us all the same, and we are not the same!"

A few months later, I saw her in court at another graduation ceremony, sitting with fellow participants also unable to access VA services because of substance use–related dishonorable discharges and who had similarly struggled with the court program. I thought she was going to be okay: she looked healthy and expressed gratitude to the court for helping her. Tragically, her sobriety did not last, and she passed away the following April, a loss felt deeply by the court community.

Over the years, I thought often of this participant, and the challenge of creating a process that is fair, which could either mean treating everyone "the same" or allowing for different approaches to relapses. This participant struggled in the military, and it was also clear that being forced to conform was harder for her than for others. Her anger at being asked to stay in jail, and the reality of her substance use and its consequences, reveal the stakes of treating participants "the same," in this case, mandating sobriety and relying on jail to enforce it. Her outburst literally burst the common narrative for me, showing how the court's approach to treating participants as a unified group belied their individual stories and needs.

At the same time, this participant's exchange with the judge was not the typical example of this conflict dynamic; participants usually pushed back without such anger by emphasizing that they should not be treated the same as others. The following dialogue was more typical in Northeast as it related to mandatory drug testing, with the judge rebuking the participant over perceived disrespect. At the beginning, the probation officer reads the weekly report about the participant's compliance. The participant complains that he is being treated unfairly and, at the end of the exchange, the mentor tries to smooth over the conflict, an illustration of how conflicts were better managed in Northeast because of the different resources the court could access.

> Probation Officer: He did not submit his essay for his missing screen and also did test positive for fentanyl [on] November 15th. Continues to work on his medical marijuana card, continues with therapy. Missed a group at strength at home. We will be issuing a violation of probation.
>
> Judge: Who did you submit the essay to?
>
> Participant: My probation officer. As far as this fentanyl shit—
>
> Judge: We don't swear.
>
> Participant: I have never taken fentanyl in my life. The only thing I take is pot and antibiotics. My essay was faxed out this morning by my case worker.
>
> Judge: I don't appreciate you interrupting me. We are issuing a VOP [violation of probation]. What I will do is appoint a lawyer to represent you, who will contact you just in case this was a mistest. I appreciate your participation in MRT [moral reconation therapy].
>
> Participant: Where is my therapist? Other people have therapists, but I don't have one.
>
> Judge: Speak to [person] to straighten that out.
>
> Participant: I got screwed on my original charges.
>
> Judge: We are trying to work with you.
>
> Mentor: Overall [participant] is doing pretty well but at times his attitude slips away from him.

As is the nature of the Northeast VTC as a "model court," this conflict in which the participant compares his individual experience to court requirements did not escalate. Representative of most conflicts in this court, rather than engage in a heated exchange, the judge immediately asserted boundaries over how they were to be addressed and clarified next steps, and the mentor spoke up to calm the situation.

Still, exchanges such as this one deviate from the common narrative in which participants are grateful for the opportunity to join the court even when the court, by its nature, curtails their freedoms. They highlight the concerns that participants may have about their individual cases, both the coercion that some may feel in a program that requires them to plead guilty and the unfairness of mandatory drug testing that interferes with their daily activities.

In Southeast, the conflicts about individual vs. group identity manifested in a different way, with the judge trying to encourage buy-in by emphasizing the common story. As the following example illustrates, the judge frequently mobilized the idea of military culture and social science "evidence" that treatment courts help people stay sober and out of the criminal legal system:

> It is great to have you here and I will go over a couple things. Some things here are very similar to drug and mental health court, but this is specifically designed for veterans. The reason for that is the science has shown that there are so many unique, special, and difficult circumstances for individuals to live with. And better outcomes come when the team and participants are all comprised of veterans.
>
> *(judge, Southeast VTC)*

The jury is still out, so to speak, on whether or not VTCs are uniquely effective courts for veterans but, regardless, this judge tried to get buy-in from participants by repeating this element of the common narrative. Of the three courts, the Southeast VTC judge had the most frequent conversations about the benefit of joining the court because of shared military culture, camaraderie, and other nonmaterial benefits pushed in the common narrative. The opening vignette shows that, on occasion, participants reciprocated.

Yet, the following exchange from Southeast shows how individual circumstances can lead to very emotional arguments. Prior to this dialogue, the participant had asked the judge to allow him to come less frequently to the court. After explaining the burdens that the court was putting on his family, the judge suggested that the participant needs to prioritize the court and comply regardless of competing obligations. In the exchange, the participant's angry pushback escalated to verbal and nearly also physical confrontation:

> Judge: You have to remember this is not a family court. Family issues are difficult, but that is not what we are here for. Everyone has things that haunt them from their past. Even me. But what we have to do is stay in the present and move forward.
>
> Participant: I just want to have monthly visits, not even weekly.
>
> Judge: That is not why we are here though; this is just for treatment.
>
> Participant: It is expensive to come here. And I don't understand. I want this to make things better, but nothing is happening.
>
> Judge: Visits will be less often as the program goes along, but you have to be patient.

At this point, the participant stormed out of the court. When a mentor attempted to slow him down, he yelled, "Get out of my fucking way."

This level of emotionality and conflict was a rare but not an isolated incident at the Southeast VTC. On a weekly basis, participants expressed open anger about their personal circumstances, particularly the challenge of getting to court and meeting drug testing requirements while also holding a job and meeting other life and family responsibilities. In a locale with limited public transportation, the costs of getting to and being in court went beyond the time in the courtroom itself. These costs differed for people who lived across the city and had varied obligations.

The levels of emotionality in these courts reflect the dynamics of treating people as though they are part of a group and their comfort in asserting their individuality. In Northeast, participants largely conformed to court expectations, and deviating from the regular script was unusual. The lack of group identity in Southeast made it easier for people to speak out forcefully in defense of their preferences and against the court's efforts to make them conform.

West's conflicts related to individuation differed from Southeast's because the judge did not seek buy-in with the same strategy. In fact, the regular judge's strategy to treat participants as individuals stood out because I first observed West on a day that a substitute judge was in the courtroom. That judge spent far more time than I had seen any judge talking to each participant about their military service. As participants stood in front of him, looking anxious and fidgety, he lectured on how they should be proud of that service, and how that service indicates they can comply with what the court is asking of them. During his brief monologues about their worth and capabilities as veterans, the case workers repeatedly looked back at me wide-eyed and seemingly embarrassed, with one explaining under her breath that this was not a typical hearing.

With the permanent judge, I witnessed a subtler approach to get a participant to comply by asking if the participant "wants" to do what is asked. The example below was typical of West, where people described detailed and complex criminal legal histories:

Judge: You've already been talked to, and we have a plan so this is going to move faster than what I proposed. Is that okay?

Participant: Well, I'm not a lawyer. I don't know the law.

Judge: Well, it's not the law. It's being in jail or not. But I need you to be invested. Do you want to do this?

Participant: Yes, let's do this.

Judge: I've heard more enthusiastic responses.

Participant: Yes, I'm sure. I'm facing a felony and a strike. I'm not looking forward to three years [incarcerated]. My civil rights are destroyed. I've already been assaulted by an officer. I haven't been able to get ahold of my lawyer, and I've been informed that if I file a grievance order, they'll come and stomp me out again.

Judge: Okay, we're trying to get you in a better situation.

Participant: Let's try.

Judge: But we need you to be motivated, right? Things about your life should improve.

Participant: Should is a try word. It's not a definite word. It's an indefinite word.

Judge: You're absolutely right, and if I could guarantee it, I would.

In this exchange, common to West, the participant focused on his individual experiences and reasons for being in the criminal legal system. He was skeptical of whether the court can actually help. The judge did not promise anything, a direct contrast to the frequent guarantees proffered in Southeast.

The participant continued by asking whether the judge is a veteran, mobilizing his own veteran identity to question the court's legitimacy. The judge apologized for not being a veteran, and the participant expressed his displeasure with the court because it was presented to him as something different than all the other criminal legal processes he's experienced:

> Participant: Are you a veteran?
> Judge: No, I am not. Sorry.
> Participant: I thought this was a Veteran's Court. This has to do with Abe Lincoln. I think we're going to go to martial law soon. That means no Department of Justice, just Department of Defense. Then I'll be happy. That's the day you'll see me smiling from ear to ear. For now, since you're enforcement of the law, I'll abide by the best of my abilities. Thank you so much, sir. Anything else?
>
> *(West VTC)*

In this exchange, the participant rejects the common narrative, mentioning his disappointment with the court and the expectation that being a VTC would mean court personnel are veterans and, perhaps, he would experience the VTC differently than he had experienced other criminal legal processes. The exchange largely felt performative, as though he expected the judge's answers. Still, as he expressed disappointment both that he is in jail and that the VTC is simply a court, he added that he will comply to "the best of my abilities" with the court's requirements. He did not fight back against what the court was asking, but he did not appear to believe that it will be useful, either.

This exchange illustrates how, when operationalized, the common narrative simplifies differences between participants, specifically why they are in the criminal legal system and what they want from the court, as well as the differences between the courts themselves. The shared experience of being a veteran is an employment experience, one that is unique in many ways but one that may have less to do with a person's identity or their criminal charges than the narrative assumes. Predicating a court on veteran identity can provide not only additional resources for the participants but also ammunition for participants to push back when the court makes demands.

Resources

The dynamics over resources reveal how material inequalities make their way into court; the VTC can provide beneficial opportunities for some participants, but it cannot do so equitably because some participants have access to resources that others do not. The distinct punishment assemblage between the VTC and VA can make some participants more vulnerable, particularly to housing insecurity, and illustrate how inequalities manifest within and between courts. While the court personnel tried to engender gratitude for the court's ability to help participants access resources, many participants had needs that the court, even with its access to resources that only veterans can receive, could not help.

Since both Northeast and West accept participants ineligible for VA benefits, conflicts during hearings often emerged over resources plaguing people seeking available social services where VA-eligible participants would have little trouble. For example, one of the Northeast's VTC's first graduates, celebrated in this book's opening vignette, had no access to VA benefits because she did not meet the requirements to qualify as a veteran under federal law. Because Northeast participants had access to substance use treatments, the main dilemma they faced was stable housing. VA-eligible participants had numerous housing options, from temporary housing to loans for more permanent housing. Coming to a court hearing about a year into the program, this participant expressed sorrow over her challenge in finding a job and housing:

> I've been doing a job search and I get this fear that, okay, why even apply? You know, they just said no to housing because of my record so I get a little [down].
>
> *(Northeast VTC)*

Although the participant expressed sadness, this conversation in Northeast did not involve blame, which I often saw in the other two courts; the participant treated the court as being on the same side in wanting long-term stability. In addition to revealing the participant's individual struggles, the sadness highlights the contrast of a court that celebrates participants for being veterans, and the reality for those who cannot access VA benefits or other forms of support.

These kinds of struggles can be more complicated for participants in a VTC than in another criminal legal process because being in the court can further affect a person's access to VA benefits. For example, veterans with a criminal conviction for possession or use of an illicit substance could make one ineligible for VA housing benefits. In Northeast, participants pleading guilty to enter the court could jeopardize these benefits. In a notable conversation in Northeast, a mentor explained his frustration to the judge that he might be able to help a participant get through the program, but that he might leave the program "a homeless guy." The judge thanked the mentor for stepping in to support that veteran as well as another participant who was not eligible for VA housing benefits because of bad discharge papers (Northeast VTC). The exchange again shows how having mentors in the court helped ease tensions in Northeast, while also illustrating the challenges facing a court predicated on an identity that carries different meanings depending on discharge status.

Since Northeast VTC participants could access a comprehensive residential facility that was well integrated with the court, there were rarely conflicts about the court's treatment requirements. However, the court could not help people with more long-term needs and the availability of a residential treatment facility was not a given. When the court was worried about drug use and participants who could not find residential treatment, they kept them incarcerated. This decision contributed to conflicts common to drug treatment courts, one more indication of VTCs being "add veteran and stir" rather than a new and better model. Even those able to access treatments more quickly because of VA benefits did not always have access to a residential facility. I often saw hearings in which participants' presence was "waived" as they were traveling long distances to VA health centers with openings.

Yet, there is a flip side to the availability of resources, evidenced by the conformity dynamics within Northeast. As explained throughout this book, with its close adherence to the common narrative, the participants having problems with the expectations in Northeast appeared more deviant than the frequently struggling participants in the other two courts. Across the courts, participants in jail were often livid that they were ordered to stay in jail because the court decided that it was "safer" for them there than to be released. Typically, the judge explained this decision as related to social services: unless the participant could go immediately to a residential facility that would closely monitor them and prevent them from accessing drugs, the court preferred that the person stay in jail. Even if the participant struggled to stay sober while living in a dedicated residential facility, participants eligible for VA benefits had access to other social services that non-VA-eligible people did not.

Likewise, participants eligible for VA benefits had access to more housing opportunities, including long-term permanent housing. This meant that, even though most participants in this program appeared well supported, there were still differences based on VA eligibility. Further, for participants who were not staying at the residential facility, I observed frequent conversations about how court requirements interfered with their ability to work (particularly if the court required a GPS ankle bracelet) and their family obligations. Since the court served a large geographic area that included both rural and urban settings, transportation to and from the court posed a challenge in Northeast as it did in the other courts.

At the Southeast VTC, for the bulk of our observations all participants had to be able to access the VA to be allowed into the program, so it makes sense that the judge frequently emphasized the role of beneficence of the VA in order to encourage participants. The references to the services offered by the VA provide another example of how gratitude logics manifested in the court hearings:

> The treatment provider is the VA, and that is on a volunteer basis. We have had individuals attend the program and not understand, the VA provider is not going to mandate you stay. If you really don't want to do this, or don't have time for this today, they are not going to stop you. But because it is under [the] court, the court can order that. It is all-volunteer, they are here because they want to be here, and recognize and accept they need to be here. It is the best results for you, to bring you back [to] balance and healthy living.
>
> *(judge, Southeast VTC)*

The suggestion that this is "voluntary"—that the VA will not mandate treatment and that participants "want to be here"—articulates responsibilizing logics that participants have a choice in both joining the court and complying with its mandates with gratitude logics more specific to VTCs. The judge also emphasizes that the team "want[s] to be here," that all parties are involved due to the service they want to provide, flipping the script of "thank you for your service" to one of mutual support between the court and participants. Of course, participants in Southeast frequently expressed anger over treatment requirements, even if those requirements were presented as resources the court was helping them access.

Even if there were not explosive arguments as illustrated above, in Southeast there were frequent conflicts over what resources the participants could access because of bureaucratic processes at the VA and the availability of other resources. In the following exchange, for example, the judge celebrated the participant for "looking fabulous" and "doing great." The judge then asked what was on the participant's mind:

Participant: I'm in pain, it's annoying to talk to my doctors about it. Old pains and new pains. They know I suffer from a lot, but they are not doing anything to help me. Housing is still up in the air. They put me on a list, no one has responded to me.

Clinician: What he is speaking of, is he was flagged in the [VA] system. [The non-VA residential facility] let us know he would be in aftercare for 60–90 days.

Participant: The VA downgraded the flag, just have a warning there for behavior. (Southeast VTC)

As the participant tells it, he was struggling to get the resources he needed to stabilize his housing, which is something treatment courts often ask for in order to graduate a participant. Even though he was VA eligible, he was "flagged" for his charge of aggravated assault with a deadly weapon and battery on someone elderly. Although he was compliant with the court and frequently celebrated for following its mandates, the VTC could not change his access to housing support from the VA or the frustration he felt about how the charge affected his benefits. If the VTC mandated housing as part of its requirements, the participants faced extra pressure to both have stable housing and be able to show it to the court and to graduate from the program. Gratitude for the opportunity to be in the court can conflict with its requirements for resources that are not readily available.

The participant continued by asking the court about a previous charge for a DUI, which affected his driver's license. The judge said they would look into it but for now the participant should focus on getting nonresidential care at the non-VA facility and getting housing. At the end of this exchange, the participant reiterated the gratitude that the judge was seeking, saying, "I appreciate being put in this program. I want to be here." The judge, in turn, replied by suggesting that the participant was not being coerced, saying, "It is voluntary for those who want to make changes and it shows. It is your work, one day at a time."

These variants on the theme of gratitude, conflict, and resources also played out in West's hearings. The West VTC's judge mobilized the common narrative less overtly than did the Southeast VTC's judge, but gratitude also played an important role in this court's hearings. With so many participants to manage, and many facing housing insecurity and long-term substance use and mental health disorders, there was less time to spend on explaining or celebrating the court.

Still, the participants of the West VTC mentioned gratitude in more overt ways than did participants in the other two courts. These participants' expressions of gratitude, particularly when they referred to their military service, were notable in part because West VTC's judge and court staff avoided discussing anyone's service history. This is because, as they told me in interviews, many participants at this VTC were ashamed of their service histories. Still, these histories emerged in the West VTC because there was often a question of whether a participant would be eligible for VA benefits (an occurrence that couldn't happen, for example, at the Southeast VTC), and the participants had to be reminded that they did not leave the military on good terms.

The following exchange shows these identity dynamics in play, whereby the judge tries to figure out what resources the program could help the participant access, and the participant mobilizes their veteran identity to suggest that they will be able to comply with the program. Note that neither judge nor participant is mobilizing veteran identity to suggest that there is, can, or should be something transformative about the court, which is a central theme of the common narrative (Sherman 2024). Rather, they draw on veteran identity to discuss resources and compliance.

> Judge: Did you sign a piece of paper, so we can figure out your veteran status?
> Participant: Yes.
> Case Worker: He does have VA healthcare, so he'll be meeting with us tomorrow.
> Judge: Lucky you. They're good folks, so you'll be well taken care of. Do you think you know what you need?
> Participant: Yes, I think I know.
> Judge: We're trying to put you in charge of your own life. If you need something, don't just sit there. People think their job is to take orders from me but they're supposed to take their own life in their hands . . . no guarantees. Sometimes we won't agree but I need you to be actively involved. So, come back here in a week.
> Participant: Well, I'm good at taking orders, the military.

(West VTC)

In this exchange, the participant reciprocates the judge's efforts in a way both ambivalent and sarcastic, suggesting that their military service will aid them in complying with the court's requirements and that accessing resources is a matter of "taking orders." While not expressing gratitude or enthusiasm, the participant expresses acceptance of the judge's attempts to get buy-in. When the judge points out that the participant is "lucky" for having VA benefits, the judge is making a statement that reflects the precarity of West's participants.

While participants with VA benefits in each court had access to resources unavailable to others, in West this access was more significant because VA benefits enabled not only more social services but more clinicians—this court had two to three case managers for half the court that was VA eligible and one clinician for the other half. And, in one of the few references by participants to veteran identity, this exchange also illustrates how mobilizing one's veteran identity can help the participant and the judge communicate a shared goal.

While the difference between the VA haves and have-nots was starker in the West VTC than in the other two courts, all three courts struggled with participants who had different levels of access to resources. These differences highlight the inequality both between the courts and within them. In Northeast, where all participants could stay at the residential facility if they complied with its rules, there was less conflict related to treatment options. In Southeast, where participants were VA eligible, conflicts over resources typically emerged when the participants were unable to access VA treatments or other benefits. In West, the conflicts were compounded by the high needs and lengthy experiences that many had with seeking and obtaining substance use treatments. Even with access to services unavailable to many people who never served in the military, the conflicts in the courts emerged as they sought resources to help struggling participants.

Indebtedness

There is a fine line between gratitude and indebtedness, and hearings often displayed this tension. The dynamic of indebtedness was often illustrated by the judge articulating how the people in the court were making sacrifices on behalf of the participant, and the participant clarifying they did not want to be there to begin with. This tension reflects the fact that many participants are grateful for the support they receive in the court, but understandably find themselves frustrated with what the court is offering. Rather than gratitude, the participants articulated indebtedness, or being obligated to comply with mandates presented as benefits.

In a VTC, the typical tension of treatment court "tough love" is exacerbated by the common narrative that part of the responsibility for a participant's struggles lies with the military, by extension the state. Coupled with the responsibilizing logics—narratives that individualize participants' struggles and ask them to take responsibility for addressing them—that characterize all treatment courts, the contradictions contribute to distinct exchanges in which participants express frustration about their expectations that a VTC is just like any other criminal legal process making demands that they do not want to comply with.

This conflict dynamic of gratitude and indebtedness was frequently evident in Northeast, a court marked by conformity, where participants struggled to articulate complaints. At the Northeast VTC, unlike in the other two courts, participants who had open arguments with the judge frequently returned over the following weeks to apologize. During my early observations, I witnessed three participants, all ineligible for VA benefits and struggling with relapses, yelling at the judge. Yet, upon returning to the court after their relapses and new placements in residential facilities, they thanked the judge for the services as well as the personal care they felt from the judge and court team. The exchanges of appreciation between the participants and the Northeast judge appeared heartfelt; the participants who expressed harsh condemnations of the court returned hat in hand. They expressed chagrin for not appreciating what the court was offering and reiterated their gratitude.

While veteran identity often remained in the background of these conversations, sometimes participants drew on it to articulate their disappointment. In the following exchange in Northeast, for example, the participant mobilizes his veteran identity as he expresses concern about what he signed up for:

> Participant: I was a little upset because throughout this whole process, it's like I felt like I got a raw deal. I pleaded out to everything and then I am doing everything I'm supposed to do, I am in compliance with everything I need to do, and I asked for a weekend pass. I went to [residential facility] because I was a veteran, and I am allowed to go. I already pleaded out in the court system and then I went to [residential facility for veterans] and now they [Probation] asked me to come to the Veterans Court.

In this participant's telling, he became involved with the VTC without fully understanding what he was signing up for. He appeared grateful for the opportunity to go a residential facility for veterans, but resentful that the requirements kept on coming. His complaint reveals the irony of coercing people to take responsibility for their lives, and the added resentment embedded in the various "benefits" being offered but experienced as burdens. The conflict in this case escalated more than was usual in Northeast, as the judge pushed back at the suggestion that there was any coercion by the court.

> Judge: No, no, no one asked you. You signed up for this.
>
> Participant: I signed the paper, but it was already after I went to court. You see what I'm saying? So I wasn't released on like, you know, coming out of jail. I was getting out of jail anyway. And then I sign the paper. It was after that.
>
> Judge: I think you're confused.
>
> Participant: No, that's what happened.
>
> Judge: I think you are confused because when you were in court in [local city], you agreed to be part of the Veteran's Treatment Court.
>
> Participant: Yeah, this was after I already went to court.
>
> Judge: And in Veteran's Treatment Court, the service plan said [residential facility] and [residential facility] has a rule that they don't let you out for a weekend pass or a pass for 30 days. And you have to apply for that, and you have to ask permission for that, and that has to be, even though you are in the Veteran's Treatment Court, you have to comply with the rules at [residential facility] too.
>
> *(Northeast VTC)*

The disagreement is clear: joining the court enabled the participant to access social services, but it required him to give up his freedom in ways that he did not want. These kinds of exchange illustrate the irony of the slogan "when thank you is not enough." Participants such as this one may not want to be "thanked" in a way that further limits their freedom by restricting their movement. And, although they theoretically chose this option, it was obviously not a free choice among many options.

In a similar exchange in Southeast, the judge began the hearing by telling the participant that he was not meeting the court's requirements. The participant suggested that this was a minor issue:

I missed an appointment on Thursday but am rescheduling, it was an early meeting that had been rescheduled and I forgot about the change in time.

Instead of focusing on this particular infraction, the judge used this opportunity to get buy-in, which the participant also resisted:

Judge: Last week I was a little uncomfortable with how you presented, like you were extremely angry; and it feels the same today. Is there something you want to talk about?

Participant: No.

Judge: Your body language and demeanor is angry.

Participant: I am not going to be happy here, I will comply, but I am not going to be happy. I believe I have every reason to be angry. I am not going to read poems, or entertain people. I simply want to comply, answer questions, and move on. Is that something we can do?

(Southeast VTC)

This type of conflict was common at the Southeast VTC, whereby the participants used forceful language that mirrored the judge's. Just as this judge frequently repeated the common VTC narrative, participants explicitly rejected it. Participants articulated concerns about the court's expectations of them and vocalized a desire to just "get [the program] done," while others challenged the court's legitimacy and authority, noting that they could simply return to the regular criminal legal system rather than continue with the VTC.

In the Southeast VTC, the amplified emotions may be related to the locale and general court culture, but they also suggest heightened conflicts that may emerge when the court mobilizes the common narrative that participants should comply because the court is uniquely beneficial to them. In one particularly heated exchange, the judge pressed an emergency button for bailiffs to enter, and the judge quickly left the courtroom in what appeared to be fear for personal safety. Although the judge in this court frequently expressed the belief that the court should be a top priority in the participant's life because of the court's unique ability to support veterans, some participants made very clear that they saw the court as a hypocritical attempt to control their lives.

The fine line between gratitude and indebtedness was also evident in West. In the following example from the West VTC, where the judge did not usually ask for gratitude, the judge mentions the mentors to encourage gratitude. In this example, we see the judge explaining the hope for "positive connections," or the kind of social proximity that gratitude is supposed to engender:

> Judge: We are happy with what you are doing and the decisions you're making right now, are you going to stick with those decisions?
>
> Participant: Yes.
>
> Judge: I, of course, credit you first for making that decision; who else deserves a little credit for that?
>
> Participant: [Mentor] also deserves credit for not pressuring me but not letting me forget that it's not an option.
>
> Judge: OK, thank you for that acknowledgment, it's important that we have people working with you. One of the most important things for me is that you have positive connections from this experience, so I am glad to hear that.

The participant responded positively to the judge's efforts for buy-in, and said he wasn't being pressured. Yet, in a contradictory addition, he observes that not complying is "not an option." Here, the gratitude logics and the responsibilizing logics are designed to make participants internalize the court's judgments about their compliance intersect. The judge's efforts are bolstered by the court's additional resources—in this case the human resources of mentors—because of the popular support for veterans and the belief that they should not be treated the same as other criminal defendants. But the participant points out that this is not voluntary.

Still, at the West VTC, personnel were less committed to the common narrative and, by extension, getting buy-in from participants by emphasizing that they should be grateful or that they should even remain in the court. The West VTC's court coordinator and clinician explained their desire to avoid too much coercion when a participant wanted to leave the program, saying, "We ask them, 'Do you really want to do this?' And they go, 'No, I really don't want to do this'" (coordinator and clinician, West VTC). These VTC personnel described termination as "mutual breakup" with the participant, something they often did rather than pressure someone who did not appear interested in treatment.

While this mutuality may be one reason for the higher rates of termination at West VTC compared to the other two courts, it does not suggest a lack of success. Rather, it shows the challenges the court's participants face and the court's approach to helping those it believes it can help and not forcing those who may not want it. This approach may also explain the lower levels of overt conflict in comparison with Southeast, which continued to forcefully mobilize the common narrative to encourage compliance with gratitude even when it appeared clear that the person did not want to be indebted.

CONFLICTED GRATITUDE:
UNDERSTANDING CONFLICT IN CONTEXT

These dynamics of conflicted gratitude illustrate how the politics of worth in VTCs shape courtroom interactions. During conflict, participants reveal whether, how, and to what extent they view the VTCs' efforts as legitimate. Although the common narrative emphasizes the distinctiveness of VTCs, veteran identity is in the background more than in the foreground in everyday court interactions. Still, notions of veteran worth structure the benefits that these courts can offer, including material (e.g., social services) and human resources (e.g., mentors), as well as the ideological support that comes with the common narrative. Even when participants are grateful for increased access to services, VTCs are still part of a criminal legal system that impedes their lives in numerous ways. Conflicted gratitude helps to explain that participants may recognize that VTCs have unique legitimacy and authority because of their ideological and material foundations, but these tools do not overcome the inherent coercion in a treatment court that many participants resent.

Further, these dynamics of conflicted gratitude help reveal how VTC judges and personnel draw on participants' veteran identity to establish their legitimacy and authority with participants, and how participants do the same. Personnel try to establish rapport and community by claiming VTCs have unique abilities to help participants because they understand veterans and can help participants access social welfare benefits (especially those eligible for VA benefits). In response, participants may draw on veteran identity to question the courts' actions. In this negotiation, conflicts may arise because participants can also use their expectations of a treatment court designed just for veterans to argue for what they want.

The dynamics help reveal what Moore and Hirai (2014) articulate as "governing expectations," which can lead to "the true paradox of [responsibilizing] strategies": "the more individuals act to take care of themselves, the more they

locate themselves outside governing expectations" (9). The "governing expectations" in VTCs are that participants both comply and be grateful because they
can be in this type of court. However, as participants assert their agency, trying
to balance the many competing demands in their lives, they do not offer the
court gratitude but rather a sense of indebtedness that they resent. All involved
parties approach the "benefit" of a court with different priorities, which in turn
are shaped by the rules and regulations of each court, the local demographics,
and, most importantly, what resources the courts can access.

In some ways, conflicted gratitude is just one more manifestation of how
the "thank you" may ring hollow to veterans. The VTC training slogan "When
Thank You Is Not Enough" maps a basic premise of sociolegal studies that law
lends legitimacy to organizational practices, with largely symbolic structures
that can mask inequities and inequalities (Edelman 2016). Given that the expression "thank you for your service" already rings hollow to many veterans
struggling to reintegrate into civilian life, the effort to make the criminal legal
system embody that expression may be particularly problematic for those an-
gered or frustrated when court mandates interfere with their ability to work
and take care of their families. Such feelings may lead to what Gallagher (2006)
refers to as "disenchantment" with the law. And, if the conflicts between expectations and experiences are too great, people may simply experience disempowerment. Such disenchantment and disempowerment were evident in all
three courts.

Finally, it is important to note that conflict in these courts is not an indication of their efficacy or lack thereof. Rather, conflict helps illustrate how
law is instrumentalized to address entrenched social and political problems.
In her pioneering work on community courts in Talea, Mexico, Laura Nader
(1952) developed the idea of "harmony ideology" to point out how courts try to
"maintain the balance" to shield themselves from outside influence. Although
the incentives differ in a treatment court, the structure of a local judicial organization working to maintain harmony to avoid sending participants back to
regular state courts is a useful parallel. Nader suggests that Talea judges create
balance because the courts are a central part of a local community's social
order, and court users and judges/decision makers had complex social relationships that they wanted to sustain. Although a completely different context from
VTCs, efficacy in Talea courts, both in resolving disputes and managing conflicts that could arise, required strong relationships between court participants

and authorities, and courts had to adapt to solve quite local problems. A lack of conflict may indicate more powerful coercion, whereas a court with open conflict may reveal a flatter hierarchy in which the participants are more able to assert their preferences.

In sum, this analysis points to the ways in which actors co-create the common narrative, as well as the common narrative's contours. Conflicts are shaped by each court's rules and resources, which again reflect local and intraorganizational workgroup dynamics. While individual reactions and responses suggest limited agency on the part of the participants, that agency is based on who is allowed into a VTC, what services are available to participants, and how each court manages interactions and conflict. Even if many participants succeed, the courts' ideological and material foundations contribute to distinct VTC practices that create hierarchies *among* those deemed worthy.

Eight

WORTHY OF JUSTICE

In fall 2023, the *New York Times* published a devastating report about veterans suffering from traumatic brain injuries, allegedly caused by artillery fire from the wars in Iraq and Afghanistan (Phillips 2023). Veterans reported hearing voices, feeling unstable, and being prescribed medications that did little either to quell the symptoms or stop them. Some could access services at the VA; some had to self-medicate; some had changes in behavior while still serving that led to dishonorable discharges, making them ineligible to receive military benefits afterward. Some of these veterans struggled to find housing and, like all the participants highlighted in this book, some were prosecuted for crimes.

This article was striking in its illustration of the reality facing many veterans, and the common narrative animating the proliferation of VTCs across the country. The subtext of the article, like the many described earlier in this book, is that veterans in the criminal legal system must have been damaged by their military service. While not discounting the terrible experiences that many veterans suffered, this socially and politically accepted explanation of veterans' involvement in the criminal legal system reveals the broader dilemma of using the criminal legal system as a tool for those plagued by mental health and substance use challenges. Courts are inherently limited to tackle these issues.

The goal of this book is not to question whether VTCs should be created but, rather, to think about the creation and operationalization of the VTC concept to interrogate other questions about US society: Can and should the same kind of care and understanding given to veterans extend to other individuals and groups? Could a criminal legal system be created that does not differentiate between those whose histories of trauma include military service and those whose histories of trauma do not? Can social services be provided to people regardless of their decision to join the military or coercion through the criminal legal system? Do the differences between these courts simply point to the need for more material resources in the criminal legal system, or do they confirm that the criminal legal system should not be tasked with solving the challenges associated with poverty, substance use, mental illness, and war?

This book suggests that those interested in criminal legal reforms more broadly, from scholars to lawyers to policymakers, should view VTCs as not only a new form of therapeutic jurisprudence or a rare movement with bipartisan political support but also as an important (if imperfect) illustration of a criminal legal system that sees more people as worthy, rather than irredeemable, and as benefiting from services and support rather than punishment. Perspectives about veteran suffering, by many who may be conservative on criminal legal issues, should be intriguing—or even eye-opening—to those interested in or already working for criminal legal reform. Yet, even with this outcome in mind, the broader implications of VTCs include further entrenchment of the criminal law to address entrenched social and political problems and manage vulnerable populations, with gaping inequalities in terms of access to healthcare, housing, education, and employment. Behind the notion that veterans do not deserve punishment is the belief that others in the criminal legal system do.

For those interested in aiding veterans, this book underscores that well-intentioned policies require effective implementation, and implementation requires close attention to social and political dynamics in a given locale. Moreover, it points to the opportunities and the challenges of implementing an intervention that may be too little, too late for some who chose to join the military and suffer from substance use and mental health disorders.

LEARNING FROM VTCs: THE POLITICS OF WORTH

The popularity of VTCs reveals how culture and politics intersect in the production of inequality in the United States, with VTCs illustrating the multiple ways in which inequalities compound over one's life. In his illuminating work on poverty in the US, Katz (2013) explains the persistent belief that some "poverty results from personal inadequacy" rather than from structures and circumstances beyond individual control (2). In this politics of worth, virtue and economic success become closely intertwined.

This analysis of VTCs suggests that joining the military can be a quick way to overcome the belief that one's challenging circumstances are due to personal inadequacy, rather than the ongoing evolution of economic relations in the US, growing costs of higher education and other barriers to professional advancement, as well as the lack of general social insurance that contributes to poverty and dependency (Katz 2013, 3). The ideological support that veterans receive is important, but the social services and other material benefits that ideological support reinforces are even more significant. Depending on discharge status, veterans have access to funding for education and for housing that those who never served are unable to access. And, in a country where healthcare debt is among the most likely causes of bankruptcy, access to VA healthcare is an incredible benefit for those who might otherwise not have the kind of insurance that guarantees a range of services.

Understanding these unique benefits for veterans provides an important lens into multiple forms of inequality in the United States. For example, as race-based affirmative action policies crumble with Supreme Court decisions against race-conscious education and employment policies, veterans remain a group legally entitled to preferential treatment. Moreover, my conversations over the years with veterans who had been or were currently in the criminal legal system revealed the cascading challenges that brought them into that system, and the "myth," as one VTC public defender commented, that there is something unique about veterans or VTCs in their ability to help people with substance use or mental health disorders. In my interviews at the residential facility in Northeast, for example, all veteran residents mentioned going into the military to escape difficult family situations; it was a story of push factors rather than pull factors. Similarly, veterans living in a veteran pod in a nearby jail told lengthy stories of substance use and criminalized behavior before joining the military. Illustrative that the military is not inherently criminogenic, inmates and guards frequently knew each other from youth and shared the experience of military service. And, although I witnessed only friendly interactions in the pod, a volunteer in the jail relayed that some guards who were also veterans were more judgmental of these inmates, having themselves served and having integrated into civilian life without problems. These complex social dynamics mirror the contradiction of creating criminal legal options for people based on the premise that the military is both noble and harmful when, for many, joining the military is an economic choice.

These dynamics of inequality, central to the politics of worth, have additional implications beyond the experience of veterans in the criminal legal system. Given the massive role that the criminal legal system plays in US society, it should be no surprise that internal shifts within that system can affect how people with criminal legal contact are viewed. In theory, treatment courts can change how people view certain people and certain crimes, as their approach to avoiding retribution is predicated on shifting notions of blameworthiness. Just as drug treatment courts present criminal defendants as suffering from illness and prostitution courts refocus people engaged in sex work as victims, altering understandings of the criminalized act, VTCs engage in similar meaning making based on a politically constructed identity. Whether or to what extent VTCs effectively destigmatize veterans in the criminal legal system more broadly is research to be done, but my conversations with VTC proponents over the years have included many examples of people facing resistance in giving a "get out of jail free card" to veterans and then finding support when the VTC eventually opened.

In these ways, VTCs help illustrate that when the meaning produced by the criminal legal system—specifically that people who commit crimes are bad or deviant—contradicts the meaning produced by other institutions, a reconciliation of meanings must occur. These latter institutions, which include the VA and media that celebrate narratives about veteran worth, are powerful. VTCs facilitate this reconciliation process, potentially helping to destigmatize people who have both served in the military and engaged in criminalized behaviors.

Beyond shifting understandings of veterans, VTCs bridge different US institutions and, thus, have the potential to shift meanings about both the causes of criminalized behavior and what to do about it. Crimes involving substance use and/or mental health challenges long confounded courts because of law's reliance on the concept of intent. As Valverde (1998) explains, cases involving mind-altering substances confuse courts because they affect personal will, or the connection between mind and body. Drug courts have helped to shift the narrative of substance use from a personal failing and deviance toward an illness that mitigates allocations of personal responsibility for either drug use or actions committed under the influence. One concern is that this approach can "widen the net" of criminal legal defendants by pushing people into treatment courts when they might otherwise have their cases dismissed (Phelps 2013; Stitt 2022). Another is that this approach still individualizes social and political problems and puts the onus of responsibility for deviant behavior on the people using drugs or suffering from mental health disorders (Perez, Leifman, and Estrada 2003; Tiger 2012). Moreover, labeling people suffering from addiction and in the criminal legal system as both "bad" and "sick" reinforces the policy argument that coercion is required for sobriety (ibid.). VTCs complicated this logic by attributing the "bad" and the "sick" to a socially acceptable life choice of joining the military.

This politics of worth—deciding who deserves public investment—is also structured by broader societal beliefs about trauma. On the one hand, the successful integration of VTCs into the criminal legal system opens the door for recognizing that trauma plays a vital role in explaining, if not defending, criminal legal behaviors (Liebert 2022; Knudsen and Wingenfeld 2016). VTCs can change perceptions of veterans who suffer from substance use and mental health disorders, while providing conceptual tools to shift other inequalities that plague the criminal legal system. Given that VTC personnel acknowledge that many VTC participants suffered adverse events in their youths, VTCs may help these personnel integrate different understandings of trauma into their other criminal legal work and local jurisdictions. Even if personnel do not believe they can cure trauma, they approach people suffering from trauma differently than people whose behavior they cannot explain with the same medically recognized concept.

The conundrum is that VTCs, by distinguishing veterans from others in the criminal legal system, may instead perpetuate the stigmatization of criminal legal defendants who did not join the military. Providing veterans with criminal legal benefits that are unavailable to nonveterans simultaneously privileges entering the military over other life choices, and reifies the use of criminal law to manage the complex social and political problems contributing to substance use and mental health disorders. Finally, VTCs also legitimize the idea that the military—and not underfunded social public infrastructure such as education and healthcare—is the cause of VTC participants' troubles. This paradoxical assumption about military service as both noble and harmful is part and parcel of the common story, which contributes to the complex dynamics of conflicted gratitude that characterize court interactions.

VTCs AND INEQUALITY

In these ways, VTCs both illustrate and help contribute to stratification among different social groups. Stratification can occur through both identification—cultural processes that generate individual and group identities and confer meaning upon those identities—and rationalization—processes that generate and apply universal, impersonal rules to individuals and groups (Lamont, Beljean, and Clair 2014). Identification here means defining veterans as their own social group, and rationalization allows for distinct rules for veterans in the criminal legal system.

While the study of stratification often reveals why certain groups become systematically disadvantaged, this book reveals the complementary processes of how groups may become systematically advantaged. Lamont (2023) articulates this concept through the idea of "recognition chains" involving both ideological and material resources, which is illustrated both in the cultural meaning of the veteran in US society and the social safety net they have. Social recognition, or destigmatization, is one pathway for designated groups to rise in social status (Clair, Daniel, and Lamont 2016). In this pathway, new social constructs contribute to new material resources (Lamont 2023). When people perceive that there is a "linked fate" between themselves and a group that has been stigmatized, it is easier for the stigma to lift (Lamont et al. 2014).

VTCs illustrate an effort to destigmatize the presence of veterans in the criminal legal system, and the success of that effort reflects the politics of militarism and social welfare in US society. This book's findings about the practices and politics of VTCs reveal broader processes of social stratification by highlighting how cultural beliefs, manifested through distinct organizational practices and material resources, delineate worthy from unworthy members of society. Situating the analysis of VTCs in the history of the Veterans Administration illustrates how policies that privilege veterans for social services created the foundation for the development of VTCs.

Yet, the concurrent celebration of the military and attribution of criminal legal involvement to it makes sense in the way it maps on to the racialized hierarchies that characterize US criminal legal and social welfare organizations. When a person's criminal legal involvement is seen as situational, rather than characterological, they are treated as less blameworthy (Liebert 2022). In the US, this situational/characterological divide in the criminal legal system is highly racialized. Given the overrepresentation of African Americans in the US criminal legal system, the attribution of blame or lack thereof as it relates to trauma is critical for understanding mass incarceration in the US. The criminal legal system's treatment of combat trauma as compared to community violence, sometimes labeled urban survival syndrome (Clarke 2001), reveals the contradiction of the state taking responsibility for veterans' exposure to violence but not people exposed to violence in urban centers where, arguably, the state also bears responsibility because of, among other historical practices and policies (e.g., slavery), racially disparate access to capital and housing (Liebert 2022).

Further, it is well known that adverse events such as psychological, sexual, and physical abuse, or exposure to others being abused in childhood, significantly increase the likelihood for a person to become addicted to drugs (Dube et al. 2003) and/or become involved in the criminal-legal system. One study, for example, suggests that every additional adverse childhood event increases the likelihood of becoming a serious and chronic violent offender by thirty-five percent, even when controlling for other risk factors (Fox et al. 2015). Yet, these kinds of adverse events have less influence in mitigating blameworthiness than military service in traditional courts, even though the data linking military service to criminalized behaviors is ambiguous at best.

These contradictions may be the reason that, despite their ambitious goals and proliferation, VTCs have clear limitations in their ability to help people with substance use and mental health disorders. The exorbitant cost of higher education and the long-standing (though shifting) correlation between educational attainment and earning potential mean that people from families without financial resources for higher education have few options after high school. Further, racialized minorities, particularly African Americans and Latinos, are more likely to join the military than their white counterparts, in large part because of their greater barriers to social mobility, including both education and secure immigration status (Lutz 2008). The VA predicts that by 2040, 40 percent of the military will be racially minoritized populations (US Department of Veterans Affairs 2020), a percentage not wholly distinct from the overall percentage of racialized minorities in the US population. However, with persistent disparities in criminal legal contact for racialized minorities, veterans may soon reemerge as a group disproportionately involved in the criminal legal system. This makes VTCs more important to understand, because their popularity as a criminal legal reform will likely continue.

These statistics about racialized groups in the military also underscore that understanding the politics of worth as it applies to veterans is increasingly important to understanding inequalities in the US and, potentially, strategies to ameliorate them. One takeaway from this study is that the presence of a dedicated provider such as the VA is necessary but not sufficient to help criminal legal defendants access services. The differences between these VTCs also illustrate how, even though veterans receive social services unavailable to most Americans, the services are still woefully inadequate. Illustrative of broader social problems, the courts struggled to support the many needs of people facing a growing housing crisis in the US, the challenge of pursuing educational opportunities without external financial support, and the wide availability of highly addictive drugs that plague both rural and urban communities.

The argument here is not a race to the bottom in which all criminal legal defendants only receive punitive outcomes. Likewise, it is not a call for all people accused of crimes or suffering from severe substance use and mental health challenges to have unfettered liberty. It is, rather, a call to consider the worth of all involved in the criminal legal system, from victims to defendants, and to integrate social services more firmly into institutions beyond the criminal legal system.

Various court personnel, VTC advocates, and media accounts attempt to rationalize their courts' incongruities by broadening their concept of veteran worth: a participant is a "veteran" and worthy of special regard simply because they chose to enlist in the military. This is regardless of whether the participant saw combat or experienced trauma during military service. But an alternative to this rationale—adopted by VTC personnel in West—is to simply abandon the fiction that all VTC participants are somehow uniquely worthy. Instead, it is enough that the VTC concept can be used to help at least some of the many people whose trauma—physical, emotional, or psychological—land them in the criminal legal system.

BRINGING THE VA INTO THE CARCERAL STATE

In addition to providing insights into the politics of worth and inequality in the criminal legal system, the opportunities and challenges outlined throughout this book underscore the dilemma of a judicial organization that relies on a federal agency that has its own distinctions between those worthy and unworthy of social services. The assemblage exemplified by VTCs reveals how inequalities can both compound and shift as more state institutions become engaged in punishment.

The sociological concept of bricolage (Lévi-Strauss 1966) helps make sense of these dynamics.[1] In art, bricolage involves the mixing together of different mediums to create something entirely new. In the social sciences, the term refers to reusing available materials and tools to solve new problems and challenges (Phillimore et al. 2019). VTCs, likewise, blend existing criminal legal and social welfare infrastructures to address the challenge facing veterans in legal trouble. However, even when they use the VA, which is not involved in other treatment courts, VTCs are not a *new* solution to an enduring problem. The idea of adding veterans to treatment courts does not change the nature or efficacy of the primary institution—the criminal court—and the disparities it can entrench when used as a tool of social control.

Despite the potentially beneficial developments, a close look at the realities of VTCs underscores how social inequalities manifest and reproduce themselves even through seemingly benevolent reforms that, by their nature, delineate people based on beliefs about not what they have done but on who they are. And, while social services could be available to all people regardless of their criminal legal involvement, the VA's embrace of the criminal legal system through its involvement with VTCs shows how legitimate it has become to use criminal law to help people access social services. With federal funding to support the VA's staff who work in VTCs, the VA increasingly has an incentive to support the establishment and use of treatment courts, further entrenching the use of criminal law to manage and support vulnerable populations.

There are broader implications of this politics of worth that privileges military service not necessarily for what one experienced during service but for assumptions about the quality of people who join the military. Criminal law is not supposed to treat people differently based on who they are but on what they have done. Criminal courts restrict evidence that may create a bias against or in favor of a criminal legal defendant based on their identities rather than their actions. Yet, in the politics of worth that characterize VTCs, this central logic dissipates in favor of a general assumption that a person who joined the military deserves preferential treatment in court for the fact that they enlisted. This kind of malleability mixed with privilege can distort the legitimacy and authority of the law (Nonet and Selznick 1978).

Further, VTCs do not change the nature of the VA, but they offer new challenges for this federal bureaucracy as well as the courts they help. Recognizing that many people with substance use disorders and mental health challenges end up in the criminal legal system, the VA's engagement with criminal law makes sense. The organization is designed to provide services to veterans who need it, and it is adapting to the challenge that comes from blending social service logics with criminal legal logics. This "double agent" dynamic—serving the patient and the court—exists for all clinicians working within the criminal legal system (Castellano 2011), but since VA has its own rules and regulations, it is less nimble than a local social service agency. In addition, the ability of the VA to help veterans in the criminal legal system largely depends on their discharge status, fostering a unique status hierarchy that does not impact treatment courts—VTC or other—relying on the same treatment options for all participants.

Although there may be problems with this new punishment assemblage, it offers a striking opportunity. The VA only recently expanded its reach to help veterans with criminal legal problems, but this powerful federal institution now increasingly operates in a way that connects poverty, civil law, and criminal law. The Veterans Justice Outreach Program started in the homelessness programming and was focused on criminal law. However, criminal law problems are rarely isolated from civil problems and the VA is now offering funding to organizations that help qualifying veterans with legal aid for civil justice problems. Making the connection between civil law and criminal law is crucial for people who are struggling; this new program reflects an access to justice paradigm that recognizes the significant impacts of civil law on inequality (Sandefur 2009).

In these ways, the VA's expansion into the legal arena could prove influential in the provision of legal services beyond helping veterans. It could inspire other social service providers who may be reluctant to engage in the legal system yet could greatly help people suffering from common civil legal challenges related to housing and healthcare. Interestingly, several recipients of VA funding for civil legal services also support criminal defense work, if that work is related to homelessness. These kinds of services may hopefully change understandings of what brings people into the criminal legal system, and what they need to get out of it. More broadly, the VA's evolving approach to veterans with legal challenges illustrates how much need exists for legal services, and how veterans continue to gain access to important social services unavailable to most Americans.

INSTITUTIONALIZING VTCs

Beyond illustrating how inequalities manifest in US institutions, VTCs also provide insights into how ideas take hold and materialize into new organizations. The proliferation of VTCs over twenty years reveals how they have been infused with social value beyond their original purpose, or what sociologists call institutionalized (Selznick 1957). VTCs have the backing at every level of government, despite concerns that they may not materially benefit participants (Baldwin and Brooke 2019), and despite evidence that the special treatment does not make veterans more compliant with the court system (Atkin-Plunk, Armstrong, and Dalbir 2021; Tsai et al. 2018).

This book suggests that VTCs' appeal may have less to do with their success in helping veterans and more to do with the entrenchment of the broader institutions of the military and the criminal legal system in providing opportunities for people who are struggling. One measure of institutionalization is expendability, meaning an organization that is not institutionalized will cease to exist if there is a better way to fulfill the goals. The value ascribed to VTCs—evident in their proliferation and ongoing resources dedicated to them regardless of evidence of their efficacy—stems from both the power of the US military and criminal legal institutions. VTCs are not the cause but a symptom of how the military and criminal legal system have become central in managing vulnerable members of society.

One concern with institutionalization is that, when an organization or certain practices are taken for granted, they may be adopted regardless of their efficacy (Rahim 2024; Johnson, Dowd, and Ridgeway 2006). As Rahim (2024) explains, "Once practices have the veneer of legitimacy, they can sustain their status through the power of circular reasoning: the practices are deemed legitimate because most organizations have adopted them, but most organizations have adopted them because they have been deemed legitimate" (9). The "rapid expansion" of VTCs (Baldwin and Brooke 2019) indicates that the VA's involvement in the criminal legal system, and modeling veterans' treatment courts on the drug treatment court model, is increasingly accepted, and that acceptance in and of itself will perpetuate VTC creation.

Rather than solely lament the glaring need to increase and strengthen educational opportunities and social services in the US, this book also offers pragmatic insights for those looking to create VTCs. These observations about the politics of worth through VTCs highlight the general opportunities and challenges facing VTCs in trying to help veterans leave their legal troubles behind, and for criminal legal reforms more broadly. Some criminal legal reform movements treat with suspicion any intervention for people with substance use and/ or mental health disorders, regardless of the reason for their challenges, and instead call for decriminalization, defunding, and a corresponding increase in social services. This book attempts a more moderate approach. Echoing Miller (2021) in his remarkable examination of mass incarceration's radiating harms, in the near and long term there will be people who exert their power in ways that harm others, and jails and criminal courts are not soon to disappear. People who care about the rise in substance use and homelessness, particularly in cities with extreme wealth disparities and housing shortages, have made compelling arguments that, despite the relationship between contemporary mass incarceration and the war on drugs (see, e.g., Lynch 2012), decriminalization and legalization of substance use does not reduce harm in the way reformers hoped (Joshi, Rivera, and Cerda 2023). Thus, learning from different criminal legal reforms can be beneficial for those in the criminal legal system or looking to change it.

The three VTCs explored in this book are strikingly different from one another, meaning that a person joining a VTC in one jurisdiction is making a markedly different calculation than someone joining a VTC in another. How long is the court's program? What does the program entail? Does the person even have the option of not joining the VTC? Anyone interested in creating or joining a VTC needs to recognize differences among VTCs' actual practices.

This insight is important for those interested in not only best practices but "standardizing VTC practices," a call that I frequently heard at All Rise conferences and see in literature on the varieties of VTCs in the country. As a theoretical matter, when an organization has goals and operations that are not precise, it is vulnerable to external influences that may affect its efficacy and efficiency (Selznick 1957). While it is of course vital to avoid practices known to cause harm, the challenge of standardization lies in the social and political milieus that characterize local jurisdictions. Criminal legal and social service practices evolve over the years in response to local needs. Standardization may help overcome some of the differences that exist in VTCs, but it could also undermine what makes a VTC effective in any given community.

Assuming that abolition of criminal legal processes is not forthcoming, the practical question is not whether to create VTCs, but how.

The clearest finding from this study is that "best practices' invariably mean more material resources. In every All Rise presentation on best practices, there was an audible sigh from participants when the presenter described the additional work that case managers and social service providers should do to make sure that participants are being diagnosed and treated properly by the court. While best practices mean better social services, these court personnel have no control over what social services are available. For those looking for solutions within their resource constraints, I hope that this book provides a baseline understanding of the conditions under which a jurisdiction might create a VTC (or any treatment court) and what VTC (or any treatment court) proponents must do to create a court that has the best chance of helping its participants. Recognizing that VTCs must continuously establish their legitimacy with funders, policymakers, court personnel, and even court participants, there are certain steps that proponents can take to improve their VTC's success in meeting their goals.

Most importantly, this book reveals that VTCs are only as effective as their access to social services for participants, particularly residential facilities. This is one reason that the VA wants to be central in the creation and implementation of VTCs. The issue is that many people who served in the military may not have access to VA benefits. This means that courts must build relationships with both the VA *and* other local service providers to facilitate the necessary support. Even then, VA-eligible veterans may have court requirements that the VA cannot fulfill. Ideally, a VTC will have access to and a strong relationship with a non-VA residential facility to which it can refer all participants.

In addition, the findings about workgroup dynamics across the three cases suggest the need for collaborative and dedicated teams with specialized knowledge about social services available to veterans. Finding personnel with experience in the military or positive sentiment toward veterans will obviously benefit participants. Although a court may have little control over staff turnover, which can occur for any number of reasons, retaining dedicated personnel adds to a court's stability. The judge obviously sets the tone of the court and establishes legitimacy with participants, and the judge's approach and ability to establish rapport with the participants are critical. Throughout my research, I observed eight VTC judges, each bringing their own approach to the unique benchcraft required in a VTC. The judges all cared deeply about the veteran participants, but they exhibited different strengths in managing the team. Further, despite the common narrative's emphasis on the value of military culture in the courtrooms, there is little evidence in my study to suggest that a judge should emphasize participants' military service or military culture in hearings, or even needs to be a veteran to develop rapport with the participants.

The clinicians in a VTC do most of the heavy lifting related to compliance and thus need to be properly supported, dedicated to the work, and familiar with the inner workings of the VA (Foley and Rowen 2022). Many of the clinicians I observed over the years had a sense of mission that carried them through the difficult work of monitoring participants, finding them services, and emotionally supporting them. This work seemed bearable because of the warm feelings that many of the clinicians expressed toward veterans, but that did not make the work less difficult. The clinicians hired from the VA support VA-eligible participants, so any VTC that hopes also to serve veterans without VA access must have the additional resources to hire an outside clinician, and should strive to reduce inequalities between participants with and without VA access.

A VTC must also have dedicated prosecution, probation, and defense personnel aligned with the VTC's goals. These goals may include sobriety, housing, and employment but also goals that are harder to define and measure, such as fostering feelings of community, camaraderie, and structure. The West VTC's early challenges included an adversarial prosecutor, which contributed to conflict in a team trying to incentivize people to get social services. It also struggled to maintain consistency with a public defender to help participants. While these types of challenges plague any treatment court, they are especially acute in VTCs, where fostering stability supports the common narrative that veterans may be in the criminal legal system *because of* the negative effects of losing the community and camaraderie they once had in the military.

The study also helps illustrate what military culture might mean in the context of a VTC. Even if there were few references to the military in the court-rooms I observed, the presence of dedicated mentors in Northeast reveals how the camaraderie and commitment that military personnel have toward one an-other can be leveraged to help people who are struggling. The idea of mentor-ship also differed across the three courts, with only the Northeast VTC having mentoring relationships that were robust outside the courtroom check-ins. That mentoring program was unique also in that nearly all the mentors were retired, making them more available to the participants. Courts looking to start a mentoring program must weigh the trade-off of having a more available but older demographic as compared to younger veterans who may have more in common with the participants but whose availability and dedication—as well as life experience—may align differently with what participants need.

But, even if a court cannot foster the robust mentorship evident in North-east, there are other practices that may help encourage participants and create the kind of community that the common narrative espouses. The VTC in the Northeast built camaraderie through the norm of participants staying to listen to everyone's hearings. People in that courtroom became familiar with one another and each other's challenges. In the other two courts, community was hard to come by, particularly at the West VTC, where participants arrived throughout the hearings and left as quickly as they could. The VTC did not want to burden its already overwhelmed participants. This difference high-lights the different goals of each court and the trade-offs any court should consider when developing its practices.

Researchers, meanwhile, can move beyond studying VTCs with the idea of best practices, as defined by All Rise, conformity to them, and efficacy. They can use theory-generating studies such as this to understand underlying mechanisms in their outcomes. For example, if VTC personnel adhere to the common story, believing that VTCs are uniquely beneficial for participants, they may be more reluctant to terminate a participant who has made clear that they do not want to be in a VTC. Likewise, a participant's experience of conflicted gratitude may contribute to their length of stay in a VTC when they might otherwise choose to terminate. In these ways, understanding the experi-ence of being in a VTC can help those who want to know whether or how they are effective or not.

As drug decriminalization reforms continue to pass state and federal legis-latures, often with bipartisan support, VTCs and all treatment courts will have to adapt their approaches if they want to enroll participants (Rowen 2024). Even with support for VTCs, there is growing concern that the criminal legal system is unfair and overused, and punishments for drug use may decrease to the point when there is no incentive to join a treatment court unless a person is already committed to accessing social services. People arrested for crimes related to substance use, or who have substance use or mental health disorders, may be unwilling to submit to an invasive treatment court program without the threat of incarceration. Like other organizations, these courts may evolve in a way that prioritizes their own survival as external pressures change (Battilana and Dorado 2010). The result may be an even more flexible approach that causes concern about the law's malleability and legitimacy in treating people the same way (Nonet and Selznick 1978). My observations over the years suggest that VTCs, despite beneficial ideological and material foundations, already focus on their own survival as they work within a criminal legal system that is changing rapidly.

Reform in the criminal legal system means not only creating more treatment courts but considering solutions to the inequalities that draw some people into the military in the first place and then into the criminal legal system, or the reverse pathway. The findings highlight the critical role that a well-resourced VA can play in helping veterans struggling with mental health and substance use challenges, and the benefit of more robust social services prior to military discharge. As scholars and policymakers seek to reform the criminal legal system, they may be able to learn from the story of VTCs to ask how a politics of worth might manifest were it not based on joining the military or being arrested for a crime but, rather, on helping people achieve their life goals through institutions that do not cause or contribute to physical or psychological harm.

METHODS APPENDIX

The purpose of this methods appendix is twofold. First, it reveals the evidence I rely on for my arguments. Insights that emerge over a decade of study can sometimes be hard to explain; it is not a specific observation or even a set of observations that yield deeper understanding of a social or political phenomenon. Second, this appendix is designed to help others interested in doing in-depth research on institutions and organizations learn qualitative techniques that can yield insights impossible to attain without sustained observations and triangulation. The research used for this book goes beyond what I was able to write in each chapter because I spent nearly a decade learning about VTCs in order to convey the main points articulated here—which may also help explain why there are a variety of points throughout the book.

Research methods should be designed around research questions. Yet, any honest researcher will tell you that the questions may evolve as the research continues, because we rarely know what the most interesting question and answer will be until we start doing the research. For this project, I was initially interested in how VTCs conceptualize war. My earlier research centered on transitional justice (Rowen 2017), an idea that spread around the world and has facilitated the growth of numerous interventions designed to help survivors of war. That research examined truth commissions, which are part of an international human rights regime designed to promote retribution and rehabilitation at a societal level. I have always been interested in the multiple, and often contradictory, goals that legal bodies are designed to realize, as well as thinking of militants as survivors of war. Studying veterans in the United States seemed an optimal way to continue to understand the impacts of war and the role of law to address it.

After my initial observations revealed that VTCs hearings do not contain much content about war, I designed the research around the question of how law is instrumentalized to address entrenched social and political problems, in this case poverty, substance use, mental illness, and war. The sub-questions asked how courts with competing or contradictory goals realize those goals, how treatment courts encourage compliance, and how participants respond.

After developing research questions, it is important to develop a theoretical framework with which to address them. Many studies on the criminal legal system adopt an inequality lens that expressly looks for race or gender or other identity-based inequalities in all court interactions (see, e.g., Gonzalez Van Cleve 2016). Others approach treatment courts with a more Foucauldian outlook, with control and discipline framing the analysis (see, e.g., Kaye 2020). These approaches offer important insights, but I worried that adopting such frameworks can lead to interpretations of events that see racial inequalities, for example, when there may be other types of inequalities driving the events, or viewing treatment courts as inherently bad when a different analysis would underscore the trade-offs they present.

Drawing on my initial observations and sociolegal theory about the agentic and structural dynamics of law, I developed a framework using sociolegal theories about courts as organizations and moral worth in bureaucratic decision making to make sense of the qualitative data I was going to collect. Because my initial interest was in how VTCs conceptualize war, it should be no surprise that I draw attention to the contradictions in VTCs as they treat military service as inherently noble as well as traumatic, damaging, and even criminogenic. Likewise, while I think it is important to remain skeptical and even critical of criminal legal interventions, I always try to separate the criticism of the system from the individuals working in it. Those seeking justice as well as peace must work in imperfect systems, and I have deep respect for the people who gave me their time to explain what they do and why. War is hell; those who choose or are compelled to make themselves available to fight a war or pick up the pieces afterward deserve admiration.

Along these lines, another aspect of social science is to expand from only normative concerns—such as how to improve outcomes for VTC participants—toward theoretical considerations that help illuminate broader patterns in society. This book seeks to go beyond critique to show how these courts operate and what might improve them, as well as to illustrate their broader meanings related to how the US spends its limited resources. As noted earlier, the differences between courts and the politics of worth are central to this book's larger interrogation of inequality in US institutions. Still, this research offered many practical insights about what works and what may be problematic for VTC staff and participants, and I try to stay focused on the practical implications throughout.

My research design also reflects the state of research on VTCs a decade ago. When I first started studying VTCs in 2016, there was little scholarly literature on the topic. Most research was descriptive, explaining the variety of courts across the country, or normative, arguing the value of VTCs or specific rules in VTCs. As a result, I had little theory to build my arguments on. Such a gap lends itself to a grounded interpretive approach that requires choices "based on intuitions, hunches and ideas of what is needed that have not yet been fully rationalized" (Greiffenhagen, Mair, and Sharrock 2011, 103; Babones 2016). Building from sociolegal scholars such as Feeley and Gusfield (1992), Ostrom and Hansen (2009), Eisenstein and Jacob (1991), and Kohler-Haussman (2019), I decided to focus on court processes rather than outcomes. This decision emerged from my early observation that studies about court outcomes fail to capture what goes on in a court. A purely outcome-oriented approach focused on sobriety or criminal offending can also obscure what success might look like. For example, if a court accepts people who have longer and more serious histories of substance use, they may also have higher "failure" rates, which manifest in termination from the program.

Moreover, VTCs are not created simply to help participants stay sober and avoid reoffending. Like criminal courts, VTCs have instrumental goals—to graduate participants—as well as expressive goals—to carry out justice (Eisenstein and Jacob 1991). These goals differ in both how they are understood and implemented depending on the location of the court, who works in it, and the rules they are bound by (Ostrom et al. 2007). Further, myriad courtroom actors and their different approaches, rather than rules, often determine the ways in which courts realize their problem-solving functions (Feeley and Gusfield 1992, 19).

The origins of VTCs are now well understood, articulated clearly in important works such as Douds and Ahlin's (2019) explanation of how VTCs originated and differ in their design. Although I write a similar story about their founding and differences, my intention was to write a different book that focuses on the broader social and political context in which VTCs emerged, as well as about people in the courts and what they do, rather than what they say they do. To this end, I designed the research for this book to help explain and, perhaps more so, illustrate how (some of) these courts operate.

Choosing the Courts

This book "scales up" from my initial case study of the Northeast VTC, which began in fall 2017 and ended in May 2022. In my initial observations, I had little idea about VTC variation, but it was clear to me that this court's practices reflected local needs and resources, and studying VTCs in context was necessary to understand them. To select my other two case studies for comparison, I had to rely on existing research and consider access. The first part of this conundrum was solved with the help of the VA which, in the 2010s, was itself trying to understand VTCs. Complementing early research when VTCs still numbered around a hundred in the country (McCormick-Goodhart 2014; Baldwin 2015), the VA began collecting regular surveys about VTCs as they became more popular. After I signed numerous disclosures, in 2018 the VA offered me their most recent survey data (already a few years old), which showed 52 percent of VTCs allowed individuals who were pre- or post-plea, while 17.2 percent accepted pre-plea only, and 30.6 percent accepted post-plea only. Sixty-six percent accepted both misdemeanor and felony charges; 20 percent accepted misdemeanors only; 13.7 percent accepted felonies only; and 61.9 percent accepted all violent offenses. Meanwhile, 32.5 percent of VTCs only accepted veterans eligible for VA health care (leaving veterans without eligibility to other treatment courts or the regular legal system). Further, 68.8 percent offered a mentorship program, averaging eight mentors per VTC; and 9 percent had mentor programs under development (for more on these data, see Flatley et al. 2017). These differences informed the criteria I selected for when designing this research, illustrated in Table 1.

These data captured many aspects of VTCs, but they overlooked other important differences that I understood better as the research was underway. Funding is central because certain grants require specific entry rules, treatment protocols, and sanctions. Given the well-known racially disparate outcomes that exist in other treatment courts, I hoped that examining courts with different demographics could help show how the presence or absence of racialized minorities influences the administration of justice in VTCs. One challenge, of course, is that it is difficult to identify racialized minorities from their appearance, and I did not have demographic data for all three courts. Second, the allocation of social services also reflects the presence or absence of certain racialized groups in a given locale (McGhee 2021). Given these two challenges, as well as my initial observations that racialized minorities were treated very similarly to their white counterparts in hearings, inequalities shaped by race are more in the background, a central feature of inequality in the US, than in the foreground of my analysis. It was clear to me that the two urban courts serving more racialized minorities had many more challenges than the more rural court with fewer racialized minorities in Northeast.

The main criteria I used for my case selection illustrate the varied rules and regulations for entry and graduation in all VTCs (Baldwin and Hartley 2022). What distinguishes my findings from other studies comparing divergent rules is that I do not conclude that these differences pose a problem; rather, the differences illustrate a fundamentally different understanding among court personnel about what their goals are and should be. In addition, these differences underscore how difficult it is to draw conclusions from large-N comparative, outcome-based studies. Entry rules and legal outcomes are crucial for examining how courts realize their goals, because each court has a unique set of accused criminal defendants with unique incentives to be in the court. For example, VTCs that accept participants with less than honorable discharges have different levels of access to social services. Likewise, courts that accept pre-plea can incentivize participants by offering to clear their criminal record; those accepting post-plea cannot. Post-plea participants may avoid jail or get a reduction in their probation, but their incentive to join may have more to do with access to social services than with the legal outcome.

There are other important variables in understanding court practices, which I learned while making my case selection. The presence of a mentor program may shape how a court creates a sense of social solidarity among participants; it may also reflect or foster the military culture VTCs are purported to have (Ahlin 2016). The three courts I studied varied in their mentor programs, though this was not a variable I initially selected for. The urban, rural, and regional variations make the findings of this study more generalizable—though none of the courts are representative of the geographic regions they are in, as there is just too much variability—and this variation can also shed light on how local social welfare needs and local politics shape the administration of justice in legal institutions that are promoted at the national level.

In addition, Easterly (2017) finds that many VTCs have judges who themselves are veterans and that the best predictor of the presence of a VTC is a nearby VA facility (see also Button 2017). All of my courts, likewise, had a VA health center nearby to offer services, but none of these courts had a veteran judge. The judges may have shaped court practices such as the relative absence of references to the military. However, controlling for whether the judge was a veteran or not makes the comparison of how these courts incorporate military culture more reliable. Likewise, varying the involvement of a veteran judge would have posed additional challenges, especially as West's treatment court judges often rotate.

Finally, when explaining this or any research design that requires participation by those being studied, it is critical to address access. I needed to find courts that were willing to let me write about them, with personnel open to discussing their practices, on top of the variables I was interested in. The first court I tried to work with near West decided that they did not want me to observe them. Then I found West, which was not too far from that first court, and had a completely different attitude. The personnel were incredibly generous, offering me access to data that a researcher can only hope for. Likewise, the Southeast court personnel were very accommodating, welcoming my research assistants and myself to observe court hearings. The three courts in this study were supportive of my research, but made clear that they did not want me to interview participants in the study, or to publish identifying information about the participants. I assured each court team that I would not identify the court or anyone in it as a condition of their involvement in the research and signed agreements with each of them to that effect.

For feasibility, I also needed to be able to create research teams that could do observations in places that are far from where I live and work. Southeast turned out to be the most comprehensive data on hearings because observations became part of a law school clinical program, with veteran students playing a particularly active role in going to the courthouse and both learning about the courts and offering their insights into court practices. This is due to the incredible assistance of a clinical law school instructor who helped integrate this research into student training on legal benefits for veterans. This practice of having veterans as court observers was also part of the research design. In the language of the National Science Foundation, this is a broader impact that can benefit the people VTCs are designed to help. It also made the research better, as the veterans engaged in observations were able to bring their insights to me, a nonveteran, about aspects of court interactions that may reflect military culture but are less obvious if one did not go through military training.

Court Observations

I began court observations in Northeast late 2016, attending weekly court sessions and taking notes on everything that was said during the hearings. I also took notes on scenes outside the courtroom while we waited to enter. After a year of conducting court observations myself, I trained undergraduate students to engage in observations, first hiring a student who had served in the military to conduct observations and later hiring an advanced undergraduate student to conduct virtual observations during the pandemic. During my observations, I connected with a filmmaker who filmed the first year of court hearings as well as mentor meetings that took place before the hearings. As a result, I was able to obtain verbatim transcripts from court hearings and mentor meetings from December 2015, when the court opened, to spring 2017 to complement my observations that began at that time. We also received seven court case summaries that illustrate how the court documents and tracks compliance.

For the Southeast VTC, I first attended court hearings in fall 2017, then twice more in 2018 before the research team described above took over in January 2019, with weekly or biweekly observations until the end of 2019, and then sporadic observations until spring 2021. Because of the pandemic, we switched to periodic virtual observations over summer 2020. These observations include detailed transcripts of the hearings from start to finish. We also tracked compliance, terminations, and new participants during our weekly observations, and collected information from records posted on the courtroom doors that identified each participant's charges.

I observed West periodically from fall 2017 through spring 2018, then hired a research assistant from a nearby university for weekly observations beginning in fall 2019. With feasibility in mind, I planned to start weekly West observations as Southeast observations ended. Due to the pandemic, in person observations stopped in spring 2020. As a result, we were unable to engage in the same number of observations as we were in the other two courts. When the court reopened in summer 2020, we switched to virtual observations, which we conducted through spring 2022, after which I engaged in period observations until spring 2024. For West, we also have transcripts from observations of case conferencing, also known as staffing, in which the court team discussed compliance and outcomes for each participant. West also provided me with detailed administrative records of outcomes during its first five years, as well as redacted case reports of individual participants from 2018.

Summaries of this data are in table A.1.

Even though I have this comprehensive data about the individual courts, I do not convey information from all of it in this book. One reason is because I want to respect the privacy of the people involved, both participants and those trying to help them. Except for what was conveyed in interviews and in public court hearings, I use much of the data as background information to help make sense of court decision making and broader meaning making about what the criminal legal system can do to help struggling veterans.

In observational notes on the hearings, which inform the bulk of the book's latter half, I and the research team focused primarily on what was said during the hearings, while also taking additional notes about what happened before and after the court hearings. Except for two students who struggled to docu-

TABLE A.1. Observation dates.

Court	Observation Dates	Observations Total	Supplemental Data
Northeast	Winter 2015–Spring 2022	77	Residential facility observations (12 hrs); 32 mentor meeting transcripts; court case summaries (7)
Southeast	Fall 2017–Spring 2021	97	Staffing meeting (1); public information sheet with name, demographics, charges
West	Spring 2018–Fall 2022	37	Staffing meetings (29); redacted snapshot administrative data records from 2018; redacted case reports from 2018

Source: Data collected by author

ment everything said, all students took notes verbatim and wrote comments about their observations within their transcripts. I encouraged the research assistants to document their personal impressions of hearings, and what stood out to them from the individual hearings. Before the pandemic, I held regular research team meetings with graduate and undergraduate students doing different aspects of the research, from observations to literature reviews. At the end of the semester, each student did a presentation of their research for the others. During the pandemic, I held biweekly meetings with the research assistants doing virtual observations of West and Northeast. During the year and a half that we conducted observations in Southeast, each semester I participated in meetings with the law students doing observations to introduce and then discuss the research design, to learn about their impressions, and to update them on the project. Those law students participated in weekly meetings with the clinical supervisor overseeing this research.

The pandemic posed many challenges to this research but also offered distinct opportunities. Rather than rely on a research assistant in West to finish observations, I was able to enlist the support of highly capable research assistants at UMass to conduct virtual observations and work on the coding. I was also able to observe these hearings myself despite being unable to travel. As I note in the manuscript and elsewhere (see Rowen 2024), the pandemic changed many aspects of treatment court practice, including participant engagement in hearings, surveillance, requirements, and enrollments. However, the differences between these courts, and their meanings, did not change. Rather, the pandemic amplified these differences while hearings were virtual, and the same patterns reemerged when hearings returned in person. Thus, I focus primarily on in-person observations in the manuscript to maintain consistency and accuracy.

Additional Data

Another significant source of data includes interviews with court personnel and others with specialized knowledge about VTCs. These interviews include a total of 55 people, seven of whom I interviewed multiple times over the years. At the Northeast VTC, I interviewed the judge (three times), the local district attorney and two assistant district attorneys involved in founding the VA, the defense attorney who volunteered in the court, two probation officers (one of them twice), and four clinicians (one of them three times). In addition, I conducted a focus group with four mentors. I also interviewed two staff who work on courts at the state level and who helped set up the VTC, a local politician engaged in advocacy related to VTCs in the region, a local advocate engaged in promoting social services for veterans in the area, and two researchers who work on veterans in the criminal legal system. In these interviews, I focused on how these decision-makers explained their goals and strategies, aware that their decision making is constrained by the different bureaucracies in which they work (Lipsky 2010; Maynard-Moody and Musheno 2003).

At the Southeast VTC, I interviewed the primary judge (three times), the regular substitute judge, three case managers (one of them three times), the mentor coordinator, the city's district attorney, and the city's public defender, as well as two others (one judge and one local policymaker) involved in creating the VTC. I also interviewed three people who worked for the VJO program in the city, one of whom became a regular clinician in the VTC.

At the West VTC, I interviewed the court's founding judge, the judge who oversaw the court for the time I was conducting observations (three times), two court coordinators (one of them three times), five case managers (one of them three times), three mentors, one district attorney, and one public defender. I also interviewed two veterans' services advocates in the region who worked with the VTC in West. At the national level, I interviewed three people who work for the Justice for Vets program, which trains VTC teams across the country, as well as three researchers and leaders in the Veterans Justice Office. I also interviewed two practitioners and researchers who worked with VTCs.

In addition to these interviews with court personnel, I also interviewed veterans who have suffered from homelessness, addiction, and criminal legal involvement. In spring and summer 2017, I engaged in multiple observations at a Northeast correctional facility (in a different jurisdiction and not affiliated with the Northeast VTC). I conducted one-on-one interviews with eight residents and three staff at the residential treatment facility associated with the Northeast's VTC. Those interviews were designed to answer a different research question—how Black veterans experience post-service life—but they provided important insights into inequalities that people experience before entering the military and upon leaving.

As noted above, while I was conducting research in Northeast, an inspirational veterans' advocate and clinician invited me to learn about incarcerated veterans in a nearby city, where the sheriff helped create a veterans' pod (i.e., those with military background allowed to live together in the prison) and where he visited to offer clinical support. At the pod, I interviewed six veterans and spent five hours observing people interacting in the pod. I was especially interested in the interactions between incarcerated veterans and the corrections officers, noting that some prisoner-guard dyads knew one another from high school. This kind of access is central to qualitative methods and requires sensitivity to the people working in social and political institutions, and those impacted by them. In all these settings I was a guest and worked hard to bring compassion to the people who lent their time explaining their work and experiences.

As noted in the introduction, a significant focus of my research was on why VTCs originated and spread. This required research into the largest advocacy and research organization dedicated to treatment courts, the National Association of Drug Court Professionals, rebranded in 2023 as All Rise because the treatment court model expanded far beyond drug treatment courts. Access to these meetings would not have been possible without federal funding, as the registration fee alone (not to mention travel) is close to $1,000. I attended the 2020 meeting virtually, due to the pandemic, and two others in person, one in 2021 northern Virginia and another in 2023 in Houston, Texas. In these conferences, where thousands of people come to learn about VTCs, the vast majority of them practitioners (I did not meet a single researcher except for those presenting), I was able to take notes on how presenters talk about treatment courts as well as what meeting participants ask about and how the treatment court model is understood. Presenters also provided slides on a conference website that participants could access.

I spent a total of seven full days at these conferences, choosing talks based on their relevance to VTCs. These conferences have a separate "track" for participants interested in VTCs, with an average of two panels to choose from during any given time slot, as well as a mentor "boot camp" that runs over the course of the conference. Most of the presentations in this track involved the VA, which I discuss in chapter 3. I could not be in more than one place at once, so I observed two "boot camp" sessions in the 2021 meeting but I did not participate in the full training. I also selected presentations on legal issues pertaining to VTCs—such as whether courts can mandate particular treatments or what kind of due process is necessary to sanction—and up-to-date research on treatment court efficacy. At these meetings, I also came to see the industry that treatment courts have become, with many profit-oriented drug testing companies present to advertise their work.

Over the years, I also engaged in extensive research on social services for veterans at the federal level and in the court communities I studied. Much of the chapter on the VA relies on secondary historical materials, just as the analysis of how ideas of veteran worth show up in the US entertainment industry is based on excellent social science research conducted by others. Complementing this research, my team also collected and coded media accounts from 156 newspaper articles about veterans treatment courts in the three different regions I studied. Finally, I have additional data from court observations in a VTC near West, and observations of VTC personnel explaining their courts in public events that I was able to attend over the years. All of these documents and observations are part of the database that I used to help make sense of the rapid growth of VTCs, as well as their operationalization in specific locales.

Analysis

Analyzing the copious data collected for this book was a daunting task. In part, the approach I took reflects a "do as I say, not as I do" reality of research, as I always tell students to focus on their research question and theoretical framework so that they do not spend too much time collecting and analyzing data that does not address their research questions. While I was particularly interested in how these courts balance retribution and rehabilitation, over time it became clear to me that social and political inequalities at the national and local levels were shaping, and reflected in, VTC practices more than I previously understood. Thus, the final analysis does not reflect the initial codebook, but emerged over years of reflection and refinement, with only a fraction of thematic codes making it into the book.

To analyze the data, I worked with graduate and undergraduate students to load the data on NVivo, a qualitative software program that enabled file organization and coding. We constructed three different codebooks, one for the media files, one for the interviews, and one for the observational data. One strength to this software is that we were able to both code "cases," which was information attributed to specific people. With this, we could track participants over the course of our observations, as well as attach memos to specific observations. The software also enabled us to compare how much one person spoke during a hearing which, for example, we used to illustrate the quantity that Southeast's judge spoke in comparison to Northeast.

Our approach to thematic coding was iterative, meaning we developed and refined codes as the observations continued, and revisited transcripts to capture codes that we did not previously identify. One graduate student and I originated the codebook in collaboration, and later research assistants further developed the codebook as our observations expanded to the other courthouses. Under my supervision, each research assistant trained the next research assistant in coding. I reviewed early coding to ensure reliability and met regularly with research assistants as a team to discuss their work. Each research assistant also wrote memos to describe incidents in the courts that were too complicated to capture with codes.

The detailed codebook for observations was developed to answer the initial research questions. It ballooned over time as we analyzed the data to better understand court practices. The detailed codebook was a boon to train research assistants over time but also made simplistic quantitative analysis (e.g., the number of times a code was present) difficult. Rather than explain the relative presence or absence of a particular code, I chose to write the book with narrative explanations on the relative presence of absence of codes in the different courtrooms, as well as the more granular examples of specific interactions to illustrate the codes and, more broadly, what they tell us about the courts. I cite specific examples of interviewee explanations and court interaction by relying on codes such as "anger" or "deservingness" to find quotes representative of that theme.

In addition to relying on the codebook to interpret court hearings, the book's main arguments emerged more from what was absent in the codebook than what was present. For example, we coded every time the military was mentioned in court. The vast majority of those references were about the VA—eligibility and treatment—with only a few dozen references to military service apart from introductions in Northeast. While my initial interpretation is that the military is just not particularly relevant in VTCs, my conversations with the research team, particularly the veterans working on this project, helped me think about the more subtle ways that military culture shapes court practices.

Similarly, the insights about veteran worth rely on my own interpretation of how interviewees articulated their goals and strategies. This is because the notion of veteran worth—that veterans are distinct, in a positive way, from those who did not join the military—was more noticeable in its absence than presence in hearings. Our coding suggests that veteran worth was only mentioned in an explicit way during hearings twelve times across the three courts. Yet, over the years of interviewing personnel, and coding for their explanations about what makes veterans different than other criminal legal defendants, I came to see how different parties described their work on behalf of veterans in ways that combined deservingness, affect, and different understandings of nexus as worth.

By its nature, this kind of analysis requires interpretation that reflects my personal experiences and knowledge, meaning that someone else with the same data may come to a different set of conclusions. There is, thus, an inherent element of "trust me" in such research, which also exists in any research where decisions must be made about what variables matter. The reader will need to evaluate whether the conclusions match the data presented, and they may question that data's representativeness of the corpus. While I recognize this limitation, other approaches, particularly those that are more readily replicable and falsifiable based on data such as recidivism rates, cannot yield the kinds of insights that come with an approach open to making sense of something as novel as a new treatment court based on the idea that veterans have unique needs that a court just for them can address. This kind of explanatory work requires a researcher to think beyond the courtroom observations in order to situate VTCs in the broader social and political infrastructure, and to interpret interactions in the courtroom within this larger context.

Through this approach, I tried to illuminate how beliefs about veteran worth shapes the administration of justice in VTCs and beyond, with mutually reinforcing ideological and material support for veterans but not other defendants who may have similar life experiences or reasons for being in the criminal legal system. My approach also illustrates the value of long-term observation, which is resource intensive. This book would not have been possible without the National Science Foundation and the congressional appropriation that enables that independent agency to fund the best social science. That program teaches students and professionals how to engage in scientific inquiry at the highest level, and I hope that the methods articulated here illustrate the value of good research design and a state that supports good research, as well as the flexibility required for good research execution.

NOTES

Chapter 1

1. See https://allrise.org/.

Chapter 2

1. The presenters at All Rise define high-risk and high-need individuals as typically suffering from a severe substance use or mental health disorder, or have other pressing social service needs such as chronic homelessness or lack of basic job skills. In addition, they have serious risk factors for poor outcomes in standard treatment or community supervision programs, such as having extensive criminal histories, delinquent peer affiliations, or antisocial tendencies.

2. This is true except in New York State, where state criminal legal reforms disallow judges to consider public safety when determining bail.

3. "Generally, in order to receive VA benefits and services, the Veteran's character of discharge or service must be under other than dishonorable conditions (e.g., honorable, under honorable conditions, general). However, individuals receiving undesirable, bad conduct, and other types of dishonorable discharges may qualify for VA benefits depending on a determination made by VA." See https://benefits.va.gov/benefits/character_of_discharge.asp.

Chapter 3

1. Similarly, medical professionals had to distinguish between deserving and undeserving veterans when deciding on medical benefits. Under Bureau of War Risk Insurance (BWRI) amendments, the federal government was obligated to aid those injured with "governmental medical, surgical and hospital services," but the extent of the obligation was unclear. The BWRI assessed percentages of medical impairment

as "temporary total," "permanent total," permanent partial," or temporary partial" (Adler 2000, 95). Other medical diagnoses were classified into these categories, but there was some discretion. If the injury prevented the veteran from doing their job, and they were the breadwinner of the family, then they may receive more money compared to someone with a similar injury but different vocation and different role in the family's financial structure.

2. *Justice Today* podcast, "The Story of Veterans Treatment Courts: Judge Robert Russell," US Department of Justice, Office of Justice Programs, https://bja.ojp.gov/podcast/story-of-veterans-treatment-courts#transcript--0.

3. As noted in chapter 2, the National Association for Drug Court Professionals rebranded itself as All Rise in 2023. For consistency, and to use the organization's new name, all conferences will be referred to as All Rise.

4. Organizations included the NDCI; BJA; US Department of Veterans Affairs; the Gather, Assess, Integrate, Network, and Stimulate (GAINS) Center; and the Battered Women's Justice Project.

5. In 1986, Congress mandated "means testing" for eligibility, meaning only individuals with service-connected disabilities and/or were very poor could access benefits. This changed in 1996, when congressional reforms created seven priority groups. In the aftermath of 9/11, the VA expanded eligibility further, providing support to all servicemembers who served for five years in what is commonly known as GWOT, or the Global War on Terror (i.e., Operation Enduring Freedom, Operation Iraqi Freedom, and Operation New Dawn).

6. Branches of services are the National Guard or Reserves, US Air Force, US Navy, US Marines, and US Army.

Chapter 4

1. As noted in another chapter, the National Association for Drug Court Professionals rebranded itself as All Rise in 2023. All Rise is used in this chapter to refer to the organization, no matter the year under discussion.

2. I thank West's judge for pointing out this important challenge in VTCs.

Chapter 6

1. It is a small group that falls into this category: those with honorable discharge and general discharge with less than two years of service, without a service-connected disability, and who served after 1980. There was also a challenge with those who have other than honorable discharge but have Veteran Health Administration eligibility. Strictly following state rules where the Southeast VTC is located, these veterans should not be allowed in the program. However, it's unclear if any were accepted into the VTC incorrectly (Ryan Foley, pers. comm.).

Chapter 8

1. I thank Liz Chiarello for making this excellent theoretical point.

REFERENCES

Adams, Gordon, and Shoon K. Murray, eds. 2014. *Mission Creep: The Militarization of US Foreign Policy*. Georgetown University Press.

Adler, Matthew D. 2000. "Expressive Theories of Law: A Skeptical Overview." *University of Pennsylvania Law Review* 148: 1364–495.

Ahlin, Eileen. 2016. "Military Socialization: A Motivating Factor for Seeking Treatment in a Veterans' Treatment Court." *American Journal of Criminal Justice* 41(1): 83–96.

Ahlin, Eileen M., and Anne S. Douds. 2018. "Many Shades of Green: Assessing Awareness of Differences in Mental Health Care Needs among Subpopulations of Military Veterans." *International Journal of Offender Therapy and Comparative Criminology* 62(10): 3168–84.

Ahlin, Eileen M., and Anne S. Douds. 2020. "If You Build It, Will Vets Come? An Identity Theory Approach to Expanding Veterans' Treatment Court Participation." *Criminal Justice Review* 45(3): 319–36.

Akers, Ronald L., and Christine S. Sellers. 2004. *Criminological Theories: Introduction, Evaluation, and Application*, 4th ed. Roxbury.

Alexander, Michelle. 2012. *The New Jim Crow: Mass Incarceration in the Age of Colorblindness*. New Press.

All Rise. *Best Practice Standards*. https://allrise.org/publications/adult-drug-court -best-practice-standards/ (accessed July 5, 2023).

American Bar Association. 2023. *Plea Bargaining Task Force Report*. https://www. americanbar.org/content/dam/aba/publications/criminaljustice/plea-bargain-tf-re port.pdf.

Appy, Christian G. 2015. *American Reckoning: The Vietnam War and Our National Identity*. Penguin Press.

Ashforth, Blake E., and Barrie W. Gibbs. 1990. "The Double-Edge of Organizational Legitimation." *Organization Science* 1(2): 177–94.

Atkin-Plunk, Cassandra A., Gaylene S. Armstrong, and Nicky Dalbir. 2021. "Veteran Treatment Court Clients' Perceptions of Procedural Justice and Recidivism." *Criminal Justice Policy Review* 32(5): 501–22.

Babones, Salvatore. 2016. "Interpretive Quantitative Methods for the Social Sciences." *Sociology* 50(3): 453–69.

Bacevich, Andrew J. 2013. *The New American Militarism: How Americans Are Seduced by War.* Oxford University Press.

Bachman, J. G., D. R. Segal, P. Freedman-Doan, and P. M. O'Malley. 2000. "Who Chooses Military Service? Correlates of Propensity and Enlistment in the U.S. Armed Forces." *Military Psychology* 12(1): 1–30.

Baker, Kimberly M. 2013. "Decision Making in a Hybrid Organization: A Case Study of a Southwestern Drug Court Treatment Program." *Law & Social Inquiry* 38(1): 27–54.

Baldwin, Julie M. 2015. "Investigating the Programmatic Attack: A National Survey of Veterans Treatment Courts." *Journal of Criminal Law and Criminology* 105(3): 705–52.

Baldwin, Julie M., and Erika J. Brooke. 2019. "Pausing in the Wake of Rapid Adoption: A Call to Critically Examine the Veterans Treatment Court Concept." *Journal of Offender Rehabilitation* 58(1): 1–29.

Baldwin, Julie M., and Richard D. Hartley. 2022. *Final Report: National Institute of Justice's Multisite Evaluation of Veterans Treatment Courts, Systematic Assessment of implementation and Intermediate Outcomes.* National Institute of Justice.

Barker, David C., Jon Hurwitz, and Traci L. Nelson. 2008. "Of Crusades and Culture Wars: 'Messianic' Militarism and Political Conflict in the United States." *Journal of Politics* 70(2): 307–22.

Battilana, Julie, and Silvia Dorado. 2010. "Building Sustainable Hybrid Organizations: The Case of Commercial Microfinance Organizations." *Academy of Management Journal* 53(6): 1419–40.

Berman, Greg, and John Feinblatt. 2001. "Problem-Solving Courts: A Brief Primer." *Law & Policy* 23(2): 125–40.

Bhati, Avinash S., John K. Roman, and Aaron Chalfin. 2008. *To Treat or Not to Treat: Evidence on the Prospects of Expanding Treatment to Drug-Involved Offenders.* Washington, DC: Urban Institute.

Bitektine, Alex. 2011. "Toward a Theory of Social Judgments of Organizations: The Case of Legitimacy, Reputation, and Status." *Academy of Management Review* 36(1): 151–79.

Blodgett, Janet C., Tigran Avoundjian, and Andrea Finlay. 2015. "Prevalence of Mental Health Disorders among Justice-Involved Veterans." *Epidemiologic Reviews* 37(1): 163–76.

Blonigen, Daniel M., Leena Bui, Eric B. Elbogen, Janet C. Blodgett, Natalya C. Maisel, Amanda M. Midboe, Steven M. Asch, James F. McGuire, and Christine

Timko. 2016. "Risk of Recidivism among Justice-Involved Veterans." *Criminal Justice Policy Review* 27(8): 812–37.

Blonigen, Daniel M., Allison L. Rodriguez, Luisa Manfredi, Jessica Britt, Andrea Nevedal, Andrea K. Finlay, Joel Rosenthal, David Smelson, and Christine Timko. 2017. "The Availability and Utility of Services to Address Risk Factors for Recidivism among Justice-Involved Veterans." *Criminal Justice Policy Review* 28(8): 790–813.

Blonigen, Daniel M., Paige M. Shaffer, Jennifer S. Smith, Michael A. Cucciare, Christine Timko, David Smelson, Jessica Blue-Howells, Sean Clark, and Joel Rosenthal. 2021. "Recidivism Treatment for Justice-Involved Veterans: Evaluating Adoption and Sustainment of Moral Reconation Therapy in the US Veterans Health Administration." *Administration and Policy in Mental Health Services Research* 48: 992–1005.

Boggs, Carl, and Tom Pollard. 2016. *The Hollywood War Machine: U.S. Militarism and Popular Culture.* Routledge Press.

Boldt, Richard C. 1998. "Rehabilitative Punishment and the Drug Treatment Court Movement." *Washington University Law Quarterly* 76: 1205–306.

Borchek, James. 2015. "In Case of USF Vet, Judge Gregory Holder Raises Questions about Impartiality." *Tampabay.Com.* http://www.tampabay.com/news/humanin terest/in-case-of-usf-vet-judge-gregory-holder-raises-questions-about-impartial ity/2257997.

Bouffard, L. A. 2003. "Examining the Relationship between Military Service and Criminal Behavior during the Vietnam Era: A Research Note." *Criminology* 41: 491–510.

Bouffard, L.A. 2005. "The Military as a Bridging Environment in Criminal Careers: Differential Outcomes of the Military Experience." *Armed Forces and Society* 31(2): 273–95.

Bouffard, L. A., and J. H. Laub. 2004. "Jail or the Army: Does Military Service Facilitate Desistance from Crime?" In *After Crime and Punishment: Pathways to Offender Reintegration*, edited by S. Maruna and R. Immarigeon, 129–51. Willan.

Boulton, Mark. 2012. "A Price on Patriotism: The Politics and Unintended Consequences of the 1966 G.I. Bill." In *Veterans' Policies, Veterans' Politics: New Perspectives on Veterans in the Modern United States*, edited by Stephen R. Ortiz, 241–60. University Press of Florida.

Brewin, Chris R., Bernice Andrews, and John D. Valentine. 2000. "Meta-analysis of Risk Factors for Posttraumatic Stress Disorder in Trauma-Exposed Adults." *Journal of Consulting and Clinical Psychology* 68(5): 748–66.

Bronson, Jennifer, E. Ann Carson, Margaret Noonan, and Marcus Berzofsky. 2015. *Veterans in Prison and Jail 2011–2012.* Bureau of Justice Statistics. https://bjs.ojp .gov/content/pub/pdf/vpj1112.pdf.

Brooke, Erika J., and Jacinta M. Gau. 2018. "Military Service and Lifetime Arrests: Examining the Effects of the Total Military Experience on Arrests in a Sample of Prison Inmates." *Criminal Justice Policy Review* 29(1): 24–44.

Brown, W. B., R. Stanulis, B. Theis, J. Farnsworth, and D. Daniels. 2013. "The Perfect Storm: Veterans, Culture and the Criminal Justice System." *Justice Policy Journal* 10: 1–44.

Bureau of Justice Statistics. 2021. "Veterans in Prison: Survey of Prison Inmates, 2016." https://bjs.ojp.gov/library/publications/veterans-prison-survey-prison-inmates-2016.

Burns, Stacy Lee, and Mark Peyrot. 2003. "Tough Love: Nurturing and Coercing Responsibility and Recovery in California Drug Courts." *Social Problems* 50(3): 416–38.

Burns, Stacy Lee, and Mark Peyrot. 2008. "Reclaiming Discretion: Judicial Sanctioning Strategy in Court-Supervised Drug Treatment." *Journal of Contemporary Ethnography* 37(6): 720–744.

Buskaite, Justina. 2021. "Holding Out for a Hero: Understanding American Militarism from Post–9/11 Hollywood's Superhero Films." *LSE Undergraduate Political Review* 4(1): 71–79.

Butterworth, Michael L. 2014. "Public Memorializing in the Stadium: Mediated Sport, the Tenth Anniversary of 9/11, and the Illusion of Democracy." *Communication & Sport* 2: 203–24.

Butterworth, Michael L., and Stormi D. Moskal. 2009. "American Football, Flags, and 'Fun': The Bell Helicopter Armed Forces Bowl and the Rhetorical Production of Militarism." *Communication, Culture and Critique* 2(4): 411–33.

Button, Eric D. 2017. "The Diffusion of Veterans Treatment Courts: An Examination of Political, Social, and Economic Determinants at the County Level 2, 37 (December 1, 2017)." Unpublished MA thesis, University of Arkansas (on file with ScholarWorks, University of Arkansas).

Caine, A. 2009. "Fallen from Grace: Why Treatment Should Be Considered for Convicted Combat Veterans Suffering from Post Traumatic Stress Disorder." *University of Missouri Kansas City Law Review* 78: 215–40.

Cancelmo, C., D. Brown, A. Pinkham, and A. Weir. 2025. "Black Veterans' Insight on Racial Disparities in Military Administrative Separations." *Journal of Veterans Studies* 11(1): 1–15.

Carson, Ann, and Rich Kluckow. 2023. *Prisoners in 2022—Statistical Tables*. US Department of Justice, Bureau of Justice Statistics.

Cartwright, Tiffany. 2011. "To Care for Him Who Shall Have Borne the Battle: The Recent Development of Veterans Treatment Courts in America." *Stanford Law & Policy Review* 22: 295–316.

Casey, Timothy. 2004. "When Good Intentions Are Not Enough: Problem-Solving Courts and the Impending Crisis of Legitimacy." *SMU Law Review* 57: 1459–587.

Castellano, Ursula. 2011. "Courting Compliance: Case Managers as 'Double Agents' in the Mental Health Court." *Law & Social Inquiry* 36: 484–514.

Castellano, Ursula. 2017. "The Politics of Benchcraft: The Role of Judges in Mental Health Courts." *Law & Social Inquiry* 42(2): 398–422.

Castellano, Ursula, and Dana Scott. 2017. "Judging Therapeutically in a Veterans Treatment Court." *Ohio Lawyer* 31(5): 20–25.

Castille, Ronald D. 2010. "A Special Court for Veterans." *New York Times*, November 10. https://www.nytimes.com/2010/11/11/opinion/11castille.html.

Cavanaugh, Jillian M. 2010. "Helping Those Who Serve: Veterans Treatment Courts Foster Rehabilitation and Reduce Recidivism for Offending Combat Veterans." *New England Law Review* 45: 463–88.

CBS Sacramento. 2015. "Sacramento Veterans Court Gives Those Who Served Another Chance and a Helping Hand." August 21. https://www.cbsnews.com/sacramento/news/sacramento-veterans-court-gives-those-who-served-another-chance-and-a-helping-hand/.

Cheesman II, Fred L., Douglas B. Marlowe, and Kathryn J. Genthon. 2023. "Racial Differences in Drug Court Referral, Admission, and Graduation Rates: Findings from Two States and Eight Counties." *Journal of Ethnicity in Criminal Justice* 21(1): 80–102.

Clair, Matthew, Caitlin Daniel, and Michèle Lamont. 2016. "Destigmatization and Health: Cultural Constructions and the Long-Term Reduction of Stigma." *Social Science & Medicine* 165: 223–32.

Clarke, George. 2001. "Urban Survival Syndrome: A New Defense." *Law Enforcement Quarterly* 30(2): 16–17.

Collins, Erin. 2017. "Status Courts." *Georgetown Law Journal* 105(6): 1481–528.

Connecticut Veterans Legal Center. 2022. *Discretionary Injustice: How Racial Disparities in the Military's Administrative Separation System Harm Black Veterans.* https://ctveteranslegal.org/wp-content/uploads/2022/11/ Discretionary-Injustice-Report.pdf.

Council on Criminal Justice. 2024. *Veterans Justice Commission: Veterans Justice Courts Model Policy Framework.* https://counciloncj.foleon.com/veterans-commission/vjc-reports/model-policy-framework.

Crogan, Patrick. 2011. *Gameplay Mode: War, Simulation, and Technoculture.* University of Minnesota Press.

Culp, R., Tashin J. Youstin, Kristin Englander, and James Lynch. 2013. "From War to Prison: Examining the Relationship between Military Service and Criminal Activity." *Justice Quarterly* 30(4): 651–80.

Dao, James. 2013. "Deployment Factors Are Not Related to Rise in Military Suicides, Study Finds." *New York Times*, August 7. https://www.nytimes.com/2013/08/07/us/deployment-factors-found-not-related-to-military-suicide-spike.html.

Darda, Joseph. 2021. *How White Men Won the Culture Wars: A History of Veteran America.* University of California Press.

De la Peña, Mark. 2024. "Veterans Treatment Courts: Broadening Eligibility for Veterans Convicted of Violent Offenses." *Catholic University Law Review* 73: 1–30.

Delmont, Matthew F. 2022. *Half American: The Epic Story of Black Americans Fighting World War II at Home and Abroad.* Viking.

DiMaggio, Paul J., and Walter W. Powell. 1983. "The Iron Cage Revisited: Institutional Isomorphism and Collective Rationality in Organizational Fields." *American Sociological Review* 48(2): 147.

Dohrenwend, B .P., J. B. Turner, N. A. Turse, R. Lewis-Fernandez, and T. J. Yager. 2008. "War-Related Posttraumatic Stress Disorder in Black, Hispanic, and Majority White Vietnam Veterans: The Roles of Exposure and Vulnerability." *Journal of Trauma Stress* 21(2): 133–41.

Douds, Anne S., Eileen M. Ahlin, Daniel Howard, and Sarah Stigerwalt. 2017. "Varieties of Veterans' Courts: A Statewide Assessment of Veterans' Treatment Court Components." *Criminal Justice Policy Review* 28(8): 740–69.

Douds, Anne S., and Eileen M. Ahlin. 2019. *The Veterans Treatment Court Movement Striving to Serve Those Who Served*. Routledge.

Douds, Anne S., Eileen M. Ahlin, and Michael Posteraro. 2021. "Noble Intent Is Not Enough to Run Veterans Court Mentoring Programs: A Qualitative Study of Mentors' Role Orientation and Responsibilities." *Journal of Qualitative Criminal Justice & Criminology* 10(2). https://doi.org/10.21428/88de04a1.a897747a.

Douds, Anne S., and Don Hummer. 2019. "When a Veterans' Treatment Court Fails: Lessons Learned from a Qualitative Evaluation." *Victims & Offenders* 14(3): 322–43. https://doi.org/10.1080/15564886.2019.1595248.

Dube, Shanta R., Vincent J. Felitti, Maxia Dong, Daniel P. Chapman, Wayne H. Giles, and Robert F. Anda. 2003. "Childhood Abuse, Neglect, and Household Dysfunction and the Risk of Illicit Drug Use: The Adverse Childhood Experiences Study." *Pediatrics* 111(3): 564–72.

Easterly, Bianca. 2017. "The Ties That Bind Beyond the Battlefield: An Examination of the Diffusion Patterns of Veterans Treatment Courts." *Social Science Quarterly* 98(5): 1622–41. https://doi.org/10.1111/ssqu.12375.

Ebo, Bosah. 1995. "War as Popular Culture: The Gulf Conflict and the Technology of Illusionary Entertainment." *Journal of American Culture* 18(3): 19–25.

Edelman, Lauren B. 2016. *Working Law: Courts, Corporations, and Symbolic Civil Rights*. University of Chicago Press.

Edelman, Lauren B., and Mark C. Suchman. 1997. "The Legal Environments of Organizations." *Annual Review of Sociology* 23(1): 479–515.

Edwards, Barry C., Ramon Hinojosa, and Komysha Hassan. 2019. "How to Transform the Judicial System: Lessons from the Institutionalization of Veterans' Treatment Courts." *NYU Journal of Legislation and Public Policy* 21: 841–901.

Eighmey, John. 2006. "Why Do Youth Enlist? Identification of Underlying Themes." *Armed Forces & Society* 32(2): 307–28.

Eisenstein, James, Roy B. Flemming, and Peter F. Nardulli. 1988. *The Contours of Justice: Communities and Their Courts*. Little, Brown.

Eisenstein, James, and Herbert Jacob. 1991. *Felony Justice: An Organizational Analysis of Criminal Courts*. University Press of America.

Elbogen, Eric, Virginia Newton, Jennifer Vasterling, Sally Johnson, Kristy Straits-Troster, H. Ryan Wagner, and Jean Beckham. 2012. "Criminal Justice Involvement, Trauma, and Negative Affect in Iraq and Afghanistan War Era Veterans." *Journal of Consulting and Clinical Psychology* 80(6): 1097–102.

Fagan, Jeffrey, and Victoria Malkin. 2003. "Theorizing Community Justice through Community Courts." *Fordham Urban Law Journal* 30(3): 897–953.

Fagundes, Jonathan. 2024. "Long History of Leniency? A Call for a Georgia Statutory Mitigation Factor for Veterans with Post-Traumatic Stress Disorder." *Georgia Law Review* 58: 899–933.

Fassin, Didier, and Richard Rechtman. 2009. *The Empire of Trauma: An Inquiry into the Condition of Victimhood.* Translated by Rachel Gomme. Princeton University Press.

Feeley, Malcolm M., and Joseph R. Gusfield. 1992. *The Process Is the Punishment: Handling Cases in a Lower Criminal Court.* Russell Sage Foundation.

Finlay, Andrea, Mandy D. Owens, Emmeline Taylor, Amia Nash, Nicole Capdarest-Arest, Joel Rosenthal, Jessica Blue-Howells, Sean Clark, and Christine Timko. 2019. "A Scoping Review of Military Veterans Involved in the Criminal Justice System and Their Health and Healthcare." *Health & Justice* 7(1): 1–18.

Finlay, Andrea K., David Smelson, Leon Sawh, Jim McGuire, Joel Rosenthal, Jessica Blue-Howells, Christine Timko, Ingrid Binswanger, Susan M. Frayne, and Janet C. Blodgett. 2016. "U.S. Department of Veterans Affairs Veterans Justice Outreach Program: Connecting Justice-Involved Veteran with Mental Health and Substance Use Disorder Treatment." *Criminal Justice Policy Review* 27(2): 203–22.

Fischer, Mia. 2014. "Commemorating 9/11 NFL-Style: Insights into America's Culture of Militarism." *Journal of Sport and Social Issues* 38(3): 199–221.

Fisher, Thomas L., Deborah L. Burnet, Elbert S. Huang, Marshall H. Chin, and Kathleen A. Cagney. 2007. "Cultural Leverage: Interventions Using Culture to Narrow Racial Disparities in Health Care." *Medical Care Research and Review* 64(5): 243S.

Flatley, Bessie, Sean C. Clark, Joel Rosenthal, and Jessica H. Blue-Howells. 2017. *Veterans Court Inventory 2016 Update: Characteristics of and VA Involvement in Veterans Treatment Courts and Other Veteran-Focused Court Programs from the Veterans Justice Outreach Specialist Perspective.* Washington, DC: US Department of Veterans Affairs, Veterans Health Administration. https://cdn.prod.website-files.com/5a74ef119634a3000119f0fe/5cb55a6df6b746a3f1682f3c_Veterans_Court-Inventory-VJO-Fact-Sheet.pdf.

Foley, Ryan, and Jamie Rowen. 2022. "Putting the 'VA' in VTCs: How Facilitating VA Access Can Make Veterans Treatment Courts More Effective." *Wake Forest Journal of Law and Policy* 12: 61–102.

Forman, James. 2017. *Locking Up Our Own: Crime and Punishment in Black America.* Farrar, Straus and Giroux.

Fox, Aubrey, and Robert Victor Wolf. 2004. *The Future of Drug Courts: How States Are Mainstreaming the Drug Court Model.* New York: Center for Court Innovation. http://www. courtinnovation.org/publications.html#future.

Fox, Bryanna Hahn, Nicholas Perez, Elizabeth Cass, Michael T. Baglivio, and Nathan Epps. 2015. "Trauma Changes Everything: Examining the Relationship between Adverse Childhood Experiences and Serious, Violent and Chronic Juvenile Offenders." *Child Abuse & Neglect* 46: 163–73.

Friedman, Lawrence Meir. 1975. *The Legal System: A Social Science Perspective*. Russell Sage Foundation.

Gade, P. A., H. Lakhani, and M. Kimmel. 1991. "Military Service: A Good Place to Start?" *Military Psychology* 3(4): 251–67.

Gallagher, Mary E. 2006. "Mobilizing the Law in China: 'Informed Disenchantment' and the Development of Legal Consciousness." *Law and Society Review* 40(4): 783–816.

Gallagher, John M., and José B. Ashford. 2021. "Perceptions of Legal Legitimacy in Veterans Treatment Courts: A Test of a Modified Version of Procedural Justice Theory." *Law and Human Behavior* 45(2): 152–64.

Galvin, Rose. 2004. "Can Welfare Reform Make Disability Disappear?" *Australian Journal of Social Issues* 39(3): 343–55.

Garland, David. 2001. *The Culture of Control: Crime and Social Order in Contemporary Society*. University of Chicago Press.

Gibson, James L., Gregory A. Caldeira, and Vanessa A. Baird. 1998. "On the Legitimacy of National High Courts." *American Political Science Review* 92(2): 343–58.

Gibson, James L., and Michael J. Nelson. 2015. "Is the U.S. Supreme Court's Legitimacy Grounded in Performance Satisfaction and Ideology?" *American Journal of Political Science* 59(1): 162–74.

Goffman, Erving. 1974. *Frame Analysis: An Essay on the Organization of Experience*. Harper and Row.

Gonzalez Van Cleve, Nicole. 2016. *Crook County*. Stanford University Press.

Gordon, Sara. 2019. "About a Revolution: Toward Integrated Treatment in Drug and Mental Health Courts." *North Carolina Law Review* 97: 355–94.

Gordon, Suzanne. 2018. *Wounds of War: How the VA Delivers Health, Healing, and Hope to the Nation's Veterans*. Cornell University Press.

Government Accountability Office. 2016. "Veterans Justice Outreach Program: VA Could Improve Management by Establishing Performance Measures and Fully Assessing Risks." https://www.gao.gov/assets/680/676922.pdf.

Gowan, Teresa, and Sarah Whetstone. 2012. "Making the Criminal Addict: Subjectivity and Social Control in a Strong-Arm Rehab." *Punishment & Society* 14(1): 69–92.

Greiffenhagen, Christian, Michael Mair, and Wes Sharrock. 2011. "From Methodology to Methodography: A Study of Qualitative and Quantitative Reasoning in Practice." *Methodological Innovations Online* 6(3): 93–107.

H.R. Veterans Treatment Court Improvement Act of 2018. Public Law No: 115–240, September 17. VTC Improvement Act 2018–Congress.gov.

Hall, Peter, and Michèle Lamont. 2013. *Social Resilience in the Neoliberal Era*. Cambridge University Press.

Hallin, Daniel, and Todd Gitlin. 2010. "Agon and Ritual: The Gulf War as Popular Culture and as Television Drama." *Political Communication* 10(4): 411–24.

Hannah-Moffat, Kelly, and Paula Maurutto. 2012. "Shifting and Targeted Forms of Penal Governance: Bail, Punishment and Specialized Courts." *Theoretical Criminology* 16(2): 201–19.

Hartley, Richard D., and Julie Marie Baldwin. 2019. "Waging War on Recidivism among Justice-Involved Veterans: An Impact Evaluation of a Large Urban Veterans Treatment Court." *Criminal Justice Policy Review* 30(1): 52–78.

Hartwell, Stephanie W., Amy James, Jie Chen, Debra A. Pinals, Martha C. Marin, and David Smelson. 2014. "Trauma among Justice-Involved Veterans." *Professional Psychology: Research and Practice* 45(6): 425–32.

Harvard Law School. 2020. *Turned Away: How the VA Unlawfully Denies Health Care to Veterans with Bad Papers.* http://www.legalservicescenter.org/wp-content/uploads/Turn-Away-Report.pdf.

Hawkins, Michael Daly. 2009. "Coming Home: Accommodating the Special Needs of Military Veterans to the Criminal Justice System." *Ohio State Journal of Criminal Law* 7: 563–73.

He, Wuming, Junjie Qiu, Yingying Chen, and Yufang Zhong. 2022. "Gratitude Intervention Evokes Indebtedness: Moderated by Perceived Social Distance." *Frontiers in Psychology* 13 (March): 824326. https://doi.org/10.3389/FPSYG.2022.824326/BIBTEX.

Herzog, Joseph Richard, Frank Ferdik, Diane Scott, Andrew Denney, and Sabrina Conklin. 2019. "Participants' Perceptions of Veterans Treatment Courts: A Qualitative Assessment and Systems Model." *Journal of Veterans Studies* 4(2): 78–93.

Hinton, Elizabeth. 2016. *From the War on Poverty to the War on Crime: The Making of Mass Incarceration in America.* Harvard University Press.

Holland, Jack. 2011. "'When You Think of the Taliban, Think of the Nazis': Teaching Americans '9/11' in NBC's *The West Wing*." *Millennium* 40(1): 85–106.

Holland, Jack. 2012. *Selling the War on Terror: Foreign Policy Discourses after 9/11.* Routledge.

Holliday, Stephanie Brooks, Lynsay Ayer, and Lauren Skrabala. 2023. *Identifying Promising Prevention Strategies and Interventions to Support Justice-Involved Veterans: Veterans' Issues in Focus.* RAND Corporation. https://www.rand.org/pubs/perspectives/PEA1363-8.html.

Horton, Alex. 2013. "Help Veterans by Taking Them Off the Pedestal." *The Atlantic,* November 10. https://www.theatlantic.com/national/archive/2013/11/help-veterans-by-taking-them-off-the-pedestal/281316/.

Hummer, Don, James M. Byrne, Sabrina S. Rapisarda, Kelly M. Socia, and Kimberly R. Kras. 2024. "No Veteran Left Behind? Perspectives on VTC Eligibility Criteria for Justice-Involved Veterans in Multiple Jurisdictions across the United States." *Victims & Offenders* 19(1): 59–79.

Jacobson, Brynn N. H. 2013. "Addressing the Tension between the Dual Identities of the American Prostitute: Criminal and Victim; How Problem-Solving Courts Can Help." *Seattle University Law Review* 37: 1023–58.

Jalain, Caroline I., and Elizabeth L. Grossi. 2020. "Take a Load Off Fanny: Peer Mentors in Veterans Treatment Courts." *Criminal Justice Policy Review* 31(8): 1165–92.

Jenkins, Richard. 2000. "Categorization: Identity, Social Process and Epistemology." *Current Sociology* 48(3): 7–25.

Jennings, Audra. 2012. "The Emblem of Distinction: The Politics of Disability Entitlement, 1940–1950." In *Veterans' Policies, Veterans' Politics: New Perspectives on Veterans in the Modern United States*, edited by Stephen R. Ortiz, 94–118. University Press of Florida.

Johnson, Cathryn, Timothy J. Dowd, and Cecilia L. Ridgeway. 2006. "Legitimacy as a Social Process." *Annual Review of Sociology* 32: 53–78.

Johnston, E. Lea. 2012. "Theorizing Mental Health Courts." *Washington University Law Review* 89(3): 519–80.

Jones, Allison E. 2014. "Veterans Treatment Courts: Do Status-Based Problem-Solving Courts Create an Improper Privileged Class of Criminal Defendants." *Washington University Journal of Law & Policy* 43: 307.

Joshi, Spruha, Bianca D. Rivera, Magdalena Cerdá, et al. 2023. "One-Year Association of Drug Possession Law Change with Fatal Drug Overdose in Oregon and Washington." *JAMA Psychiatry* 80(12): 1277–83.

Junger, Sebastian. 2016. *Tribe: On Homecoming and Belonging.* Fourth Estate.

Kang, H. K., T. A. Bullman, D. J. Smolenski, N. A. Skopp, G. A. Gahm, and M. A. Reger. 2015. "Suicide Risk among 1.3 Million Veterans Who Were on Active Duty during the Iraq and Afghanistan Wars." *Annals of Epidemiology* 25(2): 96–100.

Katz, Michael B. 2013. *The Undeserving Poor: America's Enduring Confrontation with Poverty.* 2nd ed.

Kaye, Kerwin. 2013. "Rehabilitating the 'Drugs Lifestyle': Criminal Justice, Social Control, and the Cultivation of Agency." *Ethnography* 14(2): 207–32.

Kaye, Kerwin. 2020. *Enforcing Freedom: Drug Courts, Therapeutic Communities, and the Intimacies of the State.* Columbia University Press.

Keene, Jennifer. 2012. "The Long Journey Home: African American World War I Veterans and Veterans Policies." In *Veterans' Policies, Veterans' Politics: New Perspectives on Veterans in the Modern United States*, edited by Stephen R. Ortiz, 146–72. University Press of Florida.

Kessler, Ronald C., Steven G. Heeringa, Murray B. Stein, Lisa J. Colpe, Carol S. Fullerton, Irving Hwang, James A. Naifeh, et al. 2014. "Thirty-Day Prevalence of DSM-IV Mental Disorders among Nondeployed Soldiers in the US Army." *JAMA Psychiatry* 71(5): 504–13.

King, Samantha. 2008. "Offensive Lines: Sport-State Synergy in an Era of Perpetual War." *Cultural Studies, Critical Methodologies* 8(4): 527–39.

Klein, Stephen A. 2005. "Public Character and the Simulacrum: The Construction of the Soldier Patriot and Citizen Agency in *Black Hawk Down*." *Critical Studies in Media Communication* 22(5): 427–49.

Knudsen, Kraig J., and Scott Wingenfeld. 2016. "A Specialized Treatment Court for Veterans with Trauma Exposure: Implications for the Field." *Community Mental Health Journal* 52(2): 127–35. https://doi.org/10.1007/s10597-015-9845-9.

Kohler-Hausmann, Issa. 2013. "Misdemeanor Justice: Control without Conviction." *American Journal of Sociology* 119(2): 351–93.

Kohler-Hausmann, Issa. 2019. *Misdemeanorland: Criminal Courts and Social Control in an Age of Broken Windows Policing.* Princeton University Press.

Kravetz, Pamela. 2012. "Way Off Base: An Argument against Intimate Partner Violence Cases in Veterans Treatment Courts." *Veterans Law Review* 4: 124–205.

Kroeker, JoAnna. 2016. "Fresno Court Seeks to Rehabilitate, Not Incarcerate, Veterans." *Fresno Bee*, June 18. http://www.fresnobee.com/news/local/article84610522.html.

Kubacka, Kaska E., Catrin Finkenauer, Caryl E. Rusbult, and Loes Keijsers. 2011. "Maintaining Close Relationships: Gratitude as a Motivator and a Detector of Maintenance Behavior." *Personality and Social Psychology Bulletin* 37(10): 1362–75.

Kubie, Lawrence S. 1945. "How Should the Medical Care of Veterans Be Organized?" *Military Affairs* 9(2): 114–19. https://doi.org/10.2307/1982863.

Lamont, Michèle. 2018. "Addressing Recognition Gaps: Destigmatization and the Reduction of Inequality." *American Sociological Review* 83(3): 419–44.

Lamont, Michèle. 2019. "From 'Having' to 'Being': Self-Worth and the Current Crisis of American Society." *British Journal of Sociology* 70(3): 660–707.

Lamont, Michèle. 2023. *Seeing Others: How Recognition Works—And How It Can Heal a Divided World.* Simon and Schuster.

Lamont, Michele, Graziella Moraes Silva, Jessica S. Welburn, Joshua Guetzkow, Nissim Mizrachi, Hanna Herzog, and Elisa Reis. 2016. Getting Respect: Responding to Stigma and Discrimination in the United States, Brazil, and Israel. Princeton University Press.

Lamont, Michele, Stefan Beljean, and Matthew Clair. 2014 "What Is Missing? Cultural Processes and the Making of Inequality." *Socioeconomic Review* 12(3): 573–608.

LeardMann Cynthia, Teresa Powell, and Tyler Smith. 2013. "Risk Factors Associated with Suicide in Current and Former US Military Personnel." *JAMA* 310(5): 496–506. https://jamanetwork.com/journals/jama/fullarticle/1724276.

Leon, Chrysanthia, and Corey Shdaimah. 2021. "Targeted Sympathy in 'Whore Court': Criminal Justice Actors' Perceptions of Prostitution Diversion Programs." *University of Denver Law & Policy* 43(2): 126–48.

Lerman, Amy, and Vesla Weaver. 2014. *Arresting Citizenship: The Democratic Consequences of American Crime Control.* University of Chicago Press.

Lévi-Strauss, Claude. 1966. *The Savage Mind.* University of Chicago Press.

Lewis, Libby. 2008. "Vets in Legal Trouble Find Help in Buffalo Court: NPR." *National Public Radio*, April 29. https://www.npr.org/templates/story/story.php?storyId=90254410.

Liebert, Rachel. 2022. Trauma and Blameworthiness in the Criminal Legal System. *Stanford Journal of Criminal Law and Civil Liberties* 18: 215–59.

Linkler, Beth. 2011. *Wars Waste: Rehabilitation in WWI America.* Chicago: University of Chicago Press.

Lipsky, M. 2010. *Street-Level Bureaucracy: Dilemmas of the Individual in Public Service.* 30th anniversary edition. Russell Sage Foundation.

Loader, Ian, and Richard Sparks. 2013. "Unfinished Business: Legitimacy, Crime Control, and Democratic Politics." In *Legitimacy and Criminal Justice: An International Exploration,* edited by J. Tankebe and A. Liebling, 105–26. Oxford University Press.

Longman Phillip. 2012. *Best Care Anywhere: Why VA Health Care Would Work Better for Everyone.* BK Currents.

Lucas, Paul A., and Kathleen J. Hanrahan. 2016. "No Soldier Left Behind: The Veterans Court Solution." *International Journal of Law and Psychiatry* 45(March): 52–59.

Luna, Samantha, and Allison D. Redlich. 2021. "A National Survey of Veterans Treatment Court Actors." *Criminal Justice Policy Review* 32(2): 132–61.

Lutz, Amy. 2008. "Who Joins the Military? A Look at Race, Class, and Immigration Status." *Journal of Political & Military Sociology* 36(2): 167–88.

Lynch, Mona. 2011. "Mass Incarceration, Legal Change, and Locale." *Criminology & Public Policy* 10(3): 673–98.

Lynch, Mona. 2012. "Theorizing the Role of the 'War on Drugs' in US Punishment." *Theoretical Criminology* 16(2): 175–99.

Lynch, Mona, and Marisa Omori. 2014. "Legal Change and Sentencing Norms in the Wake of Booker: The Impact of Time and Place on Drug Trafficking Cases in Federal Court." *Law & Society Review* 48(2): 411–45.

Ma, Lawrence K., Richard J. Tunney, and Eamonn Ferguson. 2017. "Does Gratitude Enhance Prosociality?: A Meta-Analytic Review." *Psychological Bulletin* 143(6): 601–35.

MacLeish, Kenneth. 2020. "Damaged and Deserving: On Care in a Veteran Treatment Court." *Medical Anthropology* 39(3): 239–54.

Manela, Tony. 2016. "Negative Feelings of Gratitude." *Journal of Value Inquiry* 50(1): 129–40.

Mankowski, Mariann, Leslie E. Tower, Cynthia A. Brandt, and Kristin Mattocks. 2015. "Why Women Join the Military: Enlistment Decisions and Postdeployment Experiences of Service Members and Veterans." *Social Work* 60(4): 315–23.

Markus, Hazel, and Paula Nurius. 1986. "Possible Selves." *American Psychologist* 41(9): 954–69.

Marlowe, Douglas B., Carolyn D. Hardin, and Carson L. Fox. 2016. *Painting the Current Picture: A National Report on Drug Courts and Other Problem Solving Courts in the United States.* National Drug Court Institute.

Maynard-Moody, Steven., and Michael C. Musheno. 2003. *Cops, Teachers, Counselors: Stories from the Front Lines of Public Service.* University of Michigan Press.

McCall, Janice D., Keri L. Rodriguez, Debra Barnisin-Lange, and Adam J. Gordon. 2019. "A Qualitative Examination of the Experiences of Veterans Treatment Court Graduates in Allegheny County, Pennsylvania." *International Journal of Offender Therapy and Comparative Criminology* 63(3): 339–56.

McCall, Janice D., Jack Tsai, and Adam J. Gordon. 2018. "Veterans Treatment Court Research: Participant Characteristics, Outcomes, and Gaps in the Literature." *Journal of Offender Rehabilitation* 57(6): 384–401.

McConnell, Terrance. 2017. "Gratitude, Rights, and Moral Standouts." *Ethical Theory and Moral Practice* 20(2): 279–93.

McCormick-Goodhart, Mark. 2012. "Leaving No Veteran Behind: Policies and Perspectives on Combat Trauma, Veterans Courts, and the Rehabilitative Approach to Criminal Behavior." *Pennsylvania State Law Review* 117: 895–927.

McCoy, Candace. 2003. "The Politics of Problem-Solving: An Overview of the Origins and Development of Therapeutic Courts." *American Criminal Law Review* 40(4): 1513–655.

McCullough, Michael E., Robert A. Emmons, Shelley D. Kilpatrick, and David B. Larson. 2001. "Is Gratitude a Moral Affect?" *Psychological Bulletin* 127(2): 249–66.

McGhee, Heather. 2021. *The Sum of Us: What Racism Costs Everyone and How We Can Prosper Together*. Random House.

McPherson, Chad Michael, and Michael Sauder. 2013. "Logics in Action: Managing Institutional Complexity in a Drug Court." *Administrative Science Quarterly* 58(2): 165–96.

McSorley, Kevin. 2012. "Helmetcams, Militarized Sensation and 'Somatic War.'" *Journal of War & Culture Studies* 5(1): 47–58.

Meffert, Brienna N., Danielle M. Morabito, Danielle A. Sawicki, Catherine Hausman, Steven M. Southwick, Robert H. Pietrzak, and Adrienne J. Heinz. 2019. "US Veterans Who Do and Do Not Utilize Veterans Affairs Health Care Services: Demographic, Military, Medical, and Psychosocial Characteristics." *Primary Care Companion for CNS Disorders* 21(1). https://pmc.ncbi.nlm.nih.gov/articles/PMC6352911/pdf/nihms-999362.pdf.

Merians, Addie N., Georgina Gross, Michele R. Spoont, Chyrell D. Bellamy, Ilan Harpaz-Rotem, and Robert H. Pietrzak. 2023. "Racial and Ethnic Mental Health Disparities in U.S. Military Veterans: Results from the National Health and Resilience in Veterans Study." *Journal of Psychiatric Research* 161: 71–76.

Merriam, Eric. 2014. "Non-Uniform Justice: An Equal Protection Analysis of Veterans Treatment Courts' Exclusionary Qualification Requirements." *Mississippi Law Journal* 84: 685–750.

Mettler, Suzanne. 2012. "Forward." In *Veterans' Policies, Veterans' Politics: New Perspectives on Veterans in the Modern United States*, edited by Stephen R. Ortiz, xi–xiv. University Press of Florida.

Miller, Eric. 2004. "Embracing Addiction: Drug Courts and the False Promise of Judicial Interventionism." *Ohio State Law Journal* 65: 1479–510.

Miller, Reuben Jonathan. *Halfway Home: Race, Punishment, and the Afterlife of Mass Incarceration*. Little, Brown.

Moore, Dawn, and Hideyuki Hirai. 2014. "Outcasts, Performers and True Believers: Responsibilized Subjects of Criminal Justice." *Theoretical Criminology* 18(1): 5–19.

Moore, Delilah A. 2022. "Veteran Defendant Reasons for Opting Out of Veterans' Treatment Court." PhD diss., Walden University.

Moses, M. C. 2009. "Do Ask, Do Tell: An Examination of Veterans behind Bars." *Corrections Compendium* 34(4): 9–12.

Murphy, Jennifer. 2015. *Illness or Deviance?: Drug Courts, Drug Treatment, and the Ambiguity of Addiction*. Temple University Press.

Musheno and Ross 2008. *Deployed: How Reservists Bear the Burden in Iraq*. University of Michigan Press.

Nader, Laura. 1952. *Harmony Ideology: Justice and Control in a Zapotec Village.* Stanford University Press.

National Treatment Court Resource Center. 2022. *Treatment Court Table.* https://ntcrc.org/wp-content/uploads/2023/11/2022_NTCRC_TreatmentCourt_Count_Table.pdf.

Nevius, C. W. 2014. "Veterans Get a Court of Their Own in San Francisco." *San Francisco Chronicle*, December 24. https://www.sfchronicle.com/bayarea/nevius/article/Veterans-get-a-court-of-their-own-in-S-F-5978431.php#/0.

Nichter, Brandon, Ryan Holliday, Lindsey L. Monteith, Peter J. Na, Melanie L. Hill, Alexander C. Kline, Sonya B. Norman, and Robert H. Pietrzak. 2022. "Military Sexual Trauma in the United States: Results from a Population-Based Study." *Journal of Affective Disorders* 306: 19–27.

Nolan, James L. 2002. *Drug Courts in Theory and in Practice.* Walter de Gruyter.

Nolan, James L. 2009. *Reinventing Justice: The American Drug Court Movement.* Princeton University Press.

Nolan, James L. 2010. "Freedom, Social Control, and the Problem-Solving Court Movement." In *Social Control: Informal, Legal, and Medical*, edited by J.J. Chriss, 65–89. Emerald.

Nonet, Philippe, and Phillip Selznick. 1978. *Law and Society in Transition: Toward Responsive Law.* Harper & Row.

Obinger, Herbert, Klaus Peterson, and Peter Starke, eds. 2018. *Warfare and Welfare: Military Conflict and Welfare State Development in Western Countries.* Oxford University Press.

O'Hear, Michael. 2009. "Rethinking Drug Courts: Restorative Justice as a Response to Racial Injustice." *Stanford Law and Policy Review* 20: 479–80.

Oishi, Shigehiro, Minkyung Koo, Nangyeon Lim, and Eunkook M. Suh. 2019. "When Gratitude Evokes Indebtedness." *Applied Psychology: Health and Well-Being* 11(2): 286–303.

Orak, U., K. Kelton, M. G. Vaughn, J. Tsai, and R. H. Pietrzak. 2023. "Homelessness and Contact with the Criminal Legal System among U.S. Combat Veterans: An Exploration of Potential Mediating Factors." *Criminal Justice & Behavior* 50(3): 392–409.

Ortiz, Stephen R., ed. 2012. *Veterans' Policies, Veterans' Politics: New Perspectives on Veterans in the Modern United States.* University Press of Florida.

Ostrom, Brian, and Roger A. Hanson. 2009. "Understanding and Diagnosing Court Culture." *Court Review* 45(4): 104–9.

Ostrom, Brian J., Charles W. Ostrom, Roger A. Hanson, and Matthew Kleiman. 2007. *Trial Courts as Organizations.* Temple University Press.

Payne, Matthew T., 2016. *Playing War: Military Video Games after 9/11.* NYU Press.

Peng, Cong, Rob M. A. Nelissen, and Marcel Zeelenberg. 2018. "Reconsidering the Roles of Gratitude and Indebtedness in Social Exchange." *Cognition and Emotion* 32(4): 760–72.

Perez, Alina, Steven Leifman, and Ana Estrada. 2003. "Reversing the Criminalization of Mental Illness." *Crime & Delinquency* 49(1): 62–78.

Perlin, M. L. 2013. "'John Brown Went Off to War': Considering Veterans' Courts as Problem-Solving Courts." *Nova Law Review* 37(3): 445–77.

Pew Research Center. 2019. "Little Public Support for Reductions in Federal Spending." https://www.pewresearch.org/politics/2019/04/11/little-public-support-for-re ductions-in-federal-spending/.

Peyrot, Mark. 1991. "Institutional and Organizational Dynamics in Community-Based Drug Abuse Treatment." *Social Problems* 38(1): 20–33.

Phelps Michelle. 2013. "The Paradox of Probation: Community Supervision in the Age of Mass Imprisonment." *Law and Policy* 35(1/2): 51–80.

Phillimore, Jenny, Hannah Bradby, Michi Knecht, Beatriz Padilla, and Simon Pemberton. 2019. "Bricolage as Conceptual Tool for Understanding Access to Healthcare in Superdiverse Populations." *Social Theory & Health* 17: 231–52.

Phillips, Dave. 2023. "U.S. Troops Still Train on Weapons with Known Risk of Brain Injury." *New York Times*, November 26. https://www.nytimes.com/2023/11/26/us /military-brain-injury-rocket-launcher.html.

Piehowski, Victoria. 2022. "We Broke 'em, We Fix 'em: Trauma as Causal Story for Veterans Treatment Court." Presentation at Law and Society Studies Association, Lisbon, Portugal.

Powell, Walter W., and Paul J. DiMaggio. 1991. *The New Institutionalism in Organizational Analysis*. University of Chicago Press.

Putnam, Robert. 2000. *Bowling Alone: The Collapse and Revival of American Community*. Simon and Schuster.

Rahim, Asad. 2024. "The Legitimacy Trap." *Boston University Law Review* 104: 1–71.

Rapisarda, Sabrina S., Kimberly R. Kras, Grace LeMoyne, Don Hummer, Kelly Socia, and James M. Byrne. 2024. "Veterans Treatment Courts: A Nationwide Review of Enacting and Eligibility State Statutes." *Victims & Offenders* 19(1): 32–58.

Ray, Victor. 2018. "Militarism as a Racial Project." In *Handbook of the Sociology of Racial and Ethnic Relations*, edited by P. Batur and J. Feagin. Handbooks of Sociology and Social Research. Springer.

Revier, Kevin. 2021. "'Without Drug Court, You'll End Up in Prison or Dead': Therapeutic Surveillance and Addiction Narratives in Treatment Court." *Critical Criminology* 29(4): 915–30.

Resch, John P. 1982. "Federal Welfare for Revolutionary War Veterans." *Social Services Review* 56(2): 171–95.

Robb, David L. 2011. *Operation Hollywood: How the Pentagon Shapes and Censors the Movies*. Prometheus Books.

Robinson, Nick. 2012. "Videogames, Persuasion and the War on Terror: Escaping or Embedding the Military—Entertainment Complex?." *Political Studies* 60(3): 504–22.

Robinson, Nick, and Marcus Schulzke. 2016. "Visualizing War? Towards a Visual Analysis of Videogames and Social Media." *Perspectives on Politics* 14(4): 995–1010.

Ridgeway, Cecilia L. 2014. "Why Status Matters for Inequality." *American Sociological Review* 79(1): 1–16.

Ridgway, James. 2013. "The Origins of the Modern Veterans Benefits System from 1914–1958." *Veterans Law Review* 5: 1–55.

Rodriguez, Evan. 2024. "Engaging the Base: Using Veterans Treatment Courts in Missouri to Address Core Issues." *University of Missouri Kansas City Law Review* 92(Spring): 635–51.

Rowen, Jamie. 2017. *Searching for Truth in the Transitional Justice Movement.* Cambridge University Press.

Rowen, Jamie. 2020. "Worthy of Justice: A Veterans Treatment Court in Practice." *Law and Policy* 42(1): 78–100.

Rowen, Jamie. 2024. "Strategic Adaptation to a Crisis: Treatment Court Responses to Covid-19." *Law and Social Inquiry* 49(2): 769–96.

Rubenstein, Steve. 2019. "Court Gives Second Chance to Veterans Who Have Trouble Fitting into Society." *San Francisco Chronicle*, November 10. https://www.sfchronicle.com/bayarea/article/Court-gives-second-chance-to-veterans-who-have-14824126.php.

Rugg, Adam. 2016. "America's Game: The NFL's 'Salute to Service' Campaign, the Diffused Military Presence, and Corporate Social Responsibility." *Popular Communication* 14: 21–29.

Russell, Robert. 2009. "Veterans Treatment Court: A Proactive Approach." *New England Journal on Criminal & Civil Confinement* 35(2): 357–72.

Russell, Robert. 2015. "Veteran Treatment Courts." *Touro Law Review* 31(8): 385–401.

Sandefur, Rebecca L., ed. 2009. *Access to Justice.* Emerald Group.

Schulzke, Marcus. 2017. "Military Videogames and the Future of Ideological Warfare." *British Journal of Politics and International Relations* 19(3): 609–26.

Seamone, Evan R., Stephanie Brooks Holliday, and Shoba Sreenivasan. 2018. "Veteran Non Grata: Veteran Sex Offenders with Service-Related Mental Health Conditions and the Need to Mitigate Risk." *Virginia Journal of Criminal Law* 6(1): 182–237.

Selznick, Philip. 1957. *Leadership in Administration: A Sociological Interpretation.* Harper & Row.

Shaheen, Jack. 2009. "Hollywood's Bad Arabs." *Cairo Review* 16: 81–97. https://www.thecairoreview.com/wp-content/uploads/2015/01/CR16-Shaheen.pdf.

Shdaimah, Corey S., Chrysanthi S. Leon, and Shelly A. Wiechelt. 2023. *The Compassionate Court?: Support, Surveillance, and Survival in Prostitution Diversion Programs.* Temple University Press.

Sherman, Nicole. 2024. "'Be All That You Can Be': The Role of Identity, Pro-Social Labeling, and Narratives in Veterans Treatment Courts." *Sociological Inquiry* 94(4): 723–46.

Silk, Michael. 2013. *The Cultural Politics of Post-9/11 American Sport: Power, Pedagogy and the Popular.* Routledge.

Simon, Jonathan. 2007. *Governing through Crime: How the War on Crime Transformed American Democracy and Created a Culture of Fear.* Oxford University Press.

Simpson, Brett, Robb Willer, and Cecilia Ridgeway. 2012. "Status Hierarchies and the Organization of Collective Action." *Sociological Theory* 30(3): 149–66.

Singh, Rashmee. 2018. "'Setting a Good Example for the Ladies': Example Setting as a Technique of Penal Reform in Specialized Prostitution Court." *British Journal of Criminology* 58(3): 569–87.

Skocpol, Theda. 1993. "America's First Social Security System: The Expansion of Benefits for Civil War Veterans." *Political Science Quarterly* 108(1): 85–116.

Skocpol, Theda. 1995. *Protecting Soldiers and Mothers: The Political Origins of Social Policy in the United States.* Harvard University Press.

Slattery, Michelle, Mallory Tascha Dugger, and Theodore A. Lamb. 2013. "Catch, Treat, and Release: Veteran Treatment Courts Address the Challenges of Returning Home." *Substance Use & Misuse* 48(10): 922–32.

Smith, Jack W. 2012. "The Anchorage, Alaska Veterans Court and Recidivism: July 6, 2004–December 31, 2010." *Alaska Law Review* 29(1): 93–111.

Smith, Jeffrey Q., and Grant R. MacQueen. 2017. "Going, Going, but Not Quite Gone: Trials Continue to Decline in the Federal and State Courts. Does It Matter?" *Judicature* 101(4): 32–34.

Smith, R. Tyson, and Gala True. 2014. "Warring Identities." *Society and Mental Health* 4(2): 147–61.

Snowden, D. L., S. Oh, C. P. Salas-Wright, M. G. Vaughn, and E. King. 2017. "Military Service and Crime: New Evidence." *Social Psychiatry & Psychiatric Epidemiology* 52(5): 605–15.

Stacer, Melissa J., and Monica Solinas-Saunders. 2020. "Justice-Involved Veterans: A Critical Review and Future Research." *Critical Military Studies* 6(1): 41–66.

Stevens, Rosemary A. 2012. "The Invention, Stumbling and Reinvention of the Veterans Health Care Administration, 1918–1924." In *Veterans' Policies, Veterans' Politics: New Perspectives on Veterans in the Modern United States,* edited by Stephen R. Ortiz, 38–64. University Press of Florida.

Stitt, Mary Ellen. 2022. "Widening the Net?" Presentation at Law and Society Association, Lisbon, Portugal.

Stratton, Evelyn Lundberg, and Jessica Lagarce. 2012. "Restoring Honor: Inside Veterans' Courts." *Ohio Lawyer* 26: 24–28.

Suid, Lawrence H. 2002. *Guts and Glory: The Making of the American Military Image in Film.* University Press of Kentucky.

Sznycer, Daniel, and Aaron W. Lukaszewski. 2019. "The Emotion–Valuation Constellation: Multiple Emotions Are Governed by a Common Grammar of Social Valuation." *Evolution and Human Behavior* 40(4): 395–404.

Talesh, Shauhin. 2007. "Mental Health Court Judges as Dynamic Risk Managers: A New Conceptualization of the Role of Judges." *DePaul Law Review* 57: 93–132.

Thompson, Mark. 2016. "Military Sexual Assault Victims Discharged after Filing Complaints." *Time Magazine.* https://time.com/4340321/sexual-assault-military-discharge-women/.

Thorson, Emily A., and Michael Serazio. 2018. "Sports Fandom and Political Attitudes." *Public Opinion Quarterly* 82(2): 391–403.

Tiger, Rebecca. 2012. *Judging Addicts: Drug Courts and Coercion in the Justice System.* New York University Press.

Timko, Christine., A. Nash, M. D. Owens, E. Taylor, and A. K. Finlay. 2020. "Systematic Review of Criminal and Legal Involvement after Substance Use and Mental Health Treatment among Veterans: Building toward Needed Research." *Substance Abuse: Research & Treatment* 14: 1–13.

Tsai, Jack, Andrea Finlay, Bessie Flatley, Wesley J. Kasprow, and Sean Clark. 2018. "A National Study of Veterans Treatment Court Participants: Who Benefits and Who Recidivates." *Administration and Policy in Mental Health and Mental Health Services Research* 45(2): 236–44.

Tsai, Jack, Bessie Flatley, Wesley J. Kasprow, and Sean Clark. 2016. "Diversion of Veterans with Criminal Justice Involvement to Treatment Courts: Participant Characteristics and Outcomes." *Psychiatric Services* 68(4): 375–83.

Tsai Jack, R. H. Pietrzak, and D. Szymkowiak. 2021. "The Problem of Veteran Homelessness: An Update for the New Decade." *American Journal of Preventative Medicine* 60(6): 774–80.

Tsai, Jack, R. A. Rosenheck, W. J. Kasprow, and J. F. McGuire. 2013. "Risk of Incarceration and Other Characteristics of Iraq and Afghanistan Era Veterans in State and Federal Prisons." *Psychiatric Services* 64: 36–43.

Tyler, Tom R. 1990. *Why People Obey the Law.* Princeton University Press.

Ulmer, Jeffrey. 1997. *Social Worlds of Sentencing: Court Communities under Sentencing Guidelines.* SUNY Press.

US Department of Veterans Affairs. 2020. *National Center for Veterans Analysis and Statistics Veteran Population Projections.* https://www.va.gov/vetdata/docs/Demographics/New_Vetpop_Model/Vetpop_Infographic2020.pdf.

US Department of Veterans Affairs. 2022. "Mental Health." https://www.mental-health.va.gov/suicide_prevention/data.asp.

Valverde, Mariana. 1998. *Diseases of the Will: Alcohol and the Dilemmas of Freedom.* Cambridge University Press.

Van Dyke, K., and E. A. Orrick. 2016. "An Examination of the Influence of Veteran Status on Offense Type among an Inmate Sample." *American Journal of Criminal Justice* 42(2): 426–42.

Vaughan, Tyler J., Lisa Bell Holleran, and Rachel Brooks. 2019. "Exploring Therapeutic and Militaristic Contexts in a Veteran Treatment Court." *Criminal Justice Policy Review* 30(1): 79–101.

Watkins, Philip C., Jason Scheer, Melinda Ovnicek, and Russell Kolts. 2006. "The Debt of Gratitude: Dissociating Gratitude and Indebtedness." *Cognition and Emotion* 20(2): 217–41.

Western, Bruce. 2006. *Punishment and Inequality in America.* Russell Sage Foundation.

Wetta, Frank J., and Martin A. Novelli. 2003. "'Now a Major Motion Picture': War Films and Hollywood's New Patriotism." *Journal of Military History* 67: 861–82.

Wexler, David B., and Bruce J. Winick. 1996. *Law in a Therapeutic Key: Developments in Therapeutic Jurisprudence.* Carolina Academic Press.

Wilson, D. B., O. Mitchell, and D. L. MacKenzie. 2006. "A Systematic Review of

Drug Court Effects On Recidivism." *Journal of Experimental Criminology* 2: 459–87.

Wimmer, Andreas. 2013. *Ethnic Boundary Making: Institutions, Power, Networks.* Oxford University Press.

Winick, Bruce J., and David B. Wexler. 2003. *Judging in a Therapeutic Key: Therapeutic Jurisprudence and the Courts.* Carolina Academic Press.

Wolff, Nancy, Nicole Fabrikant, and Steven Belenko. 2011. "Mental Health Courts And Their Selection Processes: Modeling Variation for Consistency." *Law and Human Behavior* 35(5): 402–12.

Zaw, Khaing, Darrick Hamilton, and William Darity Jr. 2016. "Race, Wealth and Incarceration: Results from the National Longitudinal Survey of Youth." *Race and Social Problems* 8: 103–15.

Zozula, Christine. 2019. *Courting the Community: Legitimacy and Punishment in a Community Court.* Temple University Press.

INDEX

The authorized representative in the EU for product safety and compliance is:
Mare Nostrum Group
B.V Doelen 72
4831 GR Breda
The Netherlands

www.ingramcontent.com/pod-product-compliance
Lightning Source LLC
Chambersburg PA
CBHW020844270326
41928CB00006B/546